549.5
7
38

MANAGEMENT DEVELOPMENT THROUGH TRAINING

D1409586

CHARLES E. WATSON

Miami University
Oxford, Ohio

WITHDRAWN

Tennessee Tech. Library
Cookeville, Tenn.

ADDISON-WESLEY PUBLISHING COMPANY
Reading, Massachusetts • Menlo Park, California
London • Amsterdam • Don Mills, Ontario • Sydney

288200

Copyright © 1979 by Addison-Wesley Publishing Company, Inc. Philippines copyright 1979 by Addison-Wesley Publishing Company, Inc.

All rights reserved. No part of this publication may be reproduced, stored in a retrieval system, or transmitted, in any form or by any means, electronic, mechanical, photocopying, recording, or otherwise, without the prior written permission of the publisher. Printed in the United States of America. Published simultaneously in Canada. Library of Congress Catalog Card No. 78-52504.

ISBN 0-201-08358-2
ABCDEFGHIJ-AL-79

To Earl G. Planty

MANAGEMENT DEVELOPMENT THROUGH TRAINING

Contents

9

**ANSWERS TO COMMONLY ASKED QUESTIONS
ABOUT MANAGEMENT TRAINING 316**

Preface

This book is intended for those people who are concerned with designing and presenting classroom learning experiences for practicing managers and supervisors. It presents what I believe to be a comprehensive treatment of both the theory and practice of management training. Throughout the book I have attempted to present the key issues and problems that training professionals face and ways in which they can meet or solve them.

It is my hope that this volume will also provide training practitioners with a richer understanding of management and what it involves, as well as a thorough and more sophisticated approach to follow in carrying out training activities.

I stress the contingency approach to management and the need to teach managers to rely upon all types of practices and theories as they are appropriate.

I have attempted to convey the idea that management education should be as much an emotional experience as it is a purely logical, intellectual process if it is to produce substantial and lasting change in people. Management education must not only help trainees to acquire greater knowledge, but also help them to develop the skills and personal characteristics they need to use their knowledge. The development of diagnostic and application skills and the personal characteristics that enable managers to apply these skills involves much more than merely appealing to a person's logic.

I have also tried to stress the importance of integrating the formal classroom training effort with all other organization and management development efforts. Generally speaking, training alone cannot bring about desired change and improvement in managerial behavior on the job. But, by the same token, it cannot be ignored. In Chapter 7 I have shown some of the kinds of things that have been done successfully to get training to pay off where it counts—on the job.

There are many fine people involved in training and development whom I have had the opportunity to work with or for and who have contributed enormously to my understanding of management development and ultimately to my writing of this book. I am particularly grateful to four of the finest bosses any training director could ask to work under—Bill Moeckel, Earl Strong, Virgil James, and Bill Egloff. I am thankful to have had the chance to learn from the personal experiences of Joe Litterer, Bill McCord, George Bricker, Earl Brooks, Allison MacCullough, Chuck Davis, John Douglas, Bill Haney, and Ed Kowalczyk, who have, each in his own way, provided me with ideas that have ultimately been incorporated here.

John F. Mee has and continues to be a source of inspiration and guidance just as he has with so many others in the field of management.

Jim Healey unselfishly shared many worthwhile and important lessons and experiences and provided helpful suggestions in writing this volume.

I owe my greatest debt of thanks to "Mr. Executive Development"— Earl G. Planty. His teachings and his living example epitomize the best in not only management development, but also personal development. It is this giant in the field of management development to whom I am indebted for the ability and inspiration to write this book.

Oxford, Ohio   C. E. W.
July 1978

1

Why Management Development?

Not long ago, a former blue-chip, billion-dollar corporation found it necessary to shut down one of its principal operations. Operating costs were outrunning income and the prospects of turning a loss situation into a profit-making one appeared nil. What had once been a center of profit-producing activity, a source of income for people in the community, a source of tax revenue for the state and local governments, and, most importantly, a place of employment for hundreds of men and women was silenced. Hundreds of people were forced out of work. They suffered; their community suffered; and the state's economy suffered.

Some claimed that external economic conditions were the cause of the operation's collapse. Yet, the company's competitors, who were operating in the same economic environment, were producing handsome profits. Others pointed the finger of blame for the operation's downfall at a handful of its key managers. In reality, there were a great many who should have received the blame. Many specific causes were cited to explain why the shutdown occurred. But, to the astute observer, one underlying cause of the operation's collapse stood out—poor management.

The author's earlier visits to this operation, discussions with its key people, and first-hand observations revealed clearly that sound management practices were lacking. Long-range goals and plans, for instance, were practically nonexistent. Basic business techniques such as capital budgeting, return on investment, and pay-back period were neglected. Company–union relations were bad. On numerous occasions during its over-one-hundred-year existence, strikes had crippled the operation for several months at a time. Many of the employees (even at the highest levels) pilfered from the company or used its supplies and resources inappropriately or for personal benefit. The design of the organization was ill-conceived. The operation was heavily over-staffed. Absenteeism was far above the average for the industry and the local area. Many of those responsible for the operation's various departments were competent in their respective technical fields, many were not. However, little or no concern was raised either about those who were ill-prepared or those who performed their work poorly. For all practical purposes, the employees were secure in their jobs because competence and performance were not valued as much as loyalty to the organization and its leaders.

And yet, in spite of bad management practices, there existed within the organization an air of complacency and a prevailing attitude that the opera-tion was outstanding and that the employees were the best in their respective areas of responsibility. Moreover, a strong feeling of security existed among the operation's employees and the local community, a feeling which was exemplified by the expressed belief that, since the operation had existed for years, its viability would always continue just as it had in the past.

In terms of basic, technical competence, most of the operation's key man-agers and operatives were as able as their counterparts in competitive firms. For the most part, capital resources were not lacking. The corporation had some of the best and most modern equipment in the world, and, up until a few months before the closing, it had continued to invest in its operation. Employees were healthy, intelligent, and educated. Yet, in spite of all these assets, this operation failed.

In the past, economic conditions were such that the firm made a healthy profit, as the demand for its product was strong. Costs were practically unimportant to its success. But, over the years, competition intensified. The world and industry became increasingly complex. Thus more effective and efficient methods of forecasting, planning, coordinating, activating, and con-trolling were needed to combine the elements of productive enterprise. In this operation, they were ignored. The one (sometimes elusive) ingredient that is absolutely essential, the factor that brings money, materials, equipment, and people together and blends them to create a whole greater than the sum of the parts—namely, sound management—was missing.

A true story? Yes. Did it have to happen? No.

WHAT IS MANAGEMENT DEVELOPMENT?

Situations like the above-mentioned case will very probably continue to occur as long as organizations continue to neglect the training and development of managerial resources. Management development does not just happen as a matter of course and it cannot be left to chance. Very few people become first-rate managers simply because of their experience in one or a variety of positions. For most people, the development of managerial ability is a carefully guided process.

Moreover, the processes by which managerial ability is developed are many and must all be present in some form and to some extent. Thus management development involves more than simply attending training classes, although such classes are helpful for opening new horizons and broadening perspectives. Management development involves more than manpower and promotion planning. These activities are useful for identifying talent, alerting superiors and training staffs to developmental needs, and assuring the organization a supply of managerial talent when needed. Management development is more than a process of measuring and evaluating employee performance. Although this is a major part of development, performance appraisals without follow-up developmental planning and positive actions for improved performance often yield little more than frustration.

Management development cannot succeed if its aim is to dramatically alter personalities or values and beliefs (Drucker 1974). Attempts to completely remake someone's personality nearly always fail because most of us are resistant to change of this sort. However, management development can help people to behave effectively in various situations and to apply sound management practices consciously.

Management development is a deliberate process. It will flourish in an organization where top management believes in it, supports it, and rewards it. It will flourish under the guidance of able and skillful leaders who are looked upon with respect and who are able to coach, guide, and assist other managers in the organization in becoming competent and dedicated to developing their own subordinates. Management development involves sound selection procedures, organization and manpower planning, performance evaluations, reviews, and appraisals, and day-to-day coaching and counseling. It also involves planned learning experiences including courses, seminars, workshops, and individual reading programs. Most importantly, it involves individual desire and commitment.

Management development is self-development. People may receive careful guidance and the necessary developmental opportunities, but they must *choose* to improve if change is to occur. Through training, people can be made aware of their individual strengths and developmental needs. One participant at a management training program put it this way, "Our development will take place on our jobs and on our own time through our individual efforts. This training program allows us a chance to see where we lack, to pinpoint our needs, and to learn about various ways in which we can improve. It's up to us to do something about it."

GUIDEPOSTS TO MANAGEMENT DEVELOPMENT

Over the past three decades, American industry has distilled from combined experience a number of widely accepted Guideposts to Management Development. James (1970) has combined several of his ideas with those of Moorehead Wright, Howard Johnson, Douglas McGregor, and Alex Bavelas to produce the following list of guideposts:

1. A person's development is 90 percent the result of on-the-job experience.

2. The three most effective executive development tools are: (1) clearly defined responsibilities; (2) commensurate authority to manage; and (3) the necessary feedback of information by which one can decide for oneself how well or how poorly he or she is performing.

3. A person grows and develops to the extent that he or she exercises increasingly refined control over his or her thought processes, actions, and behavior, bringing them closer to some known and acceptable standard of performance.

4. The focus of development and educational activities must be on the individual's *work* rather than on *personality*.

5. Developing people is not a matter of making them become something; it is a matter of creating an environment in which they can grow.

6. Either people develop according to the particular demands of their lives and in line with their potential, or they do not develop at all.

7. The methods and tools used are not as important as a sincere interest in the development of people.

8. Educational courses, when properly designed and presented, can give people the kind of experience that will help them learn quickly and easily when back on the job.

9. There is no known panacea, shortcut, or miracle method for the development of management ability.

TRAINING, EDUCATION, AND DEVELOPMENT

Some people make a distinction between training and education. To them, *training* is concerned with the teaching of specific, factual, narrow-scoped subject matter and skills primarily of a motor or mechanical nature, while *education* is concerned with broader subject matter of a conceptual or theoretical nature and the development of personal attitudes and philosophies. Here, training and education will be used synonymously. The author believes that people act as integrated beings, whose knowledge, skills, and attitudes are interrelated and inseparable. To make a distinction between training and education is to ignore these interrelationships. The teaching of knowledge, skills, and attitudes cannot be compartmentalized if it is to be effective.

A distinction is sometimes made between training and development. *Training* is thought of as formal classroom learning activities, while *development* is thought of as all learning experiences, both on and off the job, including formal, classroom training. This distinction will be observed here because it serves to emphasize the notion that formal classroom learning will be minimally effective at best, if on-the-job experience and learning are not consistent with and supportive of it.

REASONS FOR TRAINING AND DEVELOPMENT

Most leaders agree that management development is a necessary requirement for the long-term success of their organization. Yet, the underlying reasons for management training and development are not widely understood. Several of the most important reasons will be considered here.

The Manager's Environment is Changing

Managers should keep themselves updated on major changes in their environment. They should understand the significance of these changes and alter their methods and practices accordingly. Management development should help managers to recognize and adapt to change. Several of the more significant changes which are making a major impact on managers include the following:

1. Technological changes, which frequently require changes in strategies, structures, and management styles and practices

2. Changes in the availability and sources of raw materials, which may cause managers to be less consumer or marketing oriented and more procurement oriented

3. Changes in public attitudes and demands, which are creating the public-oriented manager (Mee 1975)

4. Changes in strategies and organizational structures, which require different managerial skills

5. Changes in employees' values, life styles, and education levels, which call for different ways of leading and motivating employees.

Developing Technical Specialists to Become General Managers

When a person begins a professional career with an organization, her or his first assignments are usually specialized, as employment was based on some specific technical ability. However, as she or he ascends in the organization's hierarchy, the scope of responsibility widens. The individual becomes less concerned with the technical aspects of the job and more occupied with managing the efforts of others who now hold positions in the organization which she or he held previously. Unfortunately, success in handling technical assignments is no guarantee of success in handling managerial assignments.

Take for example, the case of one young man in his mid-to-late thirties. In grammar school, he excelled in math and science. In high school, he took all the courses he could in the sciences, which eventually prepared him for admission to a top-flight engineering school. The demands of college were rugged and competition was keen. But, through his efforts and abilities, he succeeded in graduating near the top of his class.

He received job offers from some of the best organizations and, after several weeks of careful deliberation, he took a position with a fast-moving electronics firm. His first assignment was as a technical assistant to one of the firm's most promising experts. Soon, because of his excellent work, he was promoted to a project of his own. Now in the role of an independent contributor, he was really able to show his ability. This he did. His next assignment was in quality control, where he was responsible for designing a quality-control system for a new product line. After three-and-a-half years in this job, he was promoted to a supervisory position in another department. He was often found working alongside his four employees. His fascination with his work grew, but at the same time he became frustrated with the amount of effort and time he was expected to spend on supervision. He disliked attending meetings, writing reports, preparing budgets, communicating up and down the organization, handling occasional personnel problems, etc., which he felt kept him from being directly involved in the work.

After a few more years, he found himself with a better title and salary and more responsibilities. He was in charge of an entire department. While he enjoyed all of this, deep down he felt that he was losing touch with his speciality and was increasingly bothered by the thought that he might someday become technically obsolete. He reacted to these pressures and the demands of his added administrative responsibilities by spending longer hours at the plant, by trying to keep involved and watch the work closely and, at the same time, by trying to fulfill his "other" (managerial) duties. There did not seem to be enough hours in the day. People weren't motivated enough. Funds and equipment were in short supply. Top management seemed more concerned with other matters. No one could keep up with his or her technical field under these conditions. A typical story?

The transition from "doing" to "managing" is a difficult process. It is doubly difficult when a person's previous experience and education are totally void of management training. Moreover, he or she no longer derives the satisfaction of seeing the fruits of his or her efforts because, as a manager, this hands-on experience is no longer available. As a manager, one is a facilitator who gets things done through others. To gain work satisfaction in this role, one must learn to enjoy influencing others and getting them to perform the work to be done.

Younger Managers Must be Developed Sooner

In years past, most people did not get promoted to management positions, especially those of considerable importance, until they were at least in their late thirties or early forties. Most managers were in the age category from 45 to 65 years. Now, however, great numbers of younger people can be found in higher-level management positions. In the future, the trend toward promoting even more comparatively younger people into management positions most likely will continue. There are a number of reasons for this.

First, there appears to have been a change in management philosophy—i.e., ability and competence are valued more than age and years of experience. Now, to a greater extent than ever before, people are judged, rewarded, and promoted more on the basis of their ability to accomplish tasks and reach predetermined objectives efficiently than on who they are and how long they have worked for the organization. As we shift toward even greater emphasis on result-oriented management, ability will become valued more than years of experience.

Second, with extremely rapid changes in technology and increasingly rapid utilization of new knowledge, college graduates are uniquely qualified for these new fields. Very often, the majority of those qualified in the new fields and competent to manage the people charged with using this new knowledge are younger people.

Third, and possibly most important, demographical data reveal a decrease in the proportion of older people (45–64 years) in the workforce and a substantial increase in the proportion of younger people (21–44 years). During the period from 1970 to 1980, the number of people between 21 and 44 years of age will increase by 17.6 million, whereas the number of people between 45 and 64 years of age will increase by only 1.6 million.

Many firms are aware of this information and are carrying out efforts to hasten the development of their younger employees for management responsibilities. Eugene Seibert (1974), vice president of personnel, the Parker Pen Company, describes what his firm did:

> Years ago we had 20 to 25 years to prepare people fresh out of college for management positions. As we look to the future, we see we do not have as much time. We feel we will have to get people ready in only 10 to 15 years. Therefore, our company has hired a specialist in management development and we are working hard, as a matter of company policy, to develop our people so they will be ready to assume management responsibilities when they are needed.

Professional Managers are Needed in all Sectors of the Economy

For many years, management training was almost exclusively confined to private business. Today this is no longer true. The need for professional managers and administrators is recognized by most large organizations such as governmental agencies, hospitals, libraries, museums, and universities, etc. Management has become recognized as necessary to the long-run success of almost any organization. Moreover, the numbers and proportions of people employed by the service industry and by federal, state, and local government has grown enormously. These factors have led to substantial efforts in non-business-management training.

Historically, advances in technology, work procedures, increased knowledge and skill of the workforce, and capital investment in better plants and equipment have combined to increase productivity. Principally these gains in productivity have been in manufacturing and agriculture as a result of massive capital investments in labor-saving machinery. Since the early 1950s, the majority of employed people in our country has shifted to nongoods-producing industries. In the early 1950s, there were almost as many people employed in goods-producing industries (e.g., agriculture, manufacturing, mining, and construction) as there were in nongoods-producing industries (e.g., wholesale and retail trade, finance, insurance, real estate, services, and federal, state, and local government). Today about two thirds of working Americans are employed in the nongoods-producing sector of the economy; this sector now accounts for more than half of our GNP.

While salaries and wages have increased dramatically for people employed in these industries, their productivity has not increased at the same rate. For example, how can government employees improve their productivity each year? Their salaries continue to increase at least as fast as those employed in other industries, creating a situation which leads to inflation. Technological improvements will probably continue to alleviate the problem, yet the prospect of solving the problem appears nil. Better management—which will lead to effective utilization of manpower, economical assignment of tasks for those employed in the nongoods-producing areas, and better organization with less duplication of effort—seems to offer substantial hope for improving productivity. The need for continuing management development in the nongoods-producing sector of the economy, which is most prone to inflation, is therefore important because of the large numbers of people employed in these areas.

Warding Off Obsolescence

It has been said that when people begin their employment they also begin a footrace between obsolescence and retirement, with the hope that they will be able to reach retirement before becoming obsolete.

The exact nature of managerial obsolescence is not known as little formal research has been conducted on it. That which has been done consists mostly of a collection of random observations and informed estimates. Mahler (1965, p. 8) has defined managerial obsolescence as "the failure of a once capable manager to achieve results that are currently expected of him." Virgil James has identified two distinct types of managerial obsolescence:

> . . . obsolescence, in which a man's skills are no longer required; and attrition, in which he loses his capacity to perform even though his skills are still applicable (Haas 1968, p. 11).

The magnitude of managerial obsolescence has only been estimated and there is little agreement as to the percentage of obsolete managers or the age group most affected. Schuler's (1965) study of obsolescence in eleven companies revealed that the problem has affected as much as 20–25 percent of some firms' executives.

Mental decline in managers leads to a leveling-off or, in extreme cases, a decline in performance. As Albert Schweitzer characterized this problem, "The tragedy of life is what dies within a man while he still lives."

The managerial-dropout problem is truly a tragedy because it need not occur. Obsolescence can be prevented. Planned actions can be taken to stop the trend toward mental decline and the resulting obsolescence in managers. Development (or regeneration) programs, which are used by many firms in an attempt to keep the mental processes of their managers alive and growing in effectiveness, often include the following:

1.   Continuing education—both formal and informal

2.   Promotions, job rotations, and demotions

3.   Regular performance evaluations and appraisals

4.   Medical checkups and physical-fitness programs

5.   Avoidance of overspecialization through job enlargement

6.   A system that rotates the assignment of assistants to executives, in order to infuse the executives with the new methods that recent graduates have learned (Drucker 1974)

The proposition that aging naturally results in mental decline is not supported by research findings. As people grow older, they may slowly deteriorate physically—e.g., the motor skills of a typical seventy-year-old individual are less than those of a twenty-year-old individual; but, in terms of mental abilities, aging does not necessarily result in decline. The following conclusions from the field of gerontology, which pertain to mental processes and aging and which contradict popularly held beliefs, strongly support the idea that training should be available to people of all ages.

1.   Intelligence does not decline with age. Longitudinal studies have concluded that IQ scores for most people remain fairly constant.

2.   Retained information is relatively unaffected by advancing age.

3.   The ability to learn does not decline with age.

4.   With advancing age, thinking processes tend to become rigid. Problem-solving ability—finding solutions to new problems where past experience is of no help—is difficult for older subjects.

Given these conclusions it should be apparent that the maintenance and improvement of mental ability is possible. Development efforts aimed at regeneration can be successful. However, rigidity of thought and an unchanging exposure to the same life experiences, where things are safe, can cause the mental processes to slow down. Planty (1976) puts it this way:

> Minds and hearts not exposed to novelty die prematurely. It is unthinking habit which destroys.

WHAT MANAGEMENT TRAINING CAN DO

Many of the disappointments experienced when exposing people to management training have been the result of unrealistic expectations. It is unrealistic to believe that management training can dramatically alter personalities and ingrained habits overnight. Dramatic changes like these do not occur as a result of a few days or even a few weeks of training. However, training can be the *beginning* of behavioral changes. When conducted properly, management training can begin a period of reflection and development by giving the individual new perspectives about and insights into self and others, organization relationships, and the business environment.

In a survey, Crotty (1974, p. 84) identified the following five major reasons for the use of management-development programs.

1.   They broaden the manager's vision and understanding in preparation for additional responsibility.

2.   They provide the manager with the latest information on business theory and practice.

3.   They stimulate a more creative and innovative approach to problem solving and decision making.

4.   They give the manager the opportunity to discuss ideas and problems with other businesspeople.

5.   They allow the manager to reflect upon and assess his or her career development and work role.

Note: These reasons are *not* unrealistic expectations for training.

Powell and Davis (1973, p. 84) conducted a survey of organizations using university management development programs. This study measured the degree of importance of the various reasons given for using these programs.

Reasons for program utilization	Importance index
Broadens the individual's interests or awareness—that is, widens her or his business perspectives	6.8
Exposes an already competent manager to new hypotheses or avenues of management thought	6.3
Prepares the individual for greater responsibility but not necessarily for promotion	5.8
Provides management training or education to an individual who was promoted through technical channels	4.9
Permits managers to interact and compare problems/solutions with managers in other areas	4.8
Prepares the individual for imminent promotion	3.6
Provides an opportunity for subordinate development while the supervisor attends a program	2.2
Checks competency of potential successor	1.2

Maximum score = 8
Minimum score = 1
Average of possible scores = 4.5

The use of programs to broaden managers' perspectives, giving them new insights, new ways of thinking, and new avenues of complex problem solving ranked as most important. Here too, unrealistic expectations along the lines of completely remaking individual personalities was avoided.

Management training can produce important benefits and, although they might not be considered miracles, they do have substantial value, including the following:

1.   It can communicate to managers corporate philosophy, policies, procedures, rules, and standards. For example, it can acquaint lower-level managers with top management's posture with regard to specific issues. It can teach people how to follow merit-rating procedures or how to handle expense vouchers, and it can acquaint managers with company standards of performance. In short, management training can provide managers with a great

amount of information which is necessary and helpful to the smooth functioning of the organization.

2.   It can teach managers how to determine the consequences of various specific managerial actions and behaviors. For example, it can teach managers the consequences different leadership styles will produce given certain situations and types of employees. It can teach managers what kinds of results occur when organizations have goals and plans and when they don't have them. It can teach them the consequences of various types of organizational designs and arrangements given particular conditions, and it can teach managers which tools are appropriate for stimulating performance under various conditions. Most importantly, it can provide managers with useful diagnostic tools for assessing the significance and implications that various forms of behavior will have in specific situations.

3.   It very often gives people the opportunity to check out their thinking with other managers and to compare the ways in which they define and solve problems. Managers frequently see this exchange of ideas with their peers as one of the most beneficial aspects of a training program. Sometimes managers find it reassuring to learn that others handle similar situations much like they do.

4.   It can stimulate thinking and provide new and deeper insights to the managers. Management training involving face-to-face discussion among attendees benefits managers as they expose one another to perspectives and views previously not thought of, understood, or even valued. Information-giving aspects of training will usually acquaint managers with new concepts. With these inputs, along with opportunities for expression, problem-solving experiences, and case-study assignments, minds are challenged and creativity is unleashed. These conditions usually stimulate imagination and thinking processes to probe to new depths previously unencountered. This also helps establish both a pattern and the will to continue thinking creatively after formal training has ended.

5.   It can get managers to look at themselves and to understand how and perhaps why they perceive themselves, others, and situations as they do. It can teach managers to become more aware of themselves and others and to increase their awareness and sensitivity to and understanding of the significance of these behaviors.

6.   It can teach managers new practices. Exposure to examples of successful management practices can provide managers with useful models to pattern their behavior after. It can teach managers, for example, how to read a balance sheet, how to conduct a performance appraisal interview, how to handle emotional employees, how to follow problem identification and problem-solving procedures, etc. It can teach the managers skills in listening, in problem solving, in explaining concepts, in writing memos, etc.

7. It can change the managers' attitudes. To some extent training has been successful in changing the managers' attitudes toward new management practices such as participative management, discipline, motivation, and so on. Management training has not succeeded in remaking personalities, brainwashing people to new philosophies, or changing inferior managers into superior ones; but it has succeeded in changing people's opinions on a limited basis.

8. It can help cause people to choose to change their behavior and become better managers.

THE EXTENT OF MANAGEMENT-DEVELOPMENT EFFORTS

The level of activity in the area of management-development training has mushroomed during the past 40–45 years. Only 3 percent of the major firms surveyed in 1935 had some type of management-development program. A similar survey, taken in 1954, reported that 50 percent of the country's top 500 companies had management-development programs. In 1961, a survey taken determined that 77 percent of the country's large companies had management-development programs for their employees (Campbell 1970).

Today, few major companies *do not* provide training for their managers and supervisors. It seems as though the industry leaders are companies most heavily involved with management-development training—e.g., DuPont (chemicals); General Motors (automotives); General Electric and Westinghouse (electric equipment); IBM and Xerox (business machines and equipment); Bell Companies (utilities); Sears (retailing); Exxon, Mobil, and Texaco (petroleum); and so on. Today, nearly every major company employs at least one specialist in management development, and many firms have training departments staffed by highly competent professionals.

The comment made by Monroe J. Rathbone, former President and Chairman of the Board of Standard Oil of New Jersey, is typical of the belief held by corporate leaders, that management development is crucial to their organizations' success.

> One of the most important jobs of any executive of any branch of our business, either our affiliated companies or any of our departments, and right on up to the board level and the chief executive level, is to perpetuate the best possible quality of management, because a corporation has an unlimited life, and its success is heavily dependent upon the quality of its management.
>
> Management turns over, dies, and goes on to other places, so that you have to keep it moving, keep it alive, keep it effective. And this doesn't just happen. Certainly 15 percent, I think, of the time of most of the higher executives is spent developing people, identifying people, planning for their future development. (Rathbone 1965, p. 44).

The American Society for Training and Development has grown from a membership of 15, when it started in 1943, to nearly 10,000 today. In 1932, Edwin Shul began the first university management-development program at M.I.T. in Cambridge, Massachusetts. This first group consisted of eight individuals who gathered to discuss business problems. Other executive programs were set up in the years that followed. Harvard University established its program in 1945, Western Ontario University in 1948, and Pittsburgh University in 1949; and, in the early 1950s, several other major universities established programs. Today, over fifty major universities conduct annual management-development programs, which are from two to eight weeks in length. Many smaller universities are also heavily involved in various forms of supervisory and management education. Hundreds of private consulting firms are currently engaged in management-development activities. Today, training is "big business" and a major concern of top leaders from all kinds of organizations.

REFERENCES

Campbell, John P.; Dunnette, Marvin D.; Lawler, Edward E., III; and Weick, Karl E., Jr. *Managerial Behavior, Performance and Effectiveness.* New York: McGraw-Hill, 1970.

Crotty, Philip T. "Development Programs for Mature Managers." *Business Horizons,* XVII, No. 6, 1974, pp. 80–86.

Drucker, Peter F. *Management: Tasks, Responsibilities, Practices.* New York: Harper & Row, 1974.

Haas, Fredrick C. "Executive Obsolesence." American Management Association Research Study No. 90, New York, 1968.

James, Virgil A. "Guideposts to Management Development." An unpublished paper, 1970.

"Lessons in Leadership Part I: Deciding the Tough Ones" (a conversation with Monroe J. Rathbone). *Nation's Business,* 53, No. 6, 1965, pp. 34–52.

Mahler, Walter R. "Every Company's Problem: Managerial Obsolescence." *Personnel,* 42, No. 4, 1965, pp. 8–10.

Mee, John F. "Perspectives for the Future Manager and His Environment." Committee for Future Studies, Indiana University, Bloomington, Indiana, 1975.

Powell, Reed M., and Charles S. Davis. "Do University Executive Development Programs Pay Off?" *Business Horizons,* XVI, No. 4, 1973, pp. 81–87.

Planty, Earl G. Senior Seminar in General Management, Program Brochure, 1976.

Schuler, Stanley. "How to Keep from Going Out of Style." *Nation's Business,* 53, No. 2, 1965, pp. 66–68, 70, 72, 74, 77.

Seibert, Eugene, Vice President, Personnel, The Parker Pen Co., personal conversation, 1974.

2

A Concept of the Learning Process and Effective Management Training

After surveying much of what has occurred in the way of management train-ing, one soon discovers that a sizeable portion of the countless number of management courses, programs, seminars, and workshops have not been as successful in producing the hoped-for improvements in managerial perfor-mance as expected. All too often, people attend management training sessions and then behave and manage just as they always have when they return to their jobs. These efforts in management training have failed, but *not* because people cannot learn to change and *not* because training cannot produce observable results. These efforts have failed for two reasons. First, those who designed the program and presented the training had only an incomplete con-cept of what management is and what it involves. And second, they employed training processes and methods that were too inadequate to bring about deep-seated change in people.

INCOMPLETE CONCEPTS OF WHAT MANAGEMENT INVOLVES

Management is a complex subject. It has not yet developed into a well-defined, structured body of knowledge as other disciplines have. At best, its principles are only generalizations. It does not have a universally accepted vocabulary. Management literature, which exists in abundance, is disjointed and frag-mented. Those who think they understand what management "really is" are only deluding themselves. They compound their idiocy when they behave as all-knowing experts on the subject and attempt to teach others how to manage and solve given management problems. In truth, we are more able to describe what management is not, and how some management concepts are faulty or incomplete, than we are to describe precisely what it is and identify all that it contains. This is one basic reason why management education is such a difficult and complex task. As a consequence, much of it is ineffectual. If management training is to be successful, those who conduct it must have a realistic understanding of what management involves. Unfortunately, most management training people have faulty and inadequate concepts of management.

Here are five of the most common ways in which people's understanding of management can be inadequate:

1. It is viewed too narrowly or one school of thought dominates.

2. It is viewed as a series of well-defined functions.

3. It is seen as a set of universal principles.

4. The contingency approach is advocated to the extreme.

5. It is seen and presented as a collection of pleasant-sounding platitudes.

One School of Thought Dominates

Professor Leavitt of Stanford University tells the story of the executive in a large corporation who, upon learning of the poor performance record of one of his production plants, employed three consulting firms to study the problem independently and recommend solutions. The first firm, which was located in a prestigious building in the best section of town and was staffed by conservatively dressed, dignified, grey-haired consultants, studied the organization, its structure, priorities, plans, and controls. Its recommendations included reorganization, new priorities, a statement of objectives, and the creation of a planning team. "If these suggestions are followed," they concluded, "the company's problem will be solved."

The second firm, which was located in the basement of a building in a poorer section of town and was staffed by individuals with advanced degrees in mathematics, operations research, and systems analysis, attacked the problem by analyzing the organization's work flow, scheduling, and use of computerized controls. Their recommendations included a revision of production schedules based on a simulation model, an advanced, computerized, quality-control procedure, and a crash course for all of the plant's managers in quantative methods. "If these procedures are followed," they concluded, "the company's problem will be solved."

The third consulting firm, which was located in a respectable but not posh section of town and was staffed by individuals with advanced degrees in psychology and the behavioral sciences, approached the problem by surveying the organization's communication networks and its employees' attitudes toward their superiors and coworkers. After reviewing these and other data, this consulting firm recommended sensitivity training and communication and interpersonal-skills workshops. "If the human interactions can become more open and authentic and if employees begin caring more about each other," they concluded, "the company's problems will be solved."

Not one of the three consulting firms was totally incorrect, yet they were all partially correct. Like the six blind men who went to see the elephant in Saxe's poem "Six Wise Men of Indostan," each consulting firm represented a different perspective of management. Each perspective had its advantages and disadvantages, but not one provided a comprehensive solution to the problem.

Just as each of the three consulting firms in this story was able to define the problem and recommend solutions only in terms of its own particular speciality and preference, so too do many management training people fall into the same trap when they design and present programs in general management. Management training that fails to provide a balance between the various schools of management thought (i.e., the management-science approach, the structural approach, and the behavioral approach) usually fails to provide trainees with the range of approaches and skills they need.* Unfortunately, attendees of "unbalanced" management programs all too often return to their jobs with the opinion that they can solve all of their management problems with the narrow body of knowledge to which they were exposed.

Management as a Series of Functions

Another deficient concept of management is that it involves the performance of a series of functions—that is, management involves merely planning, organizing, directing, and controlling. Hence, all managers will plan, organize, direct, and finally control. While this concept of management is broader than the one described previously, it has serious limitations. To be sure, the early pioneers in the field of management realized that their definitions of management as being a process of planning, organizing, directing, and controlling had limitations. This should not be taken as a criticism of their work. However, many people needlessly limit their understanding of management by constraining it with this definition. The specific criticisms of management, as being defined or conceived as a series of functions, include the following:

1.   Managing involves more than just a handful of functions. Many other activities are involved which may or may not fit into the categories of these various functions, yet they are still managerial activities (Mintzberg 1975).

---

*   The criticism here is leveled at general management courses and not at two-to-three-day seminars, which are limited to one particular area such as planning, motivation, leadership, M.B.O., communications, etc., and which have an explicit intent of improving the participants' knowledge and skills in that limited area only.

2.   All managers do not necessarily perform all of the functions and yet they are successful. The notion that managers must perform all of the functions is inconsistent with the research findings on what managers do.

3.   Managing is presented as a series of discrete functions which, when once performed, need not be reperformed. However, we know from experience that much planning, for example, is actually replanning. These functions are usually performed over and over again.

4.   This concept of managing is inconsistent with participative management approaches, which are becoming increasingly appropriate and successful. When using the functional approach, the manager plans, organizes, directs, and controls. This implies that subordinates do just what they are told. Contrary to this, participative management involves subordinates in planning and organizing and places heavy reliance on their self-direction and self-control. Thus, in these situations, managers do not do all of the planning, organizing, and controlling. Rather they see to it that these functions are accomplished.

Management Principles

Another commonly held concept of management, which is also inadequate, is that management involves a set of universal principles which are applicable and appropriate in all situations. Essentially, this concept holds that there is a right or a best way to manage, as set forth by the various principles. For example, managers should always be democratic, have close personal work relationships with their subordinates, level with everyone and encourage others to level with them, etc. This concept holds that there is a "right way" to plan, organize, and motivate. Training specialists who ascribe to this concept of management often exhibit a *messiah complex*—that is, they believe that they have the answers to all organizational problems (namely, their prescriptions for the right way to manage) and they see their mission as one of converting the "unclean heathens" to the "proper way" of managing.

Training efforts directed along this vein are nothing more than attempts to brainwash participants into believing in and practicing some set of dogmatic principles. The fallacy of all this is, of course, that there is no simple formula or best way. While these principles are often very useful, they neglect to take into consideration the unique circumstances which render them inappropriate from time to time. These so-called management principles are at best generalizations. It makes more sense to think of them as contingent principles—that is, they are generalizations that may be applied in one way or another in a situation, with due consideration given to the unique circumstances. Training efforts aimed at trying to get trainees to understand and apply dogmatic management principles are doomed to failure also because they ignore the development of diagnostic skills, which enable managers to understand situations and forecast the probable success of given actions.

Extreme Versions of the Contingency Approach

The contingency approach to management holds that managerial actions should depend on the circumstances of the situation. For example, the best style of leadership depends on the nature of the task and the people involved in the situation. This basic viewpoint is quite realistic in that it gets away from blind adherence to unbending principles. However, it is deficient insofar as it implicitly assumes that there is some best way or approach that will work. In some situations, there may not be one best managerial approach or intervention; instead there may be several that are equally good or equally bad. Moreover, some situations might be so impossible that no managerial action will work.

Extreme versions of the contingency approach state that the best approach to a management situation depends on so many factors that there are no general guidelines that managers can follow. This is the opposite extreme of the management-principles concept. When the contingency approach is followed to the extreme, finding the best way of handling a management situation becomes so important that everything is *studied* in great detail and no *action* is ever taken. If managers followed this approach, they would be so occupied with what every action depended upon that they would not have time to perform in their roles.

Pleasant-Sounding Platitudes

Some people's knowledge and understanding of management is superficial. After listening to their explanations of or lectures on management or its various aspects, the thoughtful listener soon realizes how little substance the speech actually contained. What was supposed to be a stimulating lecture was nothing more than a collection of pleasant-sounding platitudes and generalizations. The speaker did little more than entertain the audience with jokes and stories and catchy phrases and expressions, things the audience enjoyed hearing because it already believed in them. It is like saying at a police convention, "It's time to get tough on crime."

These platitudes are sound as far as they go; the trouble is that they do not go very far. They are not accompanied by in-depth explanations of what they mean and how they can be operationalized. To be useful, management theory must be comprehensive and capable of being put into practice.

A CONCEPTUAL FRAMEWORK OF THE KNOWLEDGE
AND ABILITIES NECESSARY FOR EFFECTIVE MANAGEMENT

One conceptual framework which depicts the knowledge, abilities, and skills needed by managers is presented here. This particular framework is potentially useful to training and development professionals because it does not contain the deficiencies inherent in the other concepts of management discussed earlier. It is emphasized here that this is *only one* conceptual framework of management; it is not *the one* or *the only one*. Its principal advantage over other concepts of management is that it provides a more complete identification of the critical areas and issues management training should contain and address itself to in order to be successful. This conceptual framework (Fig. 2-1) is composed of three main parts: (1) knowledge, (2) skills, and (3) personal characteristics.

Knowledge component

The knowledge component consists of (a) general knowledge, (b) technical knowledge, and (c) management knowledge. *General knowledge* contains the types of information managers might need to perform effectively in all the roles they occupy. *Technical knowledge*, while it might rightly be considered a subset of general knowledge, is designated as a separate category to emphasize its importance. Managers need technical knowledge to fulfill the technical aspects of their work. Technical knowledge includes adequate information about the organization's products and services, the methods involved in creating them, and knowledge of the managers' specialities (accounting, production, research, personnel, or whatever). *Management knowledge* can be subdivided into three areas:

1. *Management nomenclature* is a basic vocabulary of management and it includes knowledge about and a basic understanding of the concepts that compose the subject matter of management, which would include such things as line and staff, span of control, delegation, management by objectives, communication, grapevine, plans, and so on.

2. *Conceptual frameworks and models* that are useful to the understanding of the various aspects of management include such things as systems concept, planning models, Maslow's hierarchy of needs, Theory X and Theory Y, Kepner and Tregoe's problem-solving matrix, the Managerial Grid, Homan's model, Porter-Lawler's model, the accepted qualities of a goal, etc.

3. *Contingent principles* are generalizations about appropriate managerial actions and behaviors and how they would be affected by various contingencies. Contingent principles should tell how managerial actions and behavior should be modified and adapted to be appropriate in given situations. Examples of contingent principles would be statements such as the following: "In general, most managers should plan. Planning is extremely important under certain conditions (naming conditions) and probably less important under other conditions (naming conditions)." These statements would go on to tell what should be included in planning and which circumstances of a given situation should be considered.

Skills component

The skills component of the framework is composed of diagnostic skills and application skills. Diagnostic skills are primarily mental skills which are used in appraising situations, identifying their critical dimensions, determining probable consequences and the significance of the consequences of various alternative approaches, and identifying the appropriate managerial actions, etc. Application skills are performance skills which are necessary when applying management concepts or taking managerial actions. While one might know about goal setting or planning, for example, it is quite another matter to perform these activities.

Personal-characteristics component

The remaining component of the conceptual framework is the personal-characteristics component. It involves the personal attributes of an individual which enable and facilitate the performance of the diagnostic and application skills. This part of the conceptual framework might be criticized because it suggests a form of "brainwashing" in so far as it might direct training efforts at changing personal characteristics. Most thinking people will probably raise this concern. However, it is felt that the characteristics identified here are of a nature that tends to develop people in directions of greater self-determination and individual freedom. The development of these personal characteristics is not "brainwashing" or a clandestine attempt to cause people to accept a particular doctrine or to act against their best interests. Instead, these are personal characteristics that give people more insight, make them better problem solvers, help them to think and act more rationally, and help them to grow mentally and emotionally.

There are two types of personal characteristics. The first type enables and facilitates managerial diagnoses of situations. These characteristics include such things as being observant, asking, "What is going on?", the ability and inclination to take distance from oneself and to look at situations as one would analyze a case study, and being honest with oneself, etc. The second type enables and facilitates the appropriate application of contingent principles. These characteristics include such things as a belief that there is not just one best way, openness to new ideas and new methods, the ability and inclination to experiment with different ways of behaving, and the desire to learn from experience, etc.

The items depicted within the various components of this framework are not exhaustive. Many more could be added. They are, however, the principal ones within each of the areas, and they serve to identify and illustrate the nature of each and what it involves. By utilizing this conceptual framework, instructors will be much more likely to avoid the difficulties caused by the inadequate concepts of management discussed earlier. They will be able to

Knowledge provides the bases for choosing what to do.

Knowledge		
General knowledge	Technical knowledge	Management knowledge
1. Philosophy 2. Religion 3. Social Sciences 4. Language 5. Physical Sciences 6. Life Sciences 7. Fine Arts 8. Literature 9. History	1. The organization's products or services 2. The organization's methods of producing its products or services 3. Technical knowledge required to perform the job and to supervise the work of others (e.g., marketing, engineering, finance, personnel, law, research, production, etc.)	1. Management Nomenclature. A knowledge and understanding of basic management concepts (e.g., line and staff, delegation, division of labor, break-even, strategy, optimize, leadership, authority, chain of command, etc.) 2. Management Models and Conceptual Frameworks (e.g., systems concept, planning models, qualities of a good goal, Porter-Lawler model, Theory X-Theory Y, Maslow's hierarchy of needs, etc.) 3. Contingent Principles. Generalizations about management. Practices that are generally appropriate and effective under usual circumstances and a full understanding of exceptions and when and how practices must be modified to be used effectively

Fig. 2-1. A conceptual framework of the knowledge and abilities necessary for effective management.

Skills	
Diagnostic skills (thinking)	Application skills (doing)
1. Ability to read situations. To be able to understand what is going on and what the significant aspects of a situation are 2. Ability to see and understand cause-and-effect relationships in a situation. Can distinguish important from unimportant factors in a situation 3. Ability to see how self and others behave and the affects these behaviors have on others 4. Ability to perceive solvable problems and the costs and requirements of solving them 5. Ability to create alternative courses of action for handling situations and solving problems 6. Ability to perceive the probable consequences of various actions in given situations, including doing nothing, and the ability to understand the significance of each 7. Ability to choose the best alternative actions that will achieve desired results when these desired results are possible 8. Ability to arrive at accurate conclusions, given data and information	1. Ability to select and adapt managerial actions and contingent principles so that they are appropriate and effective in achieving desired results in given situations 2. Ability to apply a wide variety of contingent principles and management concepts

Personal characteristics provide the guidance and motivation for doing

Personal characteristics	
Characteristics that enable and facilitate managerial diagnoses of situations	Characteristics that enable and facilitate the appropriate application of contingent principles and management practices
1. Observant 2. Tendency to ask, "What is going on?" 3. Can take distance from self. Looks at situations involving self and analyzes them as one would analyze a case study 4. Is introspective 5. Is honest with self: recognizes own strengths, weaknesses, and shortcomings. Is objective in seeing and interpreting own behavior and the behavior of others 6. Does not believe all management problems can be solved by one school of thought. Is open to all ways of handling problems 7. Tendency to ask question, "Is this the only logical or possible conclusion that can be reached based on the data and evidences available?" 8. Asks, "What assumptions am I making? Are these assumptions correct?"	1. Believes in and is committed to the idea that there is not just one way or one best way to do things 2. Is open to new ideas and new ways of doing things 3. Experiments with new ideas and new forms of behavior. Tests reality 4. Wars on obsolesence. Keeps self mentally alive and active 5. Always learning; desires constant and timely feedback on his or her actions. Learns from his or her successes and failures

identify areas where training which is needed might otherwise be neglected, particularly in the skills and personal-characteristics areas.

Most instructors will limit training activities to management knowledge only, excluding general and technical knowledge. They do this with the assumption that managers are sufficiently knowledgeable in the other two knowledge areas. This makes good sense, generally speaking, especially in view of the fact that the time allowed for training is typically quite limited.

The thinking that underlies this conceptual framework breaks from typical concepts of management in several important ways and it includes the following propositions:

1. Management is not simply a set of normative prescriptions for behavior. There is not "one best" or "one right" way to manage. There are effective ways and ineffective ways to manage and it is the manager's task to discover or create "better ways" and to implement them.

2. There are no management principles, but there are generalizations called *contingent principles* which are useful guidelines for managers to follow in the performance of their work. They usually need to be modified and adapted to meet the unique circumstances of the situations in which they are applied.

3. Diagnostic and application skills and personal characteristics are both as important to successful management as the possession of management knowledge. Thus management training should place an emphasis on all three areas.

4. The possession of knowledge is no guarantee that it will be applied.

5. Managers' personal characteristics will determine to a large extent the degree to which and how well they diagnose situations and apply whatever knowledge they possess.

6. Managers should be able to use all three of the principle approaches to management (management sciences, behavioral sciences, and traditional administrative or structural approaches). Managers should draw upon the useful aspects of each from time to time, as each are useful and appropriate to any given situation.

7. Management is not simply a series of functions such as planning, organizing, directing, and controlling, although these are some of the things managers do. Instead, management is a creative process of continuously determining and implementing the most valuable course of action.

8. There may not always be satisfactory answers to all situations.

TRAINING PROCESSES AND METHODS
INADEQUATE TO BRING ABOUT CHANGED BEHAVIOR

[Much of what has gone on in the area of management education and training has done little more than increase people's understanding of the subject. Little of it has had a noticeable affect on their behavior. This should *not* be taken to mean that training cannot produce change or that all training has failed along these lines. Some, in fact, has been highly successful in causing observable improvements.] Why have some efforts failed and others been successful? What does it take to cause change?

[Most training efforts have merely acquainted trainees with new information and have not caused changed behavior because they have relied almost entirely on the more traditional approaches to education such as lecturing, showing and explaining, and reading. To manage is to diagnose situations and apply knowledge. It is a process of both thinking and doing. To increase a person's knowledge generally helps him or her to understand better that which he or she observes and to have an appreciation for a greater variety of management practices.] However, it does not assure that he or she can or will even want to diagnose situations and then apply management knowledge. It is one thing to know about concepts and approaches and quite another to have both the desire and ability to use them.

A few training efforts, which have taken into account the fact that skill in the application of concepts is necessary, have made provision for teaching trainees how to apply the concepts. But they too have failed because they viewed management education in a mechanistic manner. In other words, they ignored the human aspects of learning and failed to assure that the trainees accept and believe in the usefulness of what they learned. These efforts might be called the *skills approach to training*. Going one step further than traditional approaches which merely acquaint the trainee with management concepts and contingent principles, the skills approach includes: (1) having the learner practice the skill or idea; (2) providing feedback to the learner that lets her or him know how well she or he is performing the skill or applying the idea; and, (3) providing necessary information as to how to perform the skill or apply the idea more correctly where improvement is necessary. These three steps are repeated until the trainee either acquires the ability to apply the skill satisfactorily or gives up.

While it does not necessarily bring about attitude or behavioral changes, the skills approach is useful in teaching how to perform those functions or techniques to which the trainee is predisposed or at least not averse to performing—usually mechanical techniques. Just as novice sailors are probably quite willing to learn about and how to use sextants or compasses, beginning managers are likely to be willing to learn about and how to use break-even charts or PERT networks, provided they perceive them as being useful.

Like most behavior, managerial behavior is largely voluntary. The way in which a person manages, for the most part, is of his or her own choosing.* Knowledge about particular management practices is not sufficient to cause a person to apply them. Nor will a knowledge of the benefits some particular new forms of behavior be enough to cause change.

For example, a leader will not begin practicing a democratic style of supervision merely because he or she has seen the benefits it can bring. Managers will not suddenly become permissive to foster upward communications just because a training instructor tells them they should. Likewise, it is extremely unlikely for a manager to become results-oriented or achievement-minded simply because she or he has read about the benefits of management by objectives and learns how to practice this technique.

People will not attempt to practice most management approaches or apply newly learned concepts unless they hold attitudes and values that are consistent with and supportive of them. No matter how sound or useful they may seem to be, people will not be willing or able to follow new practices until they have learned about them, understood them, accepted them, and learned how to apply them.

To be effective, management training must include efforts that will cause trainees' attitudes to become consistent with and supportive of the concepts and contingent principles taught. It must also include the development of personal characteristics which will facilitate and enable managers to diagnose situations and to apply their management knowledge. Management training must address itself to the emotional and attitudinal dimensions of learning, in addition to the cognitive ones, if it is to be successful in causing changed behavior.

FOUR LEVELS OF LEARNING

Four levels of learning, which must be reached to cause voluntary and rational behavioral change, are: (1) knowing-about; (2) understanding; (3) acceptance; and (4) ability to apply. As it is used here, rational means that the individual has a solid understanding of the newly learned concepts he or she applies, including why, when, and how they should be applied. Some people, for example, learn about participative management and see it as a panacea for almost everything and as the best way to manage regardless of the situation While they accept this concept and change their behavior to practice participative management, they do so without knowing much about it. They do not know what it involves, when it is appropriate, what it demands in terms of

---

*   One's interpretation of the exact nature of this choice process will depend on where he or she lines up in the controversy brought forth by B. F. Skinner in his book, *Beyond Freedom and Dignity*, Knopf, New York, 1971.

time and superiors' or subordinates' ability, its implications to the organization, etc. They accept it, but do not understand it. This kind of behavioral change, using the word as it has been defined here, is not rational.

The four levels of learning presented here should not necessarily be construed as four successive levels, with each succeeding one being "higher" or "deeper" than the one preceding it. They should be thought of as four different types of learning. As a practical matter, however, learning typically does proceed in successive stages, beginning with *knowing-about* and ending with the *ability to apply*. As a generalization, people usually need to know about something before they can begin to understand it, to understand something before they can begin to accept it, and to accept something before they become willing to apply it.

Knowing-About

Knowing-about is a level of learning which is reached when the trainees have an awareness that some thing or concept exists; but this understanding is shallow. Their understanding of the thing or concept in question has not advanced to the point where they can use it. On a continuum representing an individual's understanding of some thing or concept, the knowing-about level would be represented as that level of understanding ranging from awareness to whatever level of understanding is necessary for the thing or concept to be of use to the person (Fig. 2-2).

The reader should thus conclude that this definition is not precise. The point on the understanding scale where the concept becomes useful is vague. How much understanding is needed before the concept is useful? What is meant by useful? In what ways is it useful? How can these things even be measured? Answers cannot be given to these questions in the abstract; and, at best, only very rough generalizations can be given in specific cases. For example, what would a person have to understand about planning before she or he could perform planning? It seems that some reasonable estimates could be made. Even though this definition and the identification of the knowing-about

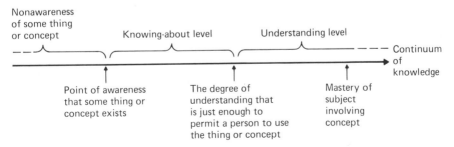

Fig. 2-2. Levels of learning: Knowing-about and understanding.

level of learning is not precise and suffers from a certain amount of ambiguity, the attempt to identify this level of learning and distinguish it from "understanding" is useful to instructors.

Understanding

Another learning level is *understanding;* it too is depicted in Fig. 2-2. It is in the range on the scale from where knowing-about ends through mastery of the concept and beyond. This definition also suffers from the same kind of inexactness as the definition of knowing-about. It is, nonetheless, useful since it tends to force instructors to specify, for each subject or concept they teach, what kinds and amounts of understanding are necessary for competent and successful usage. Two benefits are frequently associated with the effort to define knowing-about and understanding and to make a distinction between the two:

1.   It usually includes in the training giving attention to the important aspects within a subject area that are typically overlooked.

2.   It causes the instructors who design sessions and programs to think through and learn more about what they plan to teach.

Acceptance

The third level of learning, *acceptance*, is usually the most difficult to attain. It is reached when the trainee accepts the logic underlying the concepts or contingent principles and holds beliefs that are consistent or at least not averse to them. The difficult aspect often encountered in reaching this level of learning is the alteration of the trainee's values, attitudes, and beliefs so that they are more or less consistent with what is taught. This is done through the removal of incorrect assumptions, fears, doubts, mistaken beliefs, etc.

For a better understanding of what acceptance means, picture, if you will, a fairly successful manager who has practiced only one style of leadership for many years. Quite likely he or she will think that his or her method of leadership is the correct one. Any difficulties encountered in the past, he or she would probably reason, were caused simply by uncooperative people and certainly not by his or her style of leadership. Therefore, he or she is very likely to view skeptically or reject as impractical other styles of leadership to which he or she is introduced. And rightly so, as he or she sees it, for years of successful managing have reinforced his or her beliefs and habits. Thus the tell-style manager will likely view join-style leadership as abdicating all power and influence and creating chaos. Conversely, the join-style manager will most likely view the tell-style manager as a heavy-fisted personification of Captain Bligh, and perhaps even as cruel.

If trainees are presented with a choice of alternative leadership styles and have only a little knowledge about and understanding of these styles, they are not likely to accept those styles which differ from their own as being particularly useful. Supported by years of perceived success using one style, namely their own, the new style appears to be of doubtful merit. Thus the trainees are not likely to accept a new style as being useful or appropriate in any situation. Acceptance, therefore, is much more than just knowing-about and understanding. It requires intellectual and emotional understanding. Emotional understanding occurs only after attitudes, beliefs, and values are consistent with the newly learned concepts and contingent principles.

Before people are able to accept new ideas and forms of behavior, they must fully understand the underlying logic and benefits. Thinking people will not accept what they do not understand. This is particularly true when it comes to concepts that are inconsistent with currently held attitudes, values, and beliefs. In many cases, people claim that they agree with ideas or concepts and may even believe that they faithfully apply them (because they seem useful or because it is expected of them), when in fact they do not. They do not apply these ideas or concepts because they do not fully understand them intellectually and, more importantly, emotionally. In short, the concepts are not applied because they are not accepted.

Ability to Apply

The fourth level of learning, *ability to apply*, is the level of learning where individuals have the ability to diagnose situations they encounter, identify the appropriate actions or contingent principles that would be successful in these situations, modify or adapt the actions or contingent principles as necessary, and apply the principles with the necessary skills. At this level of learning, individuals have the ability to apply what they know consistently with reasonable success.

After reaching the acceptance stage of learning, most people will have the desire to apply concepts and contingent principles; however, they may not have the ability. This is often overlooked and its neglect is a major reason why many training efforts have not been successful. Some training programs bring people through the knowing-about, understanding, and even acceptance levels, but very few ever scratch the surface of the fourth level—ability to apply.

Some training efforts successfully carry people part way into the application stage of the formal training program. However, the ability to apply management concepts and contingent principles consistently and with a high degree of skill comes only through a great deal of experience and practice; generally this means on-the-job practice.

CONDITIONS FOR EFFECTIVE LEARNING

Although knowledge can be acquired in almost any psychological climate, deep intellectual and emotional understanding and acceptance of knowledge, especially new knowledge that suggests particular ways of new behavior, is reached more thoroughly and quickly in a special kind of psychological climate. Briefly, this is a climate that encourages and assists the trainees to progress through each of the four levels of learning. It is a climate in which they can assess their own values, attitudes, beliefs, and behavior openly and honestly and then choose to change in light of what they have learned about management and themselves. It is a climate in which they are not overly defensive of their own views and beliefs and will not have to constantly rationalize in order to sustain them. Rather, it is a climate that encourages active diagnoses of situations, searching for the more appropriate types of actions and behavior, willingness to experiment with these, and learning from success and failure.

The following are six principal characteristics of this learning climate:

1. Learning takes place in a group setting.

2. Openness and mutual acceptance exists between the group members and members have a strong attraction to the group.

3. The instructor is perceived by group members as being supportive and genuinely interested in their learning the concepts being taught, as well as in them as people. The instructor is enthusiastic about the concepts being taught and shows eagerness for trainees to learn them.

4. The concepts covered are sequenced in logical order and are covered at a pace that causes the acceptance of new thinking patterns and processes and the acquisition of new skills and new forms of behavior to occur gradually.

5. Trainees have a desire to know.

6. Learning is an active process. Trainees are gaining insights and making generalizations and conclusions for themselves.

Group Setting

An impactful learning environment that is conducive to changing behavior cannot, in most cases, be created for an individual in isolation. A group setting is required. When a trainee acquires new knowledge alone and is not interacting with others (for example, by reading or listening to a lecture), she or he does not have the opportunity to examine her or his own views or behavior to see where and how they are appropriate or inappropriate.

In a group setting, such as a small discussion group, individuals have the opportunity to check out their thinking with that of others, to examine their own values, beliefs, and behavior, to learn from others, and to gain a richer and deeper understanding of management concepts and contingent principles. In a group setting, individuals can see their own management styles, how they manage, and the validity and usefulness of various other management approaches which they may or may not understand, accept, or have the ability to apply. By so doing, they will most likely become prepared and willing to experiment with new ideas and different forms of behavior for the following reasons:

1. The informal atmosphere of a small group provides individuals with feelings of acceptance. In this nonthreatening environment, the trainees are with people who have similar problems at work and about equal levels of understanding of the various methods that can be used to resolve them.

2. People, even those who are not inclined to speak out, usually contribute freely in small group discussions. This occurs for a number of reasons including the following:

a) Each person is encouraged to speak and contribute ideas—formal role expectation.

b) The fear of inviting disapproval by disagreeing with the formal leader (the instructor) is absent because the instructor is not present, or, if he is, remains silent.

c) It is easier to contribute ideas in a small group than in a large group. In a large group, speakers generally feel they must speak in complete sentences or series of sentences, which form a logically sequenced presentation of a concept. In a small group setting, this feeling is not so strong and one can observe less formality in presentations of individual viewpoints.

d) In small group discussions, individuals speak voluntarily. They are not called upon to answer questions, but volunteer their thoughts as they seem appropriate.

3. Individuals are able to check out the validity and usefulness of their ideas and viewpoints in a supportive climate. Alone, the individual's thinking is typically protected from doubt and question and eventual change because it is not questioned or challenged. The individual voicing an opinion in a small discussion group usually receives feedback and, as a result, is able to understand where his or her thinking is agreeable and not agreeable with the thinking of others. Learning alone, the individual does not come face to face with expressed innermost thoughts and feelings. This does occur in the small group, which can reflect the thoughts and feelings for the individual to see.

4.   The usefulness of various management contingent principles becomes apparent more quickly when they are taught and discussed in small group settings than when the individual merely hears or reads about them. This is because contingent principles can be examined in light of the experiences of many individuals. Strong testimonials as to their usefulness, especially from one's peers, is perhaps the most powerful method for bringing about their acceptance by others. This is lateral learning, which sociologists and psychologists say affects our behavior and how we learn most of what we know.

An Atmosphere of Openness and Mutual Acceptance

An atmosphere of openness and mutual acceptance which protects group members from intolerable embarrassment and from the fear of rejection by others should exist in order to bring about the acceptance level of learning and changed behavior. In general, this openness and mutual acceptance comes when group members accept one another for who they are and when they level with each other. The leveling process involves openly expressing thoughts and feelings directly for others to view, consider, and react to honestly. When leveling, people are honest with each other.

Provided that the topics covered in a training program are relevant to the interests of the participants and provided that they understand what they are expected to do in the small group discussions, these group discussions will become attractive. Through the open exchange of ideas in such a setting, each person will become more strongly attracted to that group. Moreover, each person will sense that the others accept him or her as a member, since each has performed the necessary step of leveling to become a group member. But leveling by itself will not assure mutual acceptance. This can occur only if the leveling occurs in a group that has a permissive atmosphere as one of its norms. When this exists, all group members feel that they are fully accepted as individuals and are permitted to hold the views they do and express them without fear of rejection by others in the group. Openness and mutual acceptance are perhaps the most difficult aspects of a good learning climate to create.

When an atmosphere of openness and mutual acceptance exists in a group, its members feel that they are accepted as individuals. Each feels secure even though the views he or she expresses may not be in accord with those held by other members. Nonetheless, each person will be listened to and accepted as a person and a member of the group. The others will not only accept the individual, but will also try to understand his or her point of view. They are permissive because they allow the individual to hold whatever views he or she does. As a result, the individual feels no fear of rejection. Moreover, knowing that he or she is accepted, the individual can accept self. For some unknown reason, this frees the individual to begin to examine his or her own views and beliefs more thoroughly, openly, and honestly, and then to possibly choose to change. This kind of climate is no guarantee that an individual will choose to change, but it does not contain the barriers which typically prevent people from choosing to change—namely, rationalization and the need to protect one's self-image.

The group can also be a very powerful device for drawing its dissonant members toward its way of thinking. As the group bonds of mutual understanding strengthen and the leveling process deepens, the group becomes increasingly attractive because it meets a basic human need, that of belonging and feeling accepted. Through the ongoing exchanges of interpersonal encounters in the form of sharing ideas and experiences, particular viewpoints and values will emerge and become identified as being the group's opinion. Continued group membership then requires the acceptance of its explicitly held values and viewpoints for continued membership in good standing. The need to belong and remain a group member in good standing is often a powerful motivator, which causes dissonant members to adjust their thinking in order to conform to that of the group. Of course, if the dissonant holds views that are too different from those held by the group, she or he is likely to leave or become an isolate.

The Instructor

The trainees' perception of the instructor is also important to the learning process. The instructor should be accepted by the group if changes in thinking and behavior are to occur. The instructor should be viewed by all as one who is genuinely interested in the personal growth and enhancement of each trainee, who contributes to the group's well being, and who is supportive. A great bond of trust should exist between the group and the instructor. If these conditions exist, the instructor will be permitted by the group members to uncover new horizons of intellectual and emotional knowledge and growth, to help them to understand this knowledge, and to encourage them to accept this new knowledge by challenging their thinking, leveling with them, and reflecting the stands they take so that they can better understand themselves.

Some form of friendship should exist between the instructor and the trainees. The instructor will never be perceived as just another group member by participants, and should not try to project her/himself in this fashion. Neither should the instructor remain aloof or totally apart from the group. He or she is part of the group and plays a significant role in it. The instructor's influence on the trainees depends, to a large extent, on how they feel about him or her. If the instructor remains aloof, for example, he or she will nearly always become shut off from the group and will eventually be rejected by it. As a result, the instructor will not be able to influence the group members' thinking and beliefs, and they will not permit him or her to expose them to or enlarge their understanding of new insights and concepts. One good way for friendship to be established quickly is for the instructor to level with the trainees. In so doing, the instructor sets the pattern for them to follow as they level with each other in their group discussion sessions. If the instructor is honest and sincere, the trainees will respect and trust his or her thinking as being acceptable. They will strive to learn and will try to understand his or her point of view. Moreover, in this kind of climate, trainees will start to examine their values and beliefs more deeply and honestly than they might have otherwise.

People rarely become excited and enthusiastic over anything that appears dull. The instructors' lack of enthusiasm for their subjects is one common reason why teachers of adult-education programs fail to capture and motivate their students to learn.

Sequence and Timing of Concepts

Much of good management training involves the alteration of fixed values and attitudes which are held to some extent by all people participating in the training program. It is essential, therefore, that a program's content, sequence, and timing be such that the group will be able to change its collective, articulated beliefs and attitudes at a comfortable pace, so that the group will not become alienated from the program's aims and those who teach it. Many of the more advanced and sophisticated management concepts, particularly those in the behavioral area, cannot be appreciated or accepted unless the group fully understands and accepts the more basic concepts and has attitudes and beliefs consistent with these. When the pace of a program is such that it introduces trainees to advanced concepts quickly, before they have thoroughly understood and accepted the elementary concepts upon which the advanced ones are built, or when concepts are taught out of sequence, it is very possible that the learners will reject not only the concepts, but also the program and all who are directly associated with it. They reject the advanced concepts because they are perceived as being foolish and impractical.

This potential problem is much greater with first-level supervisory groups than it is with high-level management. Thus, because attitudes change slowly, it is important for the training to bring the group's knowledge to new levels gradually, one step at a time. One must also be sensitive to the attitudes and thinking expressed by learners at the training program and develop a feeling for the progress being made. Necessary adjustments in the program will vary from group to group and should suggest themselves to alert and thinking instructors.

A Desire to Know

A very important condition that is necessary in order for learning to occur is that the trainees' attention be focused on that which is to be learned. This thought is carried one step further and is included as the fifth characteristic of a desirable learning climate. The trainees should feel a need to know what is being presented. Most people seem to learn faster when they have a desire to know something. Therefore, it becomes important for instructors to present their material in such a way that trainees have a strong desire to know more about the subject and, as a result, will be highly motivated to learn about it.

Learning is an Active Process

Suppose that a large number of randomly selected people were asked, "What is the most penetrating and long-lasting learning experience you have ever had?" Suppose that their responses were categorized into one of the following two groups:

1. I was actively involved in doing something.

2. I was passive.

At least 99 percent of the responses would fall into the first category. Learning is more penetrating and longer lasting when trainees are actively involved —that is, when they are thinking, discussing, sharing, criticizing, solving problems, making decisions, and formulating conclusions and generalizations. An *active process* is one where learning occurs in conjunction with first-hand experience, which can include everyday experiences that take place at home and at work, as well as contrived experiences that take place in the classroom.

A number of research experiments which have investigated the relative effectiveness of various training methods provide further evidence that active trainee involvement is more impactful than passive trainee involvement. For example,

1. Group discussion is more effective than lectures in producing attitude changes in individuals.

2. Group discussion is more effective than reading in producing attitude changes in individuals.

3. The case-study method is more effective than the lecture method in producing gains in learning achievement and in modifying beliefs.

4. The case-study method is more effective than the lecture method in producing an understanding of the topics of goal setting and communications. The case-study method is also more effective than the lecture method in teaching trainees how to apply goal setting and leadership-skills motivation tools, communication, and new approaches in implementing change (Watson, 1975).

5. Laboratory training produces more behavior change in the areas of interpersonal relations and group dynamics than lectures do.

In addition to its relative effectiveness, active learning produces other important benefits. It helps people to develop many of the necessary diagnostic skills and some of the personal characteristics discussed earlier.

REACHING THE FOUR LEVELS OF LEARNING

There are, of course, many ways of causing learning to occur. To say that there is "a best way" would be incorrect. Moreover, it is equally wrong to think that the learning process and the procedures for affecting learning can be described in detail. With these cautions specified, readers should be able to understand and place into perspective the following suggestions and guidelines for causing learning to occur. These suggestions and recommendations, although strongly stated, describe in a very general sense an approach that works. This approach is based on many years of first-hand experience of a number of successful training professionals. The unique feature of this approach is that it speaks to the issue of causing each of the four levels of learning to occur, separately. This feature is helpful since different approaches are needed to cause each of the four levels of learning to occur.

Reaching the Knowing-About Level

In comparison to the other learning levels, the knowing-about level is relatively easy to reach. Perhaps the most direct and easiest ways of causing the knowing-about level to occur are by lecturing and reading. These are the methods most often used in management training. However, these methods are used almost exclusively by some training people and they fail to change behavior because, if training is to be changeful, it cannot stop at the knowing-about level. The other three levels must be reached as well. The likelihood of this happening is influenced by how the trainee arrives at the first level and his or her feelings about that which is being learned.

Specifically, trainees should sense two things as they reach the knowing-about level, which will serve as stimuli to advancement through the other three levels:

1. They should have a good idea of the probable consequences when the contingent principle being taught is not applied or is applied incorrectly in a given situation. They should also have a good idea of the probable consequences when the contingent principle being taught is applied correctly. That is, they should have some appreciation for the value or usefulness of the concept or contingent principle being taught.

2. They should have a good idea of the degree to which they understand and accept the concept. The realization of ignorance, especially ignorance of something that is important and potentially useful, is the starting point

not only for gaining wisdom, but also for becoming more successful than they already are—the source of the motivation to want to learn it.

Effective training brings people to the knowing-about level with the attitude, "I want to know more about this concept or contingent principle so that I can apply it successfully and cause the results I desire to occur." But how can this be done?

These two conditions are not likely to occur merely through hearing or reading about management concepts and contingent principles. Generally, after hearing or reading about management concepts and contingent principles, practicing managers and supervisors will nod their heads and say to themselves, "Yes, that is right," or they will shake their heads and say, "No, that is wrong." They will think to themselves, "I do that already," or, "I'd never consider doing that because my present methods are quite sound and appropriate." But, all too often, the truth of the matter is that these people either do not understand, accept, or apply what they think they do. Or they have an incorrect perception of what it is they are learning and reject it as being unsound because of their limited experience with and shallow understanding of it. When an individual thinks that he or she knows and understands something sufficiently well and rejects it for whatever reason, he or she will not be inclined to learn more about it. To this individual, to do so would simply be a waste of time and effort.

Training methods such as case studies, role-playing, management games, in-basket exercises, and simulations can cause the knowing-about level to occur and at the same time bring about these two conditions. It is recommended, therefore, that one or more of these methods be used first in the scheme of events designed to teach management concepts because they can both introduce trainees to new concepts and can demonstrate their usefulness and the degree to which trainees understand, accept, and possess the ability to apply them. Training methods that achieve these ends should precede explanations, lectures, and reading assignments so that trainees can gain wisdom in a way that has direct relevance to them—namely, through some type of experience followed by reflection on that experience. This is the approach by which diagnostic skills and personal characteristics are developed. Coming next in the scheme of things used to stimulate, foster, expand, and enrich understanding are explaining, reading and clarifying. These direct, information-conveying techniques should only be used when trainees are ready and willing to listen with interest and feel a need to know more. Explaining, reading, and clarifying are excellent techniques and can do a great deal to further knowledge and understanding, but they are only effective when the trainees are eager to know more.

Consider the following illustration of what is being advocated here. For example, instead of teaching goal-setting techniques by giving a straightforward, information-conveying type talk or by having trainees read the material, use an inductive approach. Start with a case that shows a situation beset with problems that are caused primarily because management has failed to establish goals or has done so incorrectly. Have trainees describe and diagnose the situation and try to come to understand why these problems exist. Let them discover for themselves that the problems in the case are caused by a lack of goals. Or, use a game played by two teams to achieve a similar learning experience. Have the two teams work on similar projects or activities where productivity can be measured. Set the game up so that one team has definite goals while the other team has none. Then, after a predetermined amount of time, have the two teams stop work and compare their outputs. Leave it up to the trainees to identify the differences in production and discover the reasons for them.

At first, the trainees will diagnose the situations in a very elementary and superficial fashion, as they do not have a full understanding of why there is a cause-and-effect relationship between outcomes and particular managerial actions in given situations. They will not understand how the cause-and-effect relationships operate. In some cases, trainees will barely make the connection, and, when they do, they may even be a bit unsure of the accuracy of the connection. This should not be discouraging to instructors. These weaknesses will be remedied as the other levels of learning are reached. The important thing is that level one should be reached in such a way that the trainees want to learn more.

Reaching the Understanding Level

The understanding level was previously defined as being a point at which the degree of understanding of a concept was just enough for it to be useful. To be more explicit, the understanding level, as it is defined here, is reached when two conditions exist:

1. The trainee knows why there is a cause-and-effect relationship between the correct or appropriate application of a concept or contingent principle given in a situation and the probable outcome. She or he also knows how this cause-and-effect relationship operates.

2. The trainee knows the theory underlying the concept or contingent principle sufficiently well to be able to modify or adapt it, thus making it appropriate for most given situations.

When they reach the understanding level, it is important for trainees to know the following two things, which will help motivate them to advance through the acceptance and ability-to-apply levels of learning: (1) how the application of the concept or contingent principle being learned can be helpful to them; and (2) how well they know and the extent to which they already use the concept or contingent principle.

One successful approach for effectively advancing the learning process to the understanding level and for causing trainees to realize these two additional things is by creating a situation that permits trainees to discover truths and make generalizations for themselves. This is a successful approach for a number of reasons:

1. People can understand new ideas only from their own frame of reference.

2. People understand things more fully and deeply when they discover them for themselves than when they just hear about them.

3. People remember those things which they discover for themselves longer than those things which they have merely been told about.

To reach a level of deep understanding, then, learning should be trainee-centered, not instructor-centered, which means that although the instructor is the one who establishes and manages the learning conditions, the trainees are the ones who are responsible for teaching themselves through a process of self-discovery. Instead of merely telling, the instructor arranges conditions and inspires the trainees so that they discover truths for themselves. Trainees actively discover new insights by making sense out of case studies, experiences, articles, and research findings and then arriving at their own conclusions and generalizations. This entire process of self-discovery learning can be accelerated and made richer if it is carried out in small groups. When people learn in a group, they help each other learn and clarify the new knowledge acquired. In this setting, individuals can usually see, not only how the new knowledge has meaning for them, but also how it has meaning for their peers.

The basic format of self-discovery learning is for groups to share some common experience which, together, they will analyze, discuss, and ascribe meaning to later. A learning experience may involve a case study, a role-playing exercise, an in-basket case, a management game, a management problem, etc. It is something concrete. Based upon this experience, trainees follow an inductive process and arrive at their own conclusions and generalizations. Explanations, lectures, and reading assignments follow to provide additional insight and understanding to trainees about their conclusions and generalizations. Trainees are made aware of when and where the contingent principles they have discovered will or will not hold true. And they are provided with research evidence and life experiences which provide further proof of the validity of their conclusions and how the contingent principles learned may be applied.

Some believe that case studies should not come first in the learning process. They see case studies not as a vehicle for self-discovery, but as a place where students can learn how to apply the truths or contingent principles they have acquired by means of a lecture or by reading. While this approach may seem logical on the surface, it is based on a fallacious assumption—namely, the assumption that learning is equivalent to being taught and anything that is presented logically and clearly will automatically be understood. When used in this way and when following formal lectures, case-study assignments usually degenerate into childish exercises.

The real value of the inductive approach (and this is what the case-study method was originally designed to be) lies in having trainees discover contingent principles and make generalizations for themselves through their own reasoning and discussions with others. The approach causes trainees to sense how the concept can be useful and it lets them realize the extent to which they already use the concept. Instructors help to stimulate this kind of learning by asking participants to think through, discuss, and answer specific, carefully written questions about a case study or whatever experience they are asked to understand and reflect upon. Structured guidance such as this can lead the trainees to the acquisition of particular insights which are relevant and important. It is also necessary for instructors to choose cases that are appropriate to the level and sophistication of the trainees.

The important thing is that case studies precede the formal lectures; otherwise, diagnostic skills and important personal characteristics may never be developed as they should. This is true for all levels of management from the president to first-level supervisors. Individuals in various levels of management do not learn in different ways. The basic learning format should be the same for all levels.

Consider the following illustration of how this inductive approach might be implemented to reach the understanding level. First, suppose that the trainees have reached the knowing-about level. They know that some concept exists. And suppose that they have reached this level in such a way as to have some knowledge of the probable consequences when the concept is applied appropriately and when it is applied incorrectly or not applied at all. Suppose further that the trainees sense, more or less, the extent of their understanding and acceptance of the concept. Finally, suppose that they want to know more.

A case study that depicts an organization beset with problems because of a lack of goals is used. The trainees are asked, "What are the problems and why are they caused?" After answering the questions, the knowing-about level and the conditions that accompany it should be reached. Effort should next be directed at reaching the understanding level.

This might be accomplished by having the trainees answer questions such as the following.

1. Why is whatever you claim is causing the problem doing so?

2. How is it doing it?

3. What managerial action(s) would prevent, thwart, or eliminate the problem identified?

4. Why and how would the action(s) you suggest do this?

To answer these questions, trainees will have to draw upon their own knowledge and experience and upon information contained in resource reading materials. They will most likely be more receptive to lectures about goals, goal setting, and the value of goals.

After these questions have been answered and discussed and lecture materials have been presented, the next step might be to provide trainees with a sense of how the concept or contingent principle could be useful to them and to have them see how and the extent to which they already use this knowledge. This could be accomplished through classroom discussion and probing questioning by the instructor. It might also be accomplished in a much more dramatic and impactful manner such as by having trainees participate in some kind of management-simulation exercise. Such an exercise might require the trainees to work as a team to produce a product, make a decision, or perform some ill-defined function. The instructor could observe whether the trainees saw a need to set goals and whether they actually did set goals. The type and quality of the goals set, if at all, could be examined too. By reflecting on what occurred in the exercise, trainees would obtain first-hand feedback as to the extent to which and how well they established goals.

Reaching the Acceptance Level

The acceptance level of learning is perhaps the most difficult one to achieve. To a very large extent it involves having trainees reject long-held, firm attitudes and beliefs which prevent them from trying out new forms of managerial behavior. For most people, this kind of change is possible but difficult, slow, and often psychologically painful. Some people are more prone to making this kind of change than others. Some may never change. It is important for instructors to be aware of this and to devote their attention and effort to where it will have the most impact—i.e., to those people who are least rigid and most likely to accept new attitudes and beliefs.

Knowing about and understanding a concept does not guarantee that it will be accepted. Sometimes the rejection of a concept or contingent principle is voiced honestly and openly. Very often, however, the rejection is voiced subtly. In such cases people might say, "Oh, yes, this concept is true and useful. I manage this way all the time," while deep down they reject it because it is contrary to their firmly held attitudes, values, and beliefs. So they reject it by cutting it off at the point of application and they rationalize by saying, "It won't work in my job because things are different there."

Acceptance is reached when people's values, attitudes, and beliefs are not so strongly contrary to a concept or contingent principle that they prevent them from attempting to use what they know about and understand.

One successful approach for reaching the acceptance level might be labeled *self-confrontation,* which operates as follows: Trainees are placed in a situation in which they are asked to take a stand, make a choice, or arrive at some conclusion, which then becomes a focal point for analysis. The analysis leads to the identification of one or more of the trainees' attitudes, values, or beliefs which affected their choices initially. Under the right conditions and through this approach, it is possible to discover the concepts and contingent principles that the trainees accept and those which they reject because, as the trainees perceive them, they are either consistent with or contrary to their values, attitudes, and beliefs. Self-confrontation can also occur when a person takes a stand, makes a statement, or takes an action spontaneously and not in response to a direct question or contrived situation. In both situations, this process involves having the trainees examine their actions, stands, decisions, and themselves to discover and understand more fully their own values, attitudes, and beliefs. Ultimately, most people undergoing this experience will determine for themselves the appropriateness or desirability of their own particular attitudes, values, and beliefs.

The process of reflecting, which also occurs through leveling, may be done by an instructor, one's peers within a group, or both. Each source has its own strengths and limitations. When reflecting is done by a competent instructor, that which is reflected is usually accurate. It is usually done deliberately, so that it is pertinent to that which is being taught. When reflecting is done by a peer, it is likely to be done spontaneously and haphazardly and without regard for any particular learning objective. However, reflecting that is done by peers is often perceived as being less threatening and is better accepted than if it were done by an instructor.

The process of reflecting to people their stands, decisions, and actions should not be attempted by an amateur instructor. There is no place for cruelty in this process either. People are often quite unaware of how their behavior is felt or interpreted by others. Thus reflections can be revealing and also shocking to those who see, for the first time, how others perceive them and respond to their actions. This very often challenges people's self-images and, because healthy people strive to think well of themselves, causes them either to feel hurt or become hostile or both. The hostility will usually be directed at the source of the reflecting. Instructors must accept these hurt and hostile feelings as natural. Actually they are desirable because they signal that the person has seen and understood that which has been reflected.

If a person feels that the instructor, or the person who did the reflecting, understands and has an acceptance and appreciation of his or her hurt or hostile feelings, he or she will begin to change. The process of accepting and understanding other people's feelings and letting them know it releases the forces which have prevented them from changing, thus enabling them to select to change.

Consider the following illustration of how this approach might be implemented. Suppose that the concept being taught is leadership styles. And suppose that the trainees have reached both the knowing-about and the understanding levels. Now the task is to get the trainees to accept the validity and usefulness of all the styles, as each might be appropriate to given situations. This will essentially involve getting the *autocratic* managers to *reject* attitudes, values, and beliefs that prevent them from using the participative leadership styles and getting the *democratic* managers to *change* attitudes, values, and beliefs that prevent them from using authoritarian styles. The ultimate objective in this particular situation is to get the trainees to accept the idea that all the styles can be useful and that they should practice each style when appropriate, instead of only the one or two they are in the habit of using. One approach to this might involve the following:

1. The trainees take a self-administered diagnostic test to identify their most dominant leadership style. From this, the trainees would become more consciously aware of their style and the values and perceptions that support it.

2. The trainees engage in a management game or a series of role-playing exercises during which their behaviors are observed. The trainees then analyze their behavior to see for themselves where and how their leadership styles are or are not effective. It should be pointed out to the trainees when problems resulted because they used an inappropriate style. This not only permits trainees to have an even greater appreciation of cause-and-effect relationships between the style they use and the results caused by it, but it also allows them to become more aware of their own behaviors and the consequences of them. More importantly, it causes the trainees to question some of their assumptions, attitudes, and approaches.

3. The trainees study a case which requires a stand, decision, or action. The instructor reflects back to the trainees what they chose, decided, or did, and classifies it in terms of a leadership style. For example, in a given case situation the instructor would ask the trainees how they would handle it. The instructor would then examine one or several responses, which may be written on a chalkboard, and ask, "Would these answers be likely to come from a laissez-faire, an autocratic, or a democratic manager?" He might even go further and ask the group to speculate as to what the probable consequences of the various answers might be. The first question is useful for allowing trainees to see themselves. The second question leads to greater insight as to cause-and-effect relationships and also causes trainees to question the appropriateness of their values, attitudes, and beliefs.

4. The group discusses what has occurred in 1, 2, and 3 above. This accomplishes several things:

  a) it allows people to vent feelings caused by seeing themselves;

  b) it permits trainees to learn from each other about the usefulness of the leadership styles that are different from their own (thus autocratic managers learn from democratic managers how they are successful in particular situations and vice versa);

c) it gives the instructor an opportunity to restate the comments made by trainees so that they can see their feelings and attitudes more clearly. For example, a trainee might make the comment, "The boss in the case should have exercised tighter control." The instructor should pick up on this comment and restate it, perhaps more dramatically, "What I hear you saying is the boss should really take charge." Then, putting her/himself in the role of the boss, the instructor might continue the reflecting process and act out what the trainee has recommended for the boss depicted in the case. (Instructor playing the part of the boss in the case.) "We don't have time for dilly-dallying. Someone has to call the shots around here and its going to be me. Now, let's not hear any back talk. When I give an order it will be obeyed—or else!"

While doing this, the instructor must be perceived as being supportive of the trainees and genuinely interested in them as people. If trainees perceive the instructor in this light and not as someone who is being cruel to them for no reason, they will listen and accept what he or she is reflecting and the materials being taught.

Repeated reflecting on stands the individual trainee takes is the key to bringing about acceptance because it allows the trainee to see for her/himself how well she or he understands, believes, and applies management concepts and contingent principles. Full acceptance is probably never reached by only one reflection. Generally, the reflecting has to be repeated several times before people truly begin to accept the principle to an extent that will cause them to conscientiously apply it on their own. The reflecting process is impactful since it permits trainees to learn about themselves more fully than if they were learning from lectures or reading. This cycle is depicted in Fig. 2–3.

Reaching the Ability-to-Apply Level

Ability-to-apply level requires that the trainees have knowledge, self-confidence, and a willingness to try. Much of the knowledge required to apply management concepts and contingent principles can be acquired at the formal training program, as can some self-confidence and willingness. However, the fine, subtle points of the ability to apply concepts and principles completely and properly can be acquired only on the job. These are gained through practice as trainees discover what works best in their particular situations. The trainees' self-confidence and willingness to try, when encouraged by supervisors, will begin to grow rapidly as a result of successful application.

People returning to the job from a training program face several formidable challenges—the challenge to adequately understand and believe in the concepts and contingent principles they learned; the challenge to keep their minds active and constantly aware of and sensitive to the situations in which they should apply what they learned; the challenge to believe that the concepts

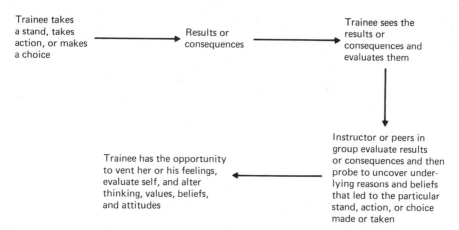

Fig. 2-3. The reflecting process.

and contingent principles they know, understand, and accept will really work on their jobs; and the challenge posed by the sometimes negative, possibly hostile attitudes of bosses, employees, and even peers toward their newly acquired knowledge and their desire to apply it. Each of these challenges must be overcome if the trainees are to apply successfully what they know and believe in. The ways in which the ability-to-apply level can be reached will be discussed further in Chapter 7.

SUMMARY

The process of learning new ways to manage is complex. It requires more than appealing to people's logic as traditional education does. Rather, it requires a *total approach,* which includes altering values, attitudes, and beliefs, in addition to systematically supplying logical information in the form of data, facts, theories, procedures, rules, principles, axioms, and points-of-view. Thus, in addition to the logical and rational aspects, there is the emotional aspect to learning. Management training can be successful and bear worthwhile results in the form of behavioral change by employing this total approach.

Some people might feel that this approach amounts to a type of brain-washing aimed at manipulating trainees to accept some given set of principles or techniques. It is not this at all. Rather, this approach is truly educational since it helps trainees become better able to diagnose situations, to understand themselves and others, to enlarge their range of behaviors, to break out of fixed patterns of behavior, and to become better able to apply a wide range of contingent principles.

REFERENCES

Mintzberg, Henry. "The Manager's Job: Folklore and Fact." *Harvard Business Review*, 53, No. 4, 1975, pp. 49–61.

Shepard, Herbert A., and Bennis, Warren G. "A Theory of Training by Group Methods." *Human Relations*, IX, No. 4, 1956, pp. 403–414.

Watson, Charles E. "The Case-Study Method and Learning Effectiveness." *College Student Journal*, 9, No. 2, 1975, pp. 109–116.

3

Identifying Needs and Formulating Training Objectives

Most managers could probably improve the ways in which they perform their jobs. Moreover, there are probably many ways in which managers could improve their job performance; however, economical use of time and resources would scarcely permit this. Thus the accurate identification of the most important training needs is of great value because it pinpoints those particular areas where improvement is most needed. For example, accounting managers who know relatively little about their technical field, but who are extremely able managers otherwise, could likely improve performance most by acquiring more knowledge about their technical area (accounting) than by improving their knowledge and abilities in an area in which they are already competent. Managers who are highly competent in their technical field, but who are totally lost when it comes to such things as establishing priorities, planning, leading others, motivating, and communicating, will improve most through learning these skills. In other words, they might be technically proficient, but complete failures as managers. Quite obviously, then, these managers could improve most by learning how to manage.

The belief that management training should always include a particular topic because "it is important" or "every manager should know it," all too frequently leads to an ill-directed training effort. For even if there were unlimited funds and resources, which could be made available for training, and if there were an adequate amount of time that could be devoted to it, the need for training-effort efficiency would still exist. Training for the sake of training is unjustified. The expenditure of resources for training can be justified only as long as the economic and social benefits derived exceed the resources spent.

Management training is most efficient when the social and economic benefits maximally exceed the value of the resources spent. This should be the primary aim of all management-training professionals.

A CONCEPTUAL FRAMEWORK OF THE NEEDS-IDENTIFICATION PROCESS

A thorough and accurate assessment of needs must precede the design of a training intervention so that it can assist managers in improving in the areas that need it most. One approach, depicted by Fig. 3-1, encompasses the following six major steps.

Step 1 The first step involves a study of the factors external to the positions held by the persons identified for training. These factors include the dominant characteristics of the firm and its industry, as well as the values, heritage, and practices that are characteristic of and that influ-

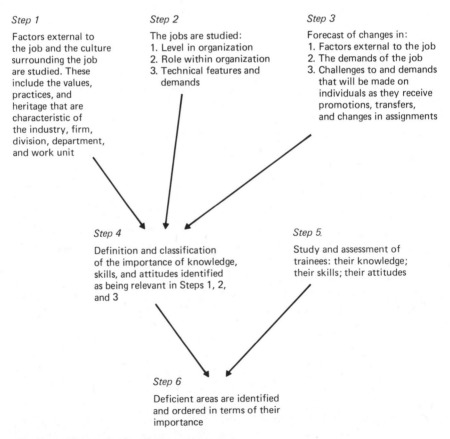

Step 1

Factors external to the job and the culture surrounding the job are studied. These include the values, practices, and heritage that are characteristic of the industry, firm, division, department, and work unit

Step 2

The jobs are studied:
1. Level in organization
2. Role within organization
3. Technical features and demands

Step 3

Forecast of changes in:
1. Factors external to the job
2. The demands of the job
3. Challenges to and demands that will be made on individuals as they receive promotions, transfers, and changes in assignments

Step 4

Definition and classification of the importance of knowledge, skills, and attitudes identified as being relevant in Steps 1, 2, and 3

Step 5.

Study and assessment of trainees: their knowledge; their skills; their attitudes

Step 6

Deficient areas are identified and ordered in terms of their importance

Fig. 3-1. The needs-identification process.

ence and are perpetuated by the industry, firm, division, department, or work unit of which they are a part. In other words, this step considers the principal characteristics of the industry and involves an overall assessment of the culture of the training population. As it is used here, *culture* refers to orientations to environmental stimuli which are (1) learned, (2) shared by others in the organization, (3) transmitted between organizational members to perpetuate their influence and to new members of the organization, and (4) symbolically derived. There are arbitrary relationships between stimuli and meanings. These orientations to environmental stimuli (the culture) must lend themselves to objective measurement.

The kinds of information gained in Step 1 include such things as the following.

1.   An assessment of the principal characteristics of the firm and the industry to which the training population belongs, including such things as the size of the firm and the industry, their growth and profitability, the markets served, the diversification of the firm, the raw materials used and their availability, the technology of the industry, the capital investment required, etc.

2.   Identification of the norms of the training population. Do they value openness, competition, quality, change? What are the accepted standards for behavior? What type of behavior is rewarded and reinforced positively? What type of behavior receives negative sanctions?

3.   An estimation of the ways in which the values, heritage, practices, etc. are consistent or inconsistent with various management concepts and contingent principles. For example, in the teaching of leadership, various leadership styles are usually covered. These range from laissez-faire to autocratic to participative management. Participative management has been found to work quite well in many instances; however, it might fail where it is strongly inconsistent with a culture. In an experiment with participative management in a Norwegian factory, it was learned that this style of management was not as successful in boosting morale and productivity as it had been in the United States partly because of different expectations held by the Norwegian workers, who did not view their participation as a proper way to behave. They functioned well under directive leadership. They expected it, but they did not get it. As a result they were unable to function productively under democratic leadership.

4.   A determination of the general characteristics of the people who find the particular culture comfortable and satisfying. For example, perhaps the culture being studied is found to be a relatively stable and risk-free one, where role expectations are well defined. If people are risk-avoiders, procedure-followers, or bureaucrats, and are uncomfortable with change, they will most likely adapt well to this type of culture.

5.   An assessment of what the members of the organization should know and the attitudes and beliefs they should hold to function effectively in the organization or a subunit of it.

Step 2   The second step involves an assessment of the positions occupied by those identified for training. The principal question to be answered here is, "What knowledge, attitudes, and skills should the incumbents possess in order to perform their jobs successfully?" Some of the important factors to consider in attempting to answer this question are the following: the level of the jobs involved (e.g., chief executive, executive, upper-middle, middle, lower-middle, first-line supervisory); the nature of the role played by the person in the position within the organization (e.g., line or staff); and the technical areas the position involves (e.g., sales, accounting, production, personnel, research, etc. or static, changing, or rapidly changing technology).

Consider the following examples of how an analysis of these three factors can provide insights that will be helpful in answering the principal question asked in this step.

Level of job as an influence

Key policymakers of large organizations should have a broad range of knowledge of the social, political, and economic forces which make up the external environment of their organization. Other key executives who occupy positions at lower levels in the organization's hierarchy are generally not so concerned with as broad a range of external factors as those above them. They may need to be knowledgeable in only a few areas. The amount of knowledge of the firm's external environment required of those at successively lower levels typically is less and less.

George Terry has attempted to show in Fig. 3–2 the relative extent to which managers at various levels need to have knowledge and skill in three areas. According to Terry (1977, p. 9),

> Managerial jobs at the top organizational level usually necessitate relatively more human and conceptual knowledge and skill than technical knowledge and skill, but at the lower organizational level the need is for more technical and human and less conceptual knowledge and skill.

Role within the organization as an influence

A maintenance supervisor with 40 people reporting directly to him or her will most likely need to be more proficient in establishing and communicating specific goals and following up with various control techniques to assure high levels of productivity than a supervisor on a production line with only a handful of immediate subordinates whose roles, responsibilities, and duties are known and understood and are relatively unchanging.

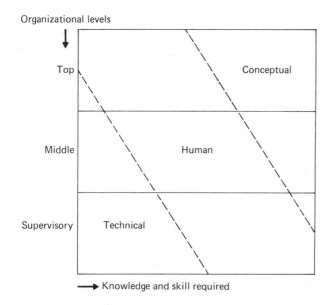

Organizational levels

Fig. 3-2. Knowledge and skill required for management varies with the organizational level. (Source: George R. Terry, *Principles of Management.* Homewood, Ill.: Richard D. Irwin, 1977, p. 9. Reprinted by permission.)

Managers in staff positions, such as training directors, do not have formal line authority over other managers in their organizations. The extent to which training directors are able to accomplish their aims, therefore, depends heavily upon their ability to win the other managers' voluntary support for training or training-related activities. Thus the training director and others in staff positions need to be particularly adept in influencing, winning approval and support, and convincing others to voluntarily comply with their aims.

Technical area of the job as an influence

Some management literature strongly suggests that the most effective ways for managing the research efforts of engineers and scientists are different from the most effective ways for managing other functional groups. Though these differences may to a large degree be due to the differences in the personality types attracted to the various technical areas, they are also due to the differences in the underlying technologies. Management practices that foster creativity, for example, are different from those practices that are effective in managing a group of production or construction workers.

Technology as an influence

Lawrence and Lorsch (1969) conducted research to identify the effect the rate of change in technologies and markets (which they labeled "environment") has on management practice. They found that effective organizational units operating in stable parts of the environment (specifically, technology and market) are more highly structured, while those in more dynamic parts of the environment are less formal.

In summary, an analysis of the jobs held by the persons identified to receive training will provide useful information and insights for determining those things which are most appropriate and most important for the prospective trainees to master.

Step 3   The third step involves a forecast of the changes that are likely to occur in the demands of the job itself by considering such questions as: What new forces and demands will arise? Which demands that exist now will fade away? Which will increase or decrease in importance? Step 3 also involves a forecast of the changes in the challenges and demands that will confront the individuals who are to receive the training as they receive promotions, transfers, or changes in assignments. An examination of career paths and career plans is helpful in doing this. Since training is future oriented—that is, its aim is to prepare people for things to come—this step is important.

Step 4   This step should carefully define the knowledge, skills, and attitudes that were identified in the first three steps and should assign some value to each according to importance. The object of the fourth step is to answer the following questions: Of the specific areas of knowledge, skills, and attitudes that have been identified as being worthy of consideration in Steps 1, 2, and 3, which are essential? Which are important? Which are of little importance for success in the positions and prospective positions of those who are designated to receive training?

Step 5   The fifth step of the process consists of a thorough study and assessment of those slated to receive training. Ideally, the first four steps should precede this one so that attention will not be wasted on unimportant areas of knowledge, skills and attitudes. The following are the questions Step 5 seeks to answer.

1.   What are the managerial behaviors of the prospective training population?

2.   Where does the training population stand with respect to the knowledge, skills, and attitudes delineated in Step 4? That is, what is their level of knowledge in the areas defined? To what extent do they possess the skills

identified in Step 4? What are their personal characteristics? Their attitudes? Their beliefs?

3. Do the prospective trainees have attitudes, values, or beliefs which are contrary to or supportive of the knowledge and skills which they should acquire?

The answers to these questions may be derived by observing the behavior of the prospective trainees, measuring their knowledge, skills, and attitudes objectively, eliciting observations and opinions from others who observe and interact with them, or combining these approaches.

Step 6 Step 6 of the process involves identifying the differences between the desired and actual—levels of knowledge, proficiency of skills, attitudes, and personal characteristics. It also involves ranking the deficiencies discovered in order of importance and answering such questions as the following: Which of the deficiencies found are most detrimental to success? Which areas, where improvement is possible, will yield the most benefits if they are improved? In short, this step aims to pinpoint the kind of training interventions that will produce the most benefits.

SUGGESTIONS FOR COLLECTING DATA

Three important considerations should be kept in mind while planning and carrying out the collection of data: (1) getting the optimal amount of data; (2) assuring that the data collected are accurate and reliable; and (3) collecting data in a manner so that those who are to support or receive the training do not become negative or hostile toward it before it begins.

The Optimal Amount of Data

Once the people who are to receive the training are identified and the information requirements for determining needs are decided upon, a determination of the various sources of the required information must be made. If in the study of needs, data are collected from all who are to receive the training, as well as from their bosses, their subordinates, and those with whom they work, obviously more of the needs will have a better chance of becoming known than if only a few people are studied or questioned. The quantity of data in the former instance would naturally be overwhelming and time would not permit it. In all likelihood, those who collect the data would have more information than they want or can use. The chances are that the value of the last bit of information obtained from the last dollar spent on collecting it would not be worth it. Therefore, data should be collected from a representative sample of those who possess the desired information instead of from all possible sources.

Accuracy and Reliability of Data

Since conclusions are only as good as the data on which they are based, it makes good sense to take measures to assure that the data are accurate and reliable. Data are accurate when they reflect the true state of affairs and are free of distortions. Data are reliable when there is consistency (agreement) between that which is collected by two or more persons or between that which one person collects at various times. The main causes of inaccurate and unreliable data are: (1) inexperienced data gatherers who are unable to distinguish between the important and the unimportant; (2) biased data gatherers who are sensitive to or only look for certain kinds of information; (3) data collection from limited sources or nonrepresentative samples; and (4) poorly designed data-collection instruments.

Avoiding the Creation of Negative Attitudes Toward Training

Since a study of needs usually requires written and verbal interaction between those closely associated with the training intervention and those who will receive the training as well as with persons closely associated with them such as their bosses, it is important that care be given to the building of positive, receptive attitudes toward the training and those who will be conducting the training. Training programs can be ineffective or never finally approved by top management or never conducted because hostile and negative attitudes toward training are engendered during the study of needs. These unfortunate situations can typically occur because of one or more of the following reasons.

1.   Those conducting the study of needs unconsciously project an attitude that they are the organization's "saviors" and they will teach the "ignorant, backward souls" how to manage. In short, they show no respect for those whom they intended to help.

2.   The study of needs uses the approach, "We will find problems and correct them." Conceptually, this is alright. However, it frequently runs into trouble because the investigators begin their study with the attitude that there are serious problems to be corrected, and they then proceed to attempt to get others to reveal these problems openly. Unaware that most people tend not to expose their shortcomings, especially to strangers, these investigators announce the intentions of their study to the unprepared people from whom they will attempt to collect data. In essence they are saying, "We are here to discover your problems. We will determine the problems you have." Such an approach will not be well received as the data collectors will understandably be interpreted as saying, "Tell us how many mistakes you made so we can see where you need to improve."

3.   Sometimes investigators neglect the fact that their studies are time consuming. Most people will tire of training or almost anything else if it involves

completing lengthy forms or questionnaires. Managers and supervisors are usually very busy people. They have many things on their minds and feel compelled to be working. At the same time, training specialists are often extremely enthusiastic about what they see as important and they fail to remember that *business* is in the business of business, and not *training*. They fail to recognize that, while training should assist managers in doing a better job, it is not their only concern. Therefore, excessive diversion from what managers perceive as important should be avoided; otherwise, it will most likely create unfavorable attitudes toward training.

4.   Unsophisticated management-development specialists believe that there is "one best way" to manage. While they may not admit that they hold to this position, their behavior strongly suggests otherwise. In essence these people think that there is a "recipe" for every situation and that they know them all. Thus they perceive the task of studying needs as one of identifying how and where managers diverge from the "one best way" or the way they would act if they were the manager. This approach is worse than simply being naive because it quite often provokes doubts in the minds of those being studied as to the credibility of those who are conducting the study and will lead the training program. Thus those who conduct assessments of needs having this perception of their task are often labeled "impractical," "too theoretical," or "unrealistic."

5.   Attitude measures, management-style assessments, and other psychological measures are often used to identify needs. These measures are helpful, often essential, to accurate assessment; however, these measures are not entirely problem free. Many people, especially those without an understanding of the behavioral sciences, have misconceptions and fears when it comes to these measures. They are suspicious of psychology and the study of human behavior and, to some extent, this is understandable. People do not want to have their behavior analyzed. They do not want others to study their inner feelings. They do not want to be psychoanalyzed. Thus, partly because of initial suspicion and misconceptions about the behavioral sciences and partly because people do not want to be studied psychologically, attempts to probe these hidden areas and inner feelings can easily be met with vigorous opposition and negative feelings.

6.   Members of organizations are generally keenly aware of what higher level management expects them to do. Their advancement and good standing depends on this. Proceeding to study training needs without open support from top management often results in overall disinterest and only minimal cooperation from those being studied, a fact sometimes overlooked.

Outsiders or relatively new employees with the assignment of identifying and studying training needs can also have a difficult time because they know very little about the organization they are to study and they are not known by top management or those they intend to study. The corporate training specialist from the home office, who goes to an operating unit in another part of the country to study needs, can run into difficulties too. People in this situation can easily become regarded as "corporate spies looking for our faults." Consider the following true episode, which was told by one who once found himself in this kind of situation.

> My first assignment as a new member in our company's training department was to identify the training needs and develop a supervisory management program for one of our operations located in the west. Coming from corporate headquarters in the east, when I arrived I was ushered into the operations manager's office as an honored guest. After the casual pleasantries and get acquainted chatter, the operations manager looked me straight in the eyes and said, "You can go ahead and make the study you need to develop a program for us, but don't you carry any stories back to the people in the home office. If you see something that needs correcting, you tell me about it first." Eager to be cooperative and fair, and realizing the importance of my acceptance and the influence his approval of me would have to the quality of the study, I quickly assured him that my intent was to be helpful and not a spy. I promised to comply with his wishes.

To earn top management's support for training, it is essential that those who conduct the study of needs, particularly outsiders, gain management's trust and confidence. As a minimum, management should be assured that whatever is uncovered in the study of needs will not go beyond the operation's premises. Such an assurance will go a long way in getting the people at all levels in the organization to cooperate with the study. If the people studying training needs are perceived as having the approval of top management, they will very likely receive the open, sincere assistance they need to complete their assignments.

This support can come almost immediately and the specialist will receive more cooperation and encounter less suspicion if he or she is announced as "one who is preparing a management training program" instead of as "one who is looking for problems."

Although word of management's approval will travel verbally, a written announcement should precede the investigator's visit so that those who receive it will have plenty of time to react to it. The announcement should explain who the visitor is, the purpose of the visit, and what will occur during the visit. It should state that the specialist is welcome and that his or her help is wanted. It should also explain that time and effort spent away from normal work duties by those in the organization to assist the visitor will be appreciated.

Employees of the organization who are already known and trusted usually will not have to overcome the suspicion barriers mentioned earlier. Nonetheless, even this study should be preceded by a written announcement containing the same information that was suggested for visitors. It should explicitly include a statement of top management's support.

Assurances and announcements are only a first step in the process of taking deliberate care to assure the collection of accurate information. Beyond this lies the need to win the confidence of those from whom the data will be gathered. Typically, feelings of fear, suspicion, and insecurity, which can cause individuals to hold back or distort information, will be experienced by employees of the organization.

One respected training professional tells of an experience he had years ago while conducting a study of organizational climate in a large hospital. He had been there two weeks when a nurse confided, "You know Mr. X, those things I told you before weren't true. I was just lying because I didn't trust you then."

This is not an unusual case. Surely a fair amount of distortions occur during all studies of needs, especially those which are conducted by outsiders or others who are relatively unknown. Earning the trust and confidence of the employees should, therefore, be the investigators' immediate priority. For if they do this, they will be not only more likely to gather the accurate information they need, but they will also establish positive attitudes toward themselves and create enthusiam for the training sessions that will follow.

METHODS OF IDENTIFYING TRAINING NEEDS

A wide variety of methods and techniques for identifying management training needs are available. Although each has its merits, none should be relied upon exclusively to provide the kinds and amounts of information that are required for an accurate and thorough assessment of needs. For this reason, competent training specialists draw upon a carefully chosen combination of methods, which have been selected on the basis of their needs and the information each method is specifically designed to gather.

Whereas the determination of training needs ought to proceed in a logical fashion, such as the six-step procedure described earlier, the actual collection of data usually will not parallel this same procedure. This is largely because the information obtained by any one method can usually be used in more than one of the six steps. It is not possible, therefore, to divide the various data collection methods into categories that correspond to the particular steps for which each can provide needed information. Another categorization scheme for classifying the data-collection methods suggested here is: (1) organizational and job analyses, and (2) human analyses.

ORGANIZATIONAL AND JOB-ANALYSES METHODS

These are assessments of nonpersonal dimensions. They seek to identify, more or less, external features that impact upon the people who are to receive the training. Some of the measures are used to study behavior, but the focus of attention should be on the demands of the organization and the job.

Organization and Industry Characteristics

An understanding of the characteristic features of a firm or the industry of which a firm is a part will provide useful insights into the environment in which prospective trainees operate. Consider the following examples.

Large firms, such as the three major automobile manufacturers, are prime targets for governmental pressures and legislation in such areas as equal employment, health and safety, full employment, environmental protection, etc. As a consequence, top management of such firms should be aware of and able to deal effectively with governmental pressures and legislation.

Small, rapidly growing and extremely profitable firms are attractive targets for takeover by large, well-financed companies. Managers of such firms may need to know how to avoid being bought out.

Firms that produce goods for the domestic markets are concerned with issues and problems different from those of firms that produce goods for foreign markets.

One technique used for identifying the important characteristics of a firm or an industry and their significance in terms of managerial abilities required is the Organization and Industry Characteristics Table (Table 3-1). When using this table, several important points should be kept in mind.

Table 3-1. Organization and industry characteristics table.

Organization/industry characteristic	*Significance of characteristic in terms of managerial abilities required*

1. Size of organization
     a) annual dollar amount of sales
     b) number of employees
     c) ranking and relative size in industry	

2. Size of industry
     a) annual dollar amount of sales
     b) firms composing industry
     c) changes	

3. Employees of organization
     a) age, education, longevity
     b) attitudes, beliefs, personal characteristics
     c) unionization	

4. Capital structure of organization
     a) level required
     b) intensity as compared to labor
     c) sources	

Table 3–1. *cont'd.*

Organization/industry characteristic	Significance of characteristic in terms of managerial abilities required

5. Capital structure of industry
   a) ownership
   b) nature of financing

6. Ownership of organization
   a) nature (stock, family, partnership)
   b) recent or prospective changes

7. Structure of organization
   a) how organized
   b) changes in structure

8. Profitability of organization
   a) current level of return on investment
   b) recent fluctuations
   c) historical fluctuations or patterns

9. Profitability of firms in industry
   a) level
   b) pattern in industry (ranking)
   c) changes

10. Growth of organization
    a) amount and areas of recent and prospective growth
    b) evolving strategies to grow

11. Growth pattern in industry
    a) new areas of activity
    b) growth of industry

12. Organization's market
    a) location and concentration
    b) size
    c) type (industrial, consumer, domestic, international)
    d) primary, secondary, tertiary, etc.

13. Pricing practices
    a) of organization
    b) in industry

Table 3-1. *cont'd.*

Organization/industry characteristic	Significance of characteristic in terms of managerial abilities required

14. Raw materials organization uses
    a) source
    b) availability
    c) fluctuations in availability and price
    d) changes

15. Organization's products and services
    a) technical content
    b) servicing required
    c) life span (life cycle)
    d) durability
    e) cost to produce
    f) age profile of product mix (life cycle)

16. Products and services produced by organizations in industry
    a) differentiation in terms of appearance, quality, durability, acceptance
    b) variety

17. Organization's side products and by-products (spin-offs)

18. Processes used by organization
    a) nature and level of technical content
    b) precision required—specialists needed
    c) changes—amount and nature

19. Processes used in industry
    a) processing secrets
    b) which firms are leaders—most advanced

20. General business conditions of industry
    a) current and prospective
    b) environmental aspects— political, social, economic
    c) relationships with other institutions

Table 3-1. *cont'd.*

Organization/industry characteristic	*Significance of characteristic in terms of managerial abilities required*

21. Historical features of organization
    a) heritage
    b) norms
    c) attitudes and philosophy

22. History of industry

23. Union-management relationships
    a) of organization
    b) industry pattern

1. The various characteristics listed for consideration in this table do not exhaust all possibilities, and others should be added and considered when appropriate. This table is only an example of what can be developed for the study of needs. A different list of characteristics would have to be developed for studying the needs of nonprofit organizations.

2. An accurate determination of the significance of each of the characteristics identified will provide those who are studying needs with the information they need for formulating training objectives. However, this is difficult. It is an extremely tricky process and it requires an uncommon level of understanding and insight.

3. Instead of just one person, a group of people who are knowledgeable of management and of the industry or firm studied should be called upon to complete a table such as the one presented in Table 3-1. Although one person may be knowledgeable, it is unlikely that she or he will be able to do as thorough a job in carrying out this exercise as a group of people would.

Position Descriptions

Carefully written job descriptions can be useful sources of information for identifying required management abilities. They should contain the following kinds of information:

1. a specific statement of the end results that should be accomplished by the person in the position and how these end results are related to the overall mission of the organization;

2. a clear identification of the amount of money, company capital resources, and personnel the person in the position has responsibility for or affects significantly;

3. other positions that report to the person in the position being described and their respective areas of responsibility;

4. ways in which the person in the position must use technical, administrative, and human-relations knowledge and skills;

5. the principal problems the person in the position is called upon to solve;

6. the degree of freedom and autonomy the person in the position has in initiating action and solving problems;

7. the nature of the policies, priorities, procedures, rules, and methods the person in the position establishes and the extent to which this person is expected to establish such; and

8. the principal areas of accountability and the key results the person in the position is responsible for achieving.

A thorough analysis of a job description will yield considerable insight into the management competencies that are required and their relative importance. The analysis will be more accurate when it is made by one who has a thorough knowledge of management and has a broad knowledge of what is required of people in similar positions in other organizations. The opinions of other managers who have had direct dealings with people who hold or who have held the position being studied can often provide helpful, supplementary information about the areas of knowledge and the abilities which those occupying the position should possess.

The identification of necessary management knowledge and abilities should go far beyond the specification of basic management functions such as planning, communicating, decision making, etc. Instead, this analysis should specify clearly the specific knowledge and abilities required. For example, instead of stating that a position requires competence in communication, the analysis should identify the particular types of communication knowledge and skills required, such as written, oral, interpersonal, or some combination thereof, and the nature of the specific circumstances within which they are used.

Behavior Recording

Concrete data that show what managers actually do may be obtained by recording on-the-job behavior. This information can be collected by observers, or managers can complete a self-description form. The former method will yield more accurate data than the latter because it does not rely on recollection and perception of time actually spent on various matters.

Horne and Lupton (1965) developed the form shown in Fig. 3-3 for a study conducted on how managers spend their time. One activity record form was completed for each work activity.

Dimensions of activity	Example
1. Methods of information exchange	1. Telephone, meeting, letter, etc.
2. Time and duration of activity	2. Time of day and time encompassed
3. Location	3. Office, plant, home, other company, etc.
4. Time relationship	4. For the past, present, or future
5. Level of relationship	5. Organizational level and unit dealt with
6. Contacts	6. Person, group, organization, etc.
7. Purpose	7. Giving, seeking, reviewing, etc. information, plans, advice, decisions, etc.
8. Functional area	8. Technical, financial, personnel, etc.
9. Managerial classification	9. Formulating, organizing, unifying, or regulating

Fig. 3-3. Work-activity form.

The data collected may be organized to show such things as the proportion of time managers spend in various methods of work, purposes, places, etc. Figures 3-4, 3-5, and 3-6 are also from the Horne and Lupton (1965) study.

These methods can reveal what the managers studied actually do and, of course, this is important because the training intervention should be designed

Method of working	Mean proportion of time spent (percent)
Talking with one other person	25
Discussion with two or more people	19
Formal meeting	10
Telephone	9
Paper work	14
Reading	10
Reflecting	2
Inspection	2
Visits	9

Fig. 3-4. Methods of work used by 66 managers.

Purpose of work activity	Mean proportion of time spent (percent)
Information transmission	42
Advice (giving, seeking, receiving)	6
Decisions (giving, reviewing, etc.)	8
Instructions	9
Plans (reviewing, coordinating, etc.)	11
Explanations	15
Other	9

Fig. 3-5. Purposes of work activities reported by 66 managers.

to be relevant to the needs of those for whom it is intended. A question that should always be asked when studying the data collected is, "Should the managers spend their time in the ways the study reveals that they do?" If training specialists simply design their programs to teach managers how to do what they are already doing, only better, they may be doing the managers a disservice because this study is not designed to show whether the managers spent their time unwisely, in nonproductive ways, or doing things they should not. In short, a study of needs that relies exclusively upon this kind of information runs the risk of concluding that the prospective trainees need to be taught to do things which they probably should not be doing in the first place.

Another problem with the behavior recording method is the diversity of data it yields and, as a consequence, it is difficult to ascribe meaning to the findings. This is especially common when higher levels of management are studied and where there is greater diversity in what managers at these levels do, as opposed to what managers at lower levels do.

Location of activity	Mean proportion of time in location (percent)
Own office	52
Own department	11
Other office in own company	16
Other department in own company	6
Another company	4
Home	4
Social	3
Anywhere else	4

Fig. 3-6. Loci of work activity reported by 66 managers.

Critical Incidents

The critical-incidents method of studying behavior is an approach that not only identifies much of what managers actually do, but also seeks to identify what they did that was effective and what they did that was ineffective. Developed by Flanagan (1954), this method attempts to identify critical job requirements. Flanagan defines *critical job requirements* as those behaviors which are crucial in making the difference between doing a job effectively and doing it ineffectively.

Critical incidents are reports or descriptions of things which those being studied did that were effective or ineffective in accomplishing parts of their job. These descriptions take the form of stories, anecdotes, reports, etc., as told by superiors, peers, or subordinates, or may be the result of first-hand observations by qualified observers. The data collected may be analyzed bit by bit, collectively, or both, in much the same manner as a case study is analyzed. It aims to provide answers to the following kinds of questions.

1.   What was done that led to effective job performance?

2.   What was done that detracted from effective job performance or led to ineffective job performance?

3.   What, if done differently, would have been more effective?

4.   What attitudes, values, abilities, knowledge, etc. (present or absent) led to success or failure?

Grievance reports are a good source of critical incidents. Many grievance reports are politically motivated by unions for various reasons; many others are legitimate complaints. While grievance reports are most directly related to first-level supervision, perceptive analyzers can often "read between the lines" as they study the grievance reports to obtain an understanding of the perceptions, climate, attitudes, and values not only of the supervisors who were directly involved, but also of higher-level managers as well. The ways in which first-level supervisors treat their subordinates more often than not suggest how higher-level management treats them. Thus an analysis of how first-level supervisors handle grievance reports can often give clues as to the strengths and weaknesses of higher-level management.

Career Path Plans

A career path may be thought of as a series of successive positions a person will typically occupy as he or she advances in the organizational hierarchy throughout his or her career. Today, many companies that are sophisticated in their manpower planning and development efforts spend a considerable amount of time and attention in laying out career path plans for promising employees. Although career path plans are primarily a manpower planning tool, they can provide management development specialists with useful insights as to the long-range training needs of key people. In other words, when training needs are formulated on the basis of career plans, they include not only a person's present development needs as they pertain to his or her current position, but also training needs that will pertain to subsequent positions he or she holds in the future. This approach offers the advantage of causing management training and development planners to take a long-range view of what they intend to accomplish and, as a consequence, tends to help them make their efforts more comprehensive and consistent over time.

There are some drawbacks to using career paths as a basis for determining long-range training needs. First, it tends to overlook the fact that most fast rising managers of today will make several changes in employment. Few start and remain with the same firm throughout their career. And second, it ignores the fact that firms change, their missions change, their organizational structures change, and the problems their managers are called upon to handle change. Consequently, career-path plans must change too.

Future Problems

As problems change so does the nature of the managerial demands change. Managerial abilities which were appropriate for solving the problems a position was called upon to solve in the past may be inadequate to meet the demands and problems the same position might face in the future. Some attention should be given to identifying and analyzing the changes that are most likely to occur and then to predicting the knowledge, attitudes, and skills that will be required to deal effectively with these changes.

Consider the following illustration of how the growth of a firm can lead to changes in the managerial competence required for success.

This firm began on a small scale in an inventor's garage. The inventor hired first one, then later, more people to produce his new product. As the product's acceptance grew, so did the organization. However, instead of changing with the new demands of leading the growing organization, the inventor persisted in doing things and running his operation just as he always had. Thus, instead of attending to matters of organization, policy making, delegation of responsibilities, training, etc., he remained heavily involved with the technical aspects of the operation, ignoring the managerial demands that emerged because of the operation's growth. A few years later his growing business, beset with financial, production, and labor problems, was forced to close.

HUMAN-ANALYSES METHODS

These are measures and assessments of the people who are to receive the training. These measures may be further divided into three areas:

1. *Observations of behavior.* These examine the people who are about to receive the training. The focus of attention is on the people and how they behave as opposed to the critical dimensions of the job. These measures are typically planned and conducted according to some preconceived procedure.

2. *Opinions.* These are less systematic than observations, although they are based on observations; these opinions are less well-planned. They can nonetheless provide helpful insights.

3. *Objective psychological measures.* These are usually paper-and-pencil diagnostic tests and inventories of knowledge, attitudes, opinions, values, and styles. They may have norms which permit comparisons with other groups of managers.

OBSERVATIONS OF BEHAVIOR

Performance Appraisals

Performance appraisals are an excellent source for identifying training needs provided they are an assessment of how well individuals accomplish specific tasks and goals as opposed to being performance appraisals that merely evaluate people on the basis of various traits. If performance appraisals are nothing more than forms that require supervisors to rate their people according to some kind of scale (e.g., excellent, very good, average, below average, poor) with respect to various traits (e.g., dependability, punctuality, neatness, judgment, job knowledge, tact, safety, initiative, etc.), they will not provide useful information about training needs for two reasons.

1. They are based on the assumption that the possession of one or more of these traits will lead to success in the job.

2. They define all of the areas in which training should occur—namely, the development of the traits specified in the performance appraisal form.

If, however, performance appraisals are assessments of how well people have accomplished predetermined objectives and they involve an analysis of what was done that was effective or ineffective, then they can yield extremely useful information about training and development needs. The degree of reliability of performance appraisals also depends on how carefully supervisors observe their subordinates' performance and whether the superiors have spent enough time in analyzing their subordinates' abilities and needs for improvement prior to the appraisal session. Superiors can obtain helpful insights by conducting periodic coaching sessions with their subordinates. In such sessions, superiors can learn how things are going from their subordinates' perspectives, what difficulties they are having, where they need help, and where they feel the need to improve.

Manager Watching

Manager watching is a technique for evaluating managerial effectiveness developed by Earl P. Strong of Pennsylvania State University, and it is essentially just what its name implies. It involves prolonged observation of an individual manager at work, which can last from a few hours to several days. The longer the period of observation, of course, the greater the amount of data collected.

The manager watchers observe the subjects' work behavior, but remain as inconspicuous as possible. They converse with the managers being watched as little as possible. When they do converse, it is usually only to gain clarification as to what is occurring. They never make on-the-spot suggestions or criticisms.

Manager watching does have some obvious limitations. First, it is hard to imagine that the presence of an observer will not affect how the person being observed will act. Yet, very often, people are so unaware of their weaknesses that they do not even attempt to conceal them and thus they remain observable. Second, it is a time consuming process. Three to five days of observation are usually required in order to provide the observer with an adequate sampling of behavior to render a valid assessment of needs. Third, this technique can be used only in cases where the subject wants to be watched and can behave more or less naturally while being observed. Observers must not be perceived as a threat to the managers' security and status within the organization. Rather, observers should be people who are thought of as supportive and able to offer the subjects useful suggestions for improvement.

Manager watchers must be knowledgeable of all phases of management, and they must also be extremely perceptive and have insight. Essentially, observers are viewing live case studies. They have to be able to see what is happening and be able to analyze and identify the effectiveness of the subjects' behavior in the various situations observed.

Interviews

Information obtained from interviews with those who are to receive training, as well as their superiors, subordinates, and others with whom they frequently interact, can yield useful insights regarding the level of sophistication of management knowledge possessed by these managers, their attitudes and value systems, as well as the overall organizational climate in which they function. Both the content of answers and the ways in which they are given should be analyzed. Interviews are usually most productive if they are structured to follow a predetermined plan to obtain specific information. They should not be overly structured, however, so as to be unable to pursue areas of importance that are not anticipated. There are, of course, innumerable questions that can be asked, and this often causes difficulties because few interviewers carefully scrutinize the questions before an interview to determine why each is asked. A well-planned interview involves, among other things, a thorough determination of the information required and carefully written questions designed to obtain it. The catch is that it is not always easy or even possible to plan these things in advance. It is usually necessary to probe further with additional questions, thought of on-the-spot, as the interview unfolds. The sample shown in Table 3–2 illustrates the general framework of a needs-analysis interview.

Table 3–2. Training-needs interview questions and the kinds of information each is designed to obtain.

1. How do you visualize your job as a manager? What do you see as your principal roles?
   a) How broad is this individual's concept of management?
   b) Which aspects of managing does she or he emphasize? Which aspects does he or she fail to see?
2. What are your main responsibilities? What major objectives are you expected to accomplish during the next year?
   a) How clearly does this individual understand his or her role within the organization? Are his or her responsibilities clear?
   b) Does this individual have well-thought-out objectives?
3. What strategies and plans do you have for accomplishing your objectives?
   a) Does this individual have a strategy? a plan?
   b) Is this plan balanced? That is, does she or he consider people, technology, and organizational structure? or ignore one or more of these aspects?
   c) How creative are these strategies and plans?
4. Why are you pursuing the particular objectives mentioned earlier? How do these objectives fit in with those of the larger organizational unit of which you are a part?
   a) Are the organization's objectives well thought out and consistent?
   b) How well are objectives and strategies communicated throughout the organization?
   c) Does this individual see how his or her objectives fit into the overall pattern of things?
5. What are the principal objectives of your boss and what strategies and plans is she or he following to reach them?
   a) Does the boss have objectives and plans?
   b) Does this individual identify with them? Does he or she have a part in them?
   c) How well have they been communicated? How well have they been accepted?
6. What are the strengths and weaknesses of your people?
   a) Does this individual emphasize strengths or weaknesses?
   b) What seem to be her or his overall assumptions about others? Does this individual ascribe to Theory X or Theory Y?

Table 3-2. *cont'd.*

    c) Do his or her people display initiative? What does this say about this individual as a manager?

    d) Does this individual seem to be utilizing his or her people to their full potential?

7. What do your people want out of their jobs?
    a) What are his or her assumptions about people?
    b) Does this individual know and understand her or his people?

8. How motivated are your people, and what do you think accounts for this?
    a) How well does this individual understand his or her people?
    b) What is their motivation level, and does he or she think about it?

9. How well-disciplined are your people?
    a) Are there discipline problems?
    b) Are there attitude problems?

10. How do you go about maintaining or increasing your people's level of motivation to do their work?
    a) What are her or his beliefs about motivation and human behavior?
    b) What kind of boss is she or he? lax, harsh and driving, or a developer?

11. What differences of opinion exist within your unit and how are they resolved?
    a) Is there conflict and how strong is it?
    b) Is conflict suppressed? Are differences of opinion resolved openly?

12. What complaints have your people brought to your attention and how did you handle them?
    a) Are people open with their feelings?
    b) Does the boss permit dissent?
    c) Are there organizational structure problems?

13. How motivated would you say you are at work? What changes, in your opinion, would help cause your level of motivation to rise?
    a) Is this person satisfied with his or her work?
    b) What elements are missing that would really turn him or her on?

14. How would you characterize the communications between you and higher levels of management? between you and your peers? between you and your subordinates?
    a) Where could communications improve and what is causing them to be less than they could be?
    b) Does the manager think he or she is an excellent communicator? What do her or his people think?

15. To what extent does your boss delegate responsibility and authority to you? Should she or he delegate more or less?
    a) Is the delegation appropriate?
    b) Are people being utilized to their capacity?

16. What could you delegate to your people?
    a) What are the strengths and weaknesses of this boss's people?
    b) What is this individual's perception of their abilities?

Table 3-2. *cont'd.*

17. What are you doing to develop the knowledge, skills and abilities of your people?
    a) Is this individual developing her or his people?
    b) How good is the unit's performance appraisal system? the unit's training system?
    c) Are people being developed?

18. What major challenges or problems have you faced during the last six to eight months and how did you handle them?
    a) What kinds of things does he or she see as problems?
    b) How good of a problem analyzer and problem solver is this individual?
    c) How creative were his or her solutions?
    d) What do the solutions suggest about his or her value system? attitudes? breadth of knowledge?

19. If your people could improve in three to five ways what would you suggest?
    a) Do this individual's development plans for subordinates jibe with these weaknesses?

20. If your boss could improve in three to five ways what would you suggest?
    a) What type of training could help here?

21. If you were in your boss's shoes how would you handle things differently?
    a) What does this suggest insofar as training needs of the boss?

22. Tell about a major change that occurred here during the past year and how it was handled.
    a) How skillfully are changes handled?
    b) What does this tell about management's knowledge and skills and attitudes?

23. How do you know if your unit is doing the kind of job it should?
    a) What kinds of controls exist?
    b) Does the manager relate what he or she does with the firm's profitability or overall success?

24. What do you see as your principal developmental needs?
    a) In which ways does the interviewee think he or she needs to improve?

The key to extracting useful insights from interview answers rests upon the interpretation of their significance. A question interviewers should keep asking themselves as they progress through the interview is, "What is the significance of the answers I hear?"

Frequently, people will conceal their true feelings and opinions. Yet, in many other cases, these feelings and opinions are not held back. Sometimes true feelings and opinions may be only somewhat concealed, yet they are visible to the alert and perceptive interviewer.

Interview data should be analyzed with respect to the framework of knowledge, skills, and personal characteristics presented in Chapter 2. By doing this, the identification of needs becomes clearer and more meaningful in terms of making learning objectives consistent with the changes in on-the-job behavior desired.

Assessment Centers

The *assessment-center method* arose out of the need for the early identification of management potential and development needs. Essentially, the assessment center involves the assessment of various areas of knowledge and skills of several individuals by a small group of trained observers using a variety of group and individual exercises.

Henry Murray of Harvard University is credited with initiating the assessment-center approach in the 1930s. Later, during the second world war, British and German armies used similar techniques to screen officer candidates. The United States Office of Strategic Services used various assessment exercises to select OSS agents.

It wasn't until the late 1950s that the first formal assessment center for selecting supervisors and managers in business was developed and put into use. Through the pioneering efforts of Douglas Bray of the American Telephone and Telegraph (AT&T), assessment centers for selecting supervisors were designed and established throughout a majority of the Bell System companies.

Although the assessment-center method has been shown to be a reasonably valid instrument for predicting the effectiveness of first-level managers, it seems reasonable to believe that it can be useful for identifying areas in which individuals at all levels of management could improve. Further training and development in one or more of the various areas which the assessment-center technique measures may or may not result in improved managerial effectiveness, depending upon the nature and demands of the job held by the individuals in question. To use the assessment center as the sole source of data for determining training needs would be foolish because it examines only a selected set of knowledge and abilities. Moreover, most of the factors examined by the assessment centers are personal characteristics, which are very difficult to change. It is much easier to cause change in a person's levels of knowledge or skill.

The AT&T assessment center spends three and a half days evaluating individuals in the following twenty-five areas (Bray and Grant 1966):

1. Organization and planning

2. Decision making

3. Creativity

4. Human-relations skills

5. Behavior flexibility

6. Personal impact

7. Tolerance of uncertainty

8. Resistance to stress

9. Scholastic aptitude

10. Range of interests

11. Inner-work standards

12. Primacy of work

13. Oral-communications skills

14. Perception of social cues

15. Self-objectivity

16. Energy

17. Realism of expectations

18. Bell System value orientation

19. Social objectivity

20. Need for advancement

21. Ability to delay gratification

22. Need for superior approval

23. Need for peer approval

24. Goal flexibility

25. Need for security

The techniques developed to reveal these variables are interviews, in-basket exercises, business games, group discussion, projective tests, paper-and-pencil tests, and personal history and biographical description.

According to McConnell and Parker (1972, p. 6–7), the American Management Association assessment center was developed to identify individuals' first-level supervisory management ability and potential, and it spends two days utilizing eight exercises to evaluate groups of twelve individuals each. The eight exercises are (1) an interview, (2) a management questionnaire, (3) an in-basket exercise, (4) a luncheon meeting with an assessor, (5) a film case, (6) a selection simulation, (7) a management-decision game, and (8) a self-evaluation of their group's performance. Unlike the AT&T assessment center, the AMA center examines abilities more specifically along the lines of management functions which include the following:

1. Functional ability—existing successfully in one's environment

2. Planning—developing a course of action to achieve an objective

3. Organizing—structuring or arranging resources to accomplish the objective of a plan

4. Controlling—maintaining adherence to a plan, and modifying it, if necessary, to achieve the desired result

5. Oral communication—transferring a thought from one person to another verbally, adjusting to audience reaction

6. Written communication—transferring a thought from one person to another in writing, without audience reaction

7. Company orientation—identifying the organization's goals and values as complementing one's own

8. Leadership—getting people to work toward reaching an objective

9. Decision making—consciously weighing and selecting one of two or more alternatives

10. Creativity—developing alternative solutions to problems

11. Initiative—introducing one's own thought or action into a situation

12. Flexibility—adjusting to changing internal and external conditions, both personal and impersonal.

Preprogram Survey

A preprogram survey is a questionnaire given to trainees several weeks before the start of a program. Its purpose is to obtain insights into their work and their level of sophistication. Most of the questions are general, which allows participants a great deal of latitude in which to express themselves. As with the interview technique, this method also requires insightful interpretation if it is to be meaningful. Its other limitations are that it requires an hour or more to complete and its scope is limited to particular areas or functions. The survey presented in Table 3–3, for example, is limited to eight areas.

OPINIONS

Opinions about the abilities of managers and their training needs can be a useful source of information provided that the opinions come from people who have had close contact with those for whom the training is being designed and who also have some appreciation for good management.

Table 3-3. Management-development preprogram survey.

We invite your best thinking. This questionnaire will provide you with an opportunity to have a direct input in the design and preparation of the management-development program you will be attending. Your thoughts and feelings are solicited with the aim of providing the course discussion leaders with a better understanding of you, your work, and what you most want out of the program. Take the necessary time to think through and complete this questionnaire so the program can be made meaningful to you and the other participants.

Return it to____(name)____by____(date)____ .

Have you been to a management-development program before?   Yes [   ]   No [   ]
If yes, which one, where, and when?

_____

_____

_____

A. The role of the manager

   1. Which aspects of your managerial responsibilities do you

      a) enjoy the most: _____

         _____

      b) enjoy the least: _____

         _____

      c) find the easiest: _____

         _____

      d) find the hardest: _____

         _____

B. Managing by objectives

   1. Do you have specific written objectives which you are accountable for achieving?   Yes [   ]   No [   ]

   2. If yes, please give one example:

      _____

      _____

      _____

   3. Does your unit have a formal management-by-objectives (MBO) system?
      Yes [   ]   No [   ]

Table 3-3. *cont'd.*

4. If yes, what do you see as the biggest problems with it?

   a) _____

   _____

   b) _____

   _____

   c) _____

   _____

5. Have you received formal instruction in management by objectives?
   Yes [   ]   No [   ]

   a) In the underlying theory of MBO?   Yes [   ]   No [   ]
   b) In the practices of MBO?   Yes [   ]   No [   ]

6. What would you most like to know about MBO?_____

   _____

   _____

C. **Planning**

   1. Think of a typical week. What proportion of your time do you think you spend in formal planning?

   _____

   2. Approximately how far into the future do the bulk of your plans extend?

   _____

   3. Give specific examples of the planning you are doing right now as a manager.

   _____

   _____

   _____

   _____

   _____

D. **Problem solving and decision making**

   1. List two or three major problems you worked on during the past year. Describe each briefly.

   a) _____

   _____

   _____

Table 3-3. *cont'd.*

b) _____

_____

_____

c) _____

_____

_____

2. Which conditions or factors make problem solving difficult for you?

_____

_____

_____

_____

3. What do you feel would be most helpful to you for doing an even better job of solving problems?

_____

_____

_____

4. Identify two or three important decisions you faced during the year.

a) _____

_____

b) _____

_____

c) _____

_____

5. What do you find to be the most difficult aspects of decision making?

_____

_____

_____

_____

Table 3-3. *cont'd.*

6. What information do you feel would help you the most in doing a better job of decision making?

_____

_____

_____

E. **Leadership**

1. Overall, are you comfortable with the leadership you receive?
   Yes [   ]   No [   ]
   Why or why not?_____

   _____

   _____

   a) Which aspects are you *most* comfortable with? _____

   _____

   b) Which aspects are you *least* comfortable with? _____

   _____

2. Overall, do you feel that the people working under you are comfortable with the leadership you provide?   Yes [   ]   No [   ]

   a) What do you think they are *most* comfortable with?_____

   _____

   _____

   b) What do you think they are *least* comfortable with?_____

   _____

   _____

3. What specifically would you like to know that would make you a better leader?

   _____

   _____

   _____

   _____

   _____

Table 3-3. *cont'd.*

F. Motivation

1. Think about each person who reports directly to you. Place an "X" on the scale below indicating the *level of motivation,* as you perceive it, of each of these people. (If you have three people, you will have three X's; five people, five X's, etc.)

Very low	Below average	Average	Above average	Very high

2. How much impact do you think you can have on the level of motivation of your subordinates? (Select one)

   a) None   [   ]
   b) Only a little   [   ]
   c) Some   [   ]
   d) Substantial   [   ]

   Why do you think this?

   _____

   _____

   _____

3. List 5 to 7 *specific things* you do now to keep or increase the level of motivation of your subordinates:

   _____

   _____

   _____

   _____

   _____

   _____

   _____

4. What questions would you most like answered about human motivation?

   _____

   _____

   _____

   _____

Table 3-3. *cont'd.*

G. Communications

1. In the past, how often have people misunderstood your writing?
   - a) Never   [   ]
   - b) Rarely   [   ]
   - c) Sometimes   [   ]
   - d) Often   [   ]
   - e) Very often   [   ]

2. How often have people misunderstood what you have said to them?
   - a) Never   [   ]
   - b) Rarely   [   ]
   - c) Sometimes   [   ]
   - d) Often   [   ]
   - e) Very often   [   ]

3. How often have you found it difficult to sell ideas to your superiors?
   - a) Very seldom   [   ]
   - b) Seldom   [   ]
   - c) Sometimes   [   ]
   - d) Often   [   ]
   - e) Very often   [   ]

4. Indicate what you feel is the predominate direction of information flow within your organization.

Downward	Mostly downward	Down and up	Down, up, and with peers

5. To what extent do you feel superiors are sharing information with those at lower levels in your organization?

Provide minimum information	Give subordinates only information superior feels they need	Give information needed and answer most questions	Seek to provide subordinates all relevant information and all information they want

6. How much *upward* communication is there in your organization?

Very little	Limited	Some	Great deal

Table 3-3. *cont'd.*

7. Where do you think communications could be improved upon most in your unit?

_____

_____

_____

8. What would you most like to know and receive assistance on, so you could do a better job of communicating?

_____

_____

_____

H. Performance appraisals

1. Does your boss formally appraise your performance on a regular basis?
Yes [   ]   No [   ]

2. Overall, are you satisfied with your company's appraisal procedure?
Yes [   ]   No [   ]
Why or why not?

_____

_____

a) Which aspects are you *most* satisfied with?

_____

_____

b) Which aspects are you *least* satisfied with?

_____

_____

3. Do you formally appraise the performance of your subordinates?
Yes [   ]   No [   ]

4. If yes, what do you feel are
a) the *most* difficult aspects of this process?

_____

_____

b) the *least* difficult aspects of this process?

_____

_____

Table 3-3. *cont'd.*

5. What would you most like assistance on, so you could do a better job of appraising subordinates and feel more comfortable about it?

_____

_____

_____

Opinions About Who Needs Training and Their Management Strengths and Weaknesses

Questionnaires are useful for obtaining relatively large samples of opinions from those who will receive training themselves or from those who have contact with these persons. Figures 3-7, 3-8, and 3-9 are sample questionnaires which seek to uncover who needs management training and their management strengths and weaknesses.

Directions: Indicate how strongly you feel that there is a need for training and improvement for the following people or groups of people in your organization by placing an "X" in the appropriate columns below.

Management training is recommended for:	Degree of need			
	Considerable	Moderate	Little	Very little
1. My immediate superior				
2. Other superiors at my boss's level (my superior's peers)				
3. Managers at levels above my boss				
4. My peers in my department				
5. My peers in other departments				
6. My subordinates				
7. The subordinates of my subordinates				
8. My peers' subordinates				

Fig. 3-7. Where is management training needed questionnaire.

Directions: For the people or groups of people listed below, briefly state their greatest management strength. That is, what do these people do most effectively in their role as managers?

Person possessing this strength	Brief statement of greatest management strength
1. My superior	
2. Superiors at the same level as my boss	
3. Managers at levels above my boss	
4. My peers in my department	
5. My subordinates	
6. Myself	

Fig. 3-8. Management-strengths questionnaire.

Directions: For those listed below, briefly state the greatest need for improvement in the way they manage. That is, what do these people most need to do better in?

Management training is recommended for:	Brief statement of greatest need for improvement in management
1. My superior	
2. Managers at the same level as my boss	
3. Managers at levels above my boss	
4. My peers in my department	
5. My subordinates	
6. Myself	

Fig. 3-9. Management-weaknesses questionnaire.

Opinions About Specific Areas in Which Managers Need to Study and Improve

Checklists of management training needs completed by superiors and those for whom the training is being designed generally provide data on specific subject areas which are perceived to be in most need of further development. The accuracy of the data obtained is, of course, limited by the perceptions of those who complete the questionnaires or checklists.

These checklists usually identify fifty or more subject areas and ask respondents to indicate the extent to which they perceive a need. Table 3–4 is one example.

Table 3–4. Survey of management-development needs.

Your assistance is required in our effort to identify the most useful subject areas for the _____ managers to study as an aid in improving their abilities in these areas. To do this, we ask that you do the following:

1. Read over the entire list of sixty-five subjects, each of which is broken into three groups.

2. Reflect on it for a minute and ask yourself,

   "In which areas do the _____ managers need to improve most?"

3. Be *very discriminating* when indicating what you feel to be the relative importance of each of the sixty-five subjects. Circle the appropriate number according to the following rating scale:

   5 = Very important
   4 = Somewhat important
   3 = No opinion
   2 = Slightly important
   1 = Not important

4. Place check marks next to the fifteen subjects that you feel are *most important*.

5. Indicate any topics omitted here which you feel should be included in the _____ management training program.

I. Subjects to expand the managers' general knowledge of business

The following subjects are taught with the aim of enlarging managers' overall understanding of business and to update their knowledge of new trends.

Topic	Rating scale of relative importance (Circle one for each topic)				
1. The enterprise system and economic change	5	4	3	2	1
2. The economy and forecasting business activity	5	4	3	2	1
3. Basic concepts and tools used in managerial finance	5	4	3	2	1
4. Managerial accounting	5	4	3	2	1
5. Business and society—management ethics	5	4	3	2	1
6. Marketing management	5	4	3	2	1
7. Production management	5	4	3	2	1
8. How to analyze and select capital investment opportunities	5	4	3	2	1
9. Cash management	5	4	3	2	1

Table 3–4. *cont'd.*

Topic	Rating scale of relative importance (Circle one for each topic)				
10. The concept of management and what it means to manage	5	4	3	2	1
11. Understanding and using accounting information	5	4	3	2	1
12. Understanding markets and the marketing function	5	4	3	2	1
13. Labor unions and the role of industrial relations	5	4	3	2	1
14. Statistical and other quantitative tools for managers	5	4	3	2	1
15. The history of management and schools of management thought	5	4	3	2	1
16. Business and government	5	4	3	2	1
17. Legal aspects of business	5	4	3	2	1
18. The personnel function in business	5	4	3	2	1
19. The computer and its uses in management	5	4	3	2	1
20. Sales forecasting and planning	5	4	3	2	1
21. Preparing and presenting oral and written reports	5	4	3	2	1
22. Management information systems	5	4	3	2	1
23. Simulation and model building	5	4	3	2	1
24. The systems concept and its application to management	5	4	3	2	1
25. Computer-assisted decision making	5	4	3	2	1

II. Subjects to change attitudes and improve managers' ability to apply management knowledge

A. Structural forces in management

This is the logical mechanical part of management. Skill in applying the structural forces brings stability, continuity, direction, and certainty. The structural forces include: setting objectives and establishing priorities; planning; policymaking; organizing, measuring, and evaluating efforts; controlling; coordinating the work activities; etc.

Topic	Rating scale of relative importance (Circle one for each topic)				
1. Long-range planning for the firm	5	4	3	2	1
2. Planning work at the departmental level	5	4	3	2	1
3. Establishing goals and standards	5	4	3	2	1

Table 3-4. *cont'd.*

Topic	Rating scale of relative importance (Circle one for each topic)				
4. Management by objectives	5	4	3	2	1
5. Organizing a company—basic theories and principles	5	4	3	2	1
6. Organizing a small unit for specific work	5	4	3	2	1
7. Management controls and their uses	5	4	3	2	1
8. Methods of attacking and solving complex problems	5	4	3	2	1
9. Job descriptions and job specifications	5	4	3	2	1
10. Production planning concepts and tools	5	4	3	2	1
11. Measuring and evaluating human performance	5	4	3	2	1
12. Financial audits and controls	5	4	3	2	1
13. Managing one's time	5	4	3	2	1
14. Decision making	5	4	3	2	1
15. Designing a business strategy	5	4	3	2	1
16. Quality control	5	4	3	2	1
17. Delegation and coordination of efforts for effectiveness	5	4	3	2	1
18. Performance standards for managers	5	4	3	2	1
19. Work measurement and methods improvement for better productivity	5	4	3	2	1
20. Troubleshooting organizational problems	5	4	3	2	1

B. Activating forces in management

This is the human part of management. It is subtle and complex, and it is based on the behavioral sciences, especially psychology. The activating forces include: management styles; leadership practices; understanding people and their interpersonal relationships; motivation; introducing and implementing change; solving conflict; counseling; inspiring creativity; discipline; communications; developing one's self and others; working with groups; etc.

Topic	Rating scale of relative importance (Circle one for each topic)				
1. Management styles	5	4	3	2	1
2. The nature of leadership: effective leadership practices	5	4	3	2	1

Table 3-4. *cont'd.*

Topic	Rating scale of relative importance (Circle one for each topic)				
3. Motivation of self and subordinates	5	4	3	2	1
4. Managing for innovation and creativity	5	4	3	2	1
5. Organizational communications	5	4	3	2	1
6. Interpersonal communications	5	4	3	2	1
7. Handling and solving interpersonal conflict	5	4	3	2	1
8. Introducing and implementing change effectively	5	4	3	2	1
9. Understanding human behavior	5	4	3	2	1
10. Training and developing subordinates	5	4	3	2	1
11. Conducting performance evaluations and coaching subordinates	5	4	3	2	1
12. Counseling subordinates	5	4	3	2	1
13. The manager's personal effectiveness and self-development for the future	5	4	3	2	1
14. Building work groups and teamwork	5	4	3	2	1
15. Dealing with a union	5	4	3	2	1
16. Discipline and climates that produce self-discipline	5	4	3	2	1
17. Managing the marginal performer	5	4	3	2	1
18. Understanding group processes and managing several large groups	5	4	3	2	1
19. Job enrichment and job enlargement	5	4	3	2	1
20. Behavioral science findings applied	5	4	3	2	1

Did you place check marks next to the fifteen topics, from all three lists, that you feel are most important?

What other topics, not listed here, do you feel should be included in the training program?

_____

_____

_____

_____

Committee Opinions

Some organizations use committees, composed of people from various departments, to study and identify training needs. More complete information can be generated if there are several committees composed of people from various management levels (e.g., a committee of supervisors, or a committee of department heads, or an executive-level committee, etc.). An important ingredient for a fruitful outcome from a committee's expression of needs is openness. Because of this, training specialists will want to consider information from a committee's efforts in light of the degree of openness and honesty of expression they perceive the committee to have.

Before attending the committee meeting, the members should be thoroughly briefed as to its purpose, what they are expected to contribute, how they should prepare, and what it is they are expected to accomplish by the end of the meeting. Without these preparations the committee meetings will degenerate into "bull-sessions." It is also helpful if all of the committee members have read some material that will provide them with a common set of terms and definitions of management functions. They should also be prepared to provide evidence and illustrations to support their claims regarding who needs what kind of training. Serious effort should be made before the meeting to prevent it from being a time where conjectures, impressions, and feelings are put forth as concrete evidences of training needs.

The major benefit of committee opinion as a method of determining needs is its acceptability to those who will be asked to support the training. In general, people tend to accept and support that which they have created.

Experts' Observations and Opinions

Some organizations find it valuable to use the services of a professional training consultant, who spends several days interviewing personnel and observing operations first-hand. The observations made by qualified consultants will provide them with a reasonably good basis for judging the sophistication of the organization's managers as compared with their counterparts in other organizations. First-hand observations are also a good source of qualitative data.

Importance and Level of Knowledge of Management Functions

This information, obtainable from large numbers of questionnaires, is useful for a number of reasons. First, it provides insights into the management knowledge and skills which are needed in particular jobs. Second, it gives some clue as to the level of knowledge people perceive they have and thus where they feel they need to improve most. And, third, it reveals some things about how those who complete the questionnaires perceive their roles as managers.

The major deficiency of this kind of measure, however, is that it is very subjective and reveals more about people's perceptions than what may actually exist.

One management-development expert gauges needs by subtracting the values in Column 3 from those in Column 2 of the questionnaire shown in Table 3–5.

Table 3–5. Importance of management functions and the extent to which they are known and used.

Directions: In columns two and three below, circle the number which gives your answer to the question asked.

0 = practically not at all
1 = a little
2 = some
3 = a great deal
4 = absolutely essential

The Structural Aspects of General Management

(Column 1) The rational, logical, and systematic aspects of general management follow:	(Column 2) How important to success on my current job is my ability in this activity?					(Column 3) Of all that is known and practiced in this activity, how much do I know and practice?				
1. Planning	0	1	2	3	4	0	1	2	3	4
2. Forecasting	0	1	2	3	4	0	1	2	3	4
3. Setting objectives	0	1	2	3	4	0	1	2	3	4
4. Organizing	0	1	2	3	4	0	1	2	3	4
5. Setting standards	0	1	2	3	4	0	1	2	3	4
6. Budgeting	0	1	2	3	4	0	1	2	3	4
7. Delegating	0	1	2	3	4	0	1	2	3	4
8. Directing	0	1	2	3	4	0	1	2	3	4
9. Measuring results	0	1	2	3	4	0	1	2	3	4
10. Controlling	0	1	2	3	4	0	1	2	3	4
11. Systematizing	0	1	2	3	4	0	1	2	3	4
12. Making policy	0	1	2	3	4	0	1	2	3	4
13. Making rules	0	1	2	3	4	0	1	2	3	4
14. Establishing procedures	0	1	2	3	4	0	1	2	3	4
15. Disciplining	0	1	2	3	4	0	1	2	3	4

Table 3–5. *cont'd.*

The Activating Aspects of General Management		
(Column 1) *The human-relations, and the emotional, psycho-logical, and behavioral aspects of general management follow:*	*(Column 2)* *How important to success on my current job is my ability in this activity?*	*(Column 3)* *Of all that is known and practiced in this field, how much do I know and practice?*
1. Communicating (both telling and listening)	0 1 2 3 4	0 1 2 3 4
2. Motivating	0 1 2 3 4	0 1 2 3 4
3. Integrating activities, units, departments	0 1 2 3 4	0 1 2 3 4
4. Introducing changes effectively	0 1 2 3 4	0 1 2 3 4
5. Satisfying basic needs of self and others	0 1 2 3 4	0 1 2 3 4
6. Counseling	0 1 2 3 4	0 1 2 3 4
7. Offering and encouraging freedom and participation in decisions	0 1 2 3 4	0 1 2 3 4
8. Developing maturity, responsibility, and acceptance of challenge and risk	0 1 2 3 4	0 1 2 3 4
9. Being sensitive to and acceptive of self; per-ceiving realistically	0 1 2 3 4	0 1 2 3 4
10. Adapting, compro-mising, and adjusting	0 1 2 3 4	0 1 2 3 4

OBJECTIVE PSYCHOLOGICAL AND KNOWLEDGE MEASURES

Management Style Identification

There is no shortage of management and leadership diagnostic instruments. Some of these instruments sample attitudes and beliefs, and draw conclusions from these data about the kinds of behavior or management style the respondent exhibits on the job. Others identify the respondents' style by asking how they typically behave in various situations. Others, still, present short case studies and situational episodes for respondents to analyze. Their management styles are deduced from their answers and recommended actions.

An important, yet rarely raised, objection to leadership styles inventories is that they frequently imply that there is a one best or most desirable style. This is the same as saying that there is a correct way or one best way to manage. On the negative side, the trouble with this is that there *is not* one best way to manage, and those people who discover that their style is something other than this go away from the diagnostic experience with guilt feelings, which may later be expressed by either aggressive or withdrawn behavior or internalization of the discomfort. On the positive side, these management style instruments can provide managers with greater insights about themselves, which may suggest explanations for their difficulties and thus become the basis for their motivation to change.

Leadership Opinion Questionnaire

The Leadership Opinion Questionnaire (LOQ) is a forty item, objective, paper-and-pencil diagnostic test that measures preferences for two independent dimensions of leadership—initiating structure and consideration. *Initiating structure* involves the managers' actions which are oriented toward defining or structuring their work groups' situation, toward getting work done and goal attainment. *Consideration* involves managerial acts which are oriented toward developing mutual trust and which reflect respect for subordinates' ideas and consideration for their feelings. The test has norms.

The Managerial Grid®

Developed by Blake and Mouton (1964), the Managerial Grid is a framework for describing managerial styles. Styles are described in terms of two dimensions: (1) concern for production and (2) concern for people. The former measures the extent to which managers emphasize and push organizational needs for production and profit. The latter measures the extent to which managers emphasize and work for human needs for mature and healthy relationships. The grid, shown in Fig. 3–10, has nine points on both axes to measure the degree of concern for each dimension.

An accurate view of one's managerial-grid style can only be gained through feedback from others who have studied him or her in a work setting.

Management-style diagnostic test

Based on Reddin's (1970) 3-D theory of managerial effectiveness, the management-style diagnostic test measures management style in terms of three dimensions. The test is a self-administered and self-scored test consisting of sixty-four pairs of questions. The theory holds that there are four more effective and four less effective styles of managing and that there is no ideal style that is perfect for every situation. The model depicts eight different managerial styles since there are eight possible combinations of the three dimensions: (1) task orientation, (2) relationship orientation, and (3) effectiveness. *Task orienta-*

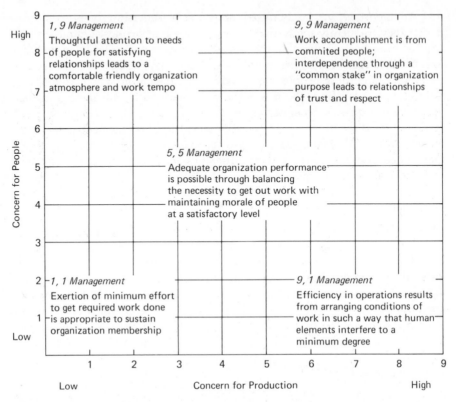

Fig. 3–10. The Managerial Grid®. (From *The Managerial Grid,* by Robert R. Blake and Jane Srygley Mouton. Houston: Gulf Publishing Company, Copyright 1964, p. 10. Reproduced by permission.)

tion reflects the extent to which managers direct their subordinates' efforts toward goal attainment. *Relationship orientation* is defined as the extent to which managers have personal job relationships. *Effectiveness* refers to the extent to which managers achieve the output requirements of their position. (See Fig. 3–11.)

Measures of Management Knowledge

There are many paper-and-pencil tests available that purport to measure management knowledge and, to a very limited extent, perhaps they do. Some of these tests measure knowledge of a number of management functional areas. Others measure only a single functional area. The problem with management knowledge tests is that the subject of management is simply too large and complex to measure one's knowledge about it adequately.

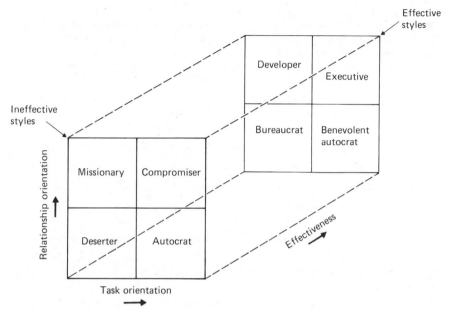

Fig. 3–11. The tri-dimensional grid. (From *Managerial Effectiveness*, by William J. Reddin. New York: McGraw-Hill, 1970. Reprinted by permission.)

How Supervise?

The purpose of *How Supervise?* is to measure the knowledge and insights supervisors have concerning practices which (according to File and Remmers, 1971) greatly influence worker efficiency and morale. The test consists of 100 items. Each item describes a situation that is common to most industrial concerns. In some of the items the respondent is asked whether she or he agrees, disagrees, or is uncertain about the statement made. In other items, she or he is asked whether the supervisory action described is desirable or undesirable. The test has norms.

Management thinking

Management Thinking is similar to *How Supervise?* but shorter. It measures knowledge in the following five functional areas:

1. Goals and planning

2. Motivation

3. Making changes

4. Leadership and developing subordinates

5. Communication. (See Table 3–6.)

Table 3-6. Management thinking.

This exercise is designed to give you an opportunity to see how your ideas and opinions on management compare with those held by other supervisors. It is not a test or a formal measure of your ability to supervise. It is only a small sample of your ideas and opinions.

Read the following thirty statements and indicate whether you agree or disagree with each. Circle *A* if you *agree* with the statement. Circle *D* if you *disagree* with the statement.

1. A   D   Completing jobs far in advance of deadlines is a sign of good planning.

2. A   D   There is a direct relationship between pay increases and productivity.

3. A   D   The main reason workers often resist change is simply because they have become comfortable with the current situation.

4. A   D   Close supervision promotes high morale.

5. A   D   Company policy need not be communicated below the supervisory level.

6. A   D   An evidence of good planning in a department is to have 100 percent of everyone's time scheduled for a week in advance.

7. A   D   Workers will do less work if they are continually watched and supervised closely.

8. A   D   Important changes are always best introduced by open written memos placed on bulletin boards.

9. A   D   Bosses should know all the answers to keep the respect of their subordinates.

10. A   D   All important communication is either spoken or written.

11. A   D   Since conditions change and problems come up in many cases, it is better not to set definite objectives to be achieved.

12. A   D   If management does not lay out goals and strict guidelines, employees will generally be passive and nothing will be accomplished.

13. A   D   Workers should usually influence the rate at which changes are implemented.

14. A   D   Managerial talent develops faster under tight supervisory control.

15. A   D   The best supervisors usually listen more than they talk.

16. A   D   It is wise to formulate only very general plans and take care of the operational problems as work progresses.

17. A   D   Motivating people is largely a job of selling your ideas and what the company demands of them.

18. A   D   Group discussion, especially where hostility to management exists, is seldom a good way to introduce change.

19. A   D   Leadership is fundamentally establishing high standards and then controlling through performance measurements to assure they are met.

Table 3–6. *cont'd.*

20. A   D   When communicating, the supervisor's sole concern should be with the facts.

21. A   D   Planning is almost impossible since it is unrealistic for one to think that troubles which might arise can be forecast.

22. A   D   In general, employees should be allowed to establish their own level of work output.

23. A   D   Supervisors who introduce change should give their primary attention to the technical and mechanical aspects so as not to slow up production.

24. A   D   There are a few people who have ability and will rise to the top, but many do not, and their advancement possibilities are limited.

25. A   D   Workers have the responsibility for understanding their supervisors' communications.

26. A   D   If workers are taught to plan, then supervisors have their planning jobs done for them.

27. A   D   The average person tends to work as little as possible.

28. A   D   Changes in company policy which are likely to be controversial and disagreed with should simply be announced from the highest level without discussion.

29. A   D   Generally, bosses should make decisions for those below them.

30. A   D   Stating a point clearly and frequently is usually the best way to get it across.

Key: The letter *A* should be circled in items 7, 13, 15, 22, and 25; the letter *D* should be circled in all other items.

(1) Goals and planning: Items 1, 6, 11, 16, 21, and 26

(2) Motivation: Items 2, 7, 12, 17, 22, and 27

(3) Making changes: Items 3, 8, 13, 18, 23, and 28

(4) Leadership and developing subordinates: Items 4, 9, 14, 19, 24, and 29

(5) Communication: Items 5, 10, 15, 20, 25, and 30

Supervisory Quiz for determining training needs

The Supervisory Quiz was developed by McLarney and Berliner (1970) to measure supervisory knowledge (not performance) in the following nineteen areas:

1. Management fundamentals

2. Organization structure

3. Policies and procedures

4. Organization dynamics

5. Communicating more effectively

6. Teamwork and cooperation

7. Planning and controlling

8. Methods improvement

9. Standards of work performance

10. Fitting people and jobs

11. Human relations

12. Training and orientation

13. Evaluating employees

14. Transfers and promotion

15. Supervisory leadership

16. Rules, discipline, tardiness, and absenteeism

17. Gripes and grievances

18. Motivation and morale

19. Tendency toward wanting to exercise (and to operate under) tight or loose supervisory control

The quiz is a hand-scored, paper-and-pencil objective test. It contains 100 statements that supervisors are asked to consider and then indicate whether they agree or disagree.

Management Behavior Descriptions

These methods serve to help indentify training needs through describing on-the-job behavior. Data are collected by easily scorable paper-and-pencil instruments, which are completed by the managers' superiors or subordinates or other close observers.

Leadership Behavior Description Questionnaire

The Ohio State Leadership Behavior Description Questionnaire (LBDQ) is much like the Leadership Opinion Questionnaire in content, but it is completed by subordinates, supervisory peers, or other close observers. It describes people's leadership styles in terms of initiating structure and consideration.

Cornelson-Strong Test

The Cornelson-Strong Self-Image Identification Test measures perceived managerial behavior in the following five areas:

1. Problem solving (or intellectual functioning)

2. Responsibility and conscientiousness (or carry-through)

3. Dominance and leadership (the tendency to emerge as the natural leader)

4. Emotional control (or balance)

5. Social competence and personal effectiveness

The intended purpose of the test is to provide managers with better self-understanding through an investigation of their perceived behavior. There are two parts to the test; one part is completed by the managers being studied and the other by their bosses. Both forms contain 100 statements describing various types of typical managerial behavior in each of the five areas mentioned above. The managers and bosses complete their respective instruments to indicate their perceptions of the extent to which the managers behave in the manner described (i.e., always, most of the time, sometimes, seldom, never). The differences in perception, as well as the behavior described, become a source for discussion and often suggest a need for improvement.

Organization-Climate Measures

The measurement of an organization's climate can provide investigators with valuable insights into probable training barriers, as well as into the abilities of the organization's management.

During the past several years, however, organization-climate measures have come under attack. Supported by good research evidence, critics point to the apparent inability of the various climate-measuring instruments to identify more than two valid dimensions: (1) structure and production orientation, and (2) consideration and people-relationship orientation. In other words, at this time, the best organization-climate measures can only discern whether the climate is "good" or "bad" in its structural and human aspects. Nonetheless, even this limited amount of information can be useful.

The Likert (1967) organization-climate measure is perhaps the best-known one. It identifies organizations as being, more or less, like one of four types of systems: (1) exploitive-authoritative; (2) benevolent-authoritative; (3) consultative, or (4) participative-group. The Likert organization-climate measure is a paper-and-pencil instrument which is completed by the organization's members, or some sample thereof. It measures eight dimensions of an organization's climate:

1. Leadership processes

2. Motivational forces

3. Communications

4. Interactions and interpersonal influences

5. Decision-making processes

6. Control processes

7. Goal setting or ordering

8. Performance goals and training.

Other organization-climate measures appear to treat the same basic kinds of issues. The better ones are Stern's (1970) Organizational Climate Index, and Payne's and Pheysey's (1971) Business Organization Climate Index.

Attitude Measures and Projective Tests

There are a host of psychological measures that are useful for measuring things such as attitudes, needs, drives, orientations, self-confidence, dependence, etc. These have not been demonstrated to be reliable predictors of managerial effectiveness. They can, at least, supplement other data collected, making its interpretation more meaningful. The measures listed here are among those most typically used.

The F-Scale

The F-Scale was originally designed to measure authoritarianism (F for potential Fascism) and it is based on the research of Adorno et al. (1950). Several other F-Scale tests have since been devised to measure authoritarianism, antidemocratic personality, ethnic prejudice, rigidity, and authority dependent persons.

The Rigidity Scale

The Rigidity Scale measures rigidity, which is defined as the tendency to persist in responses that may previously have been suitable in some situations or other but that no longer appear adequate to achieve current goals or solve current problems.

Other measures

The Thematic Apperception Test (TAT) is a projective test used to measure needs for achievement, power, and affiliation. It is a method of revealing to the trained interpreter some of the dominant drives, emotions, sentiments, complexes, and conflicts of a personality. Special value resides in its power to expose the underlying inhibited tendencies that the subject is not willing to admit or cannot admit because she or he is not conscious of them (Bellak 1951).

The Intolerance of Ambiguity Test measures the tendency to perceive ambiguous situations as sources of threat.

The Critical Thinking Test measures the ability to define problems, select pertinent information, recognize unstated assumptions, evaluate hypotheses, and make valid inferences.

The Rorschach Ink Blot Test is a measure of needs, drives, and motivations.

FORMULATING TRAINING OBJECTIVES

Specific objectives serve two important purposes: (1) they are a source of direction to channel efforts toward specific purposes; and (2) they serve as the bases for evaluating the effectiveness of these efforts. With the absence of specific objectives, efforts are usually haphazard, uncoordinated, and less effective than they might otherwise be.

An *objective* is a statement that describes a desired, future condition. It should be complete in all important detail. It is not a statement of what will be done or how it will be accomplished. Rather, it is a complete description of a desired, future condition.

Kinds of End Results

Training objectives may be written to reflect the following five different kinds of end results:

1. Reactions of participants to the learning experience and those who present it

2. Learning, in terms of changes of knowledge, skills and attitudes

3. Job behavior, changes produced by the training

4. Organizational impact, improvements in overall organizational performance

5. Additional outcomes or side benefits above and beyond those in the first four categories

It is recommended, however, that a distinction be drawn between the objectives that a training program aims to accomplish by itself and those objectives that a training program will only *assist* in getting accomplished. If this approach is followed, the objectives of a training program would be confined to the first two kinds of end results—reactions and learning. The remaining three kinds of end results would then be called *organizational* and *individual-developmental* objectives. These would require other interventions above and beyond training.

Some may criticize this approach and say, "See, training really can't do any good after all. It cannot cause meaningful change in people once they are back on the job. And here is just a sneaky attempt to let training slip away from what it purports to do—namely, improve managerial performance."

Such criticism is warranted provided two assumptions are valid: (1) that people's behavior on the job is not affected by the organization's culture and the reinforcements they receive for their behavior from the various people and elements which compose their job environment; and (2) that management development involves only formal classroom learning experiences. Both of these assumptions are absurd.

The reader will recall that in Chapter 1 a distinction was made between training and development. *Development* was defined as a systematic attempt to cause some desired behavior or performance to occur by means of a variety of both on- and off-the-job learning experiences and deliberate positive and negative reinforcements. *Training* was defined as just one, although a very important one, of the various aspects of development.

By itself, training can produce the following in people: (1) an increase in knowledge, (2) the acquisition and development of skills, and (3) changes in attitudes and beliefs. Whether this learning will, in turn, cause changes in on-the-job behavior and also improvements in the organization's performance will depend upon the support and reinforcement that the trainees receive on the job as they try to implement the things that they have learned and now accept, and upon the extent to which the performance of the organization is influenced by this new behavior. The profits earned by a firm during any one year of operations, for example, may be only slightly affected by the quality of its management because of the overriding impact of the economic and competitive forces in its environment. Over much longer periods of time, however, a firm's performance is much more a function of the quality of its management.

By making a distinction between training and development, establishing separate sets of objectives for each, as it is suggested here, and communicating this to everyone associated with the training, some very useful benefits result. Namely, attention will be called to the fact that training can produce only certain kinds of changes and, if top management wants changes in on-the-job behavior, then it will be necessary to establish an organizational climate and working environment that is supportive and positively reinforces those who received training as they apply on their jobs what they have learned. And, if top management wants improvements in organizational performance, a host of additional activities and interventions systematically designed to cause these improvements must be carried out.

This approach is not without potential problems. By separating training objectives from development objectives it becomes very easy for those people who are responsible for the achievement of these objectives to specialize in one or the other. If they do this, the likelihood of these two sets of objectives being inconsistent and incompatible becomes great. To prevent this from occurring, training objectives must be formulated in light of the development objectives, which were established earlier. Only then can these two kinds of efforts and their corresponding objectives be consistent.

Mechanics of Preparing Training Objectives

Training objectives per se, following along with what has been suggested earlier, should be written for two areas—participant reactions and learning.

Participant reactions are targets associated with how well the program ran and the degree to which everyone involved with it was satisfied. The objectives established for this area should include things such as the participants' satisfaction with the course overall, its various teachers and discussion leaders, the materials presented, the daily schedule, and the facilities and accommodations. A complete list of factors which should be included in the area of participant reactions appears in Chapter 8.

The second area of training objectives involves learning. Remember that *learning objectives* are carefully prepared statements of the learning that should occur to help correct the deficient areas identified in Step 6 of the needs identification process. Once these deficient areas are identified and ordered in terms of their importance and training specialists have identified the knowledge, skills, and attitudes that must be learned to help overcome them, specific training objectives can be formulated.

The conceptual framework of knowledge, skills, and personal characteristics necessary for effective management found in Chapter 1 can be useful in preparing learning objectives because it shows the interrelationship of the knowledge, skills, and personal characteristics that are identified as learning targets.

Learning objectives should be written so that the extent to which they have been reached can easily be determined. Statements such as, "The trainees will learn about basic principles of leadership," "We will teach management by objectives," "The trainees will understand how to plan," "The trainees will know the basic concepts of motivation," etc. refer to desired areas of learning, but they are *not* measurable end results. To help overcome the problem of having statements of learning objectives that are not measurable, the concept

---

1. Name and describe six traditional principles of organization.
2. List the steps involved in making a time study.
3. Define a system and tell what the system's concept is.
4. Explain Maslow's hierarchy of needs and tell how this concept can be useful to managers.
5. Define perception.
6. Write a goal that meets the tests of a well-written goal.
7. Demonstrate an ability to listen for and understand how another person feels by what he or she says.
8. Define and describe the psychological reasons for resistance to change.
9. Construct a break-even chart and explain how it can be used.
10. Demonstrate a willingness to use various styles of leadership, appropriately selected for different situations.
11. Explain the difference between "activities-oriented management" and "results-oriented management."
12. Identify and explain the key elements of an MBO system.

Fig. 3–12. Examples of behavioral objectives.

of *behavioral objectives* came into being. Behavioral objectives are statements of what the trainees will be able to do as a result of the training they receive. Thus, instead of relying on a vague statement, "Learners will know about management by objectives" as being the objective, several specific, measurable statements about what trainees will be able to do are formulated. These statements clearly identify key things the trainees will be able to do, and they provide demonstrable evidence that learning has occurred. (See Fig. 3–12.)

Difficulties

Nearly everyone will find that writing behavioral objectives is not easy. There is no question about it. The process is difficult and laborious. It requires considerable thought to crystallize in one's own mind exactly what it is he or she wishes to accomplish. This is a process that is foreign to many people and one in which most people have not yet developed skill. So, very often, to avoid this unpleasant exercise, all kinds of excuses will be made. For example, many people will argue that since it is so difficult to say what people will actually learn, the exercise of preparing long lists of objectives is a meaningless exercise. Still others will say that because they are professionals who have had many years of experience and already know what they are doing, for them to write out objectives is a waste of time. To some extent, these arguments have some substance. However, there is no substitute for carefully thought-through objectives.

There also seems to be some logic to the argument that one can go too far and get bogged down writing too many objectives. It is suggested, therefore, that a representative sample of key indicators be used as the set of behavioral objectives which are ultimately formulated. By doing this, the necessary exercise of clearly thinking through and defining the desired learning is accomplished in a fashion that does not become an overwhelming academic exercise. As a generalization, four to six statements (or behavioral objectives) are usually sufficient to describe the outcomes that should be reached in a typical half-day session for most topics.

Responsibility for Attainment

Training objectives should be known, understood, and accepted by both trainees and instructors. The responsibility for their attainment should be shared by both. More importantly, trainees, instructors, and top management should understand and share in the responsibility for achieving developmental objectives.

Once training objectives have been established, the next task is to plan for their achievement.

REFERENCES

Adorno, Theodor W. et al. *The Authoritarian Personality.* New York: Harper & Row, 1950.

Bellak, Leopold. *Thematic Apperception Test.* New York: The Psychological Corporation, 1951.

Blake, Robert R., and Mouton, Jane S. *The Managerial Grid.* Houston: Gulf Publishing, 1964.

Bray, Douglas W., and Grant, D. L. "The Assessment Center in the Measurement of Potential for Business Management." *Psychological Monographs* 80 (17, No. 625), 1966.

Dunnette, Marvin D. (Ed.). *Handbook of Industrial and Organizational Psychology.* Chicago: Rand-McNally, 1976.

File, Quentin W., and Remmers, H. H. *How Supervise?* New York: The Psychological Corporation, 1971.

Flanagan, John C. "Defining the Requirements of the Executive's Job." *Personnel* 28, No. 1, July 1951, pp. 28–35.

Flanagan, John C. "The Critical Incident's Technique." *Psychological Bulletin* 51, No. 4, July 1954, pp. 327–358.

Gallegos, Robert C., and Phelan, Joseph G. "Using Behavioral Objectives in Industrial Training." *Training and Development Journal,* 28, No. 4, April 1974, pp. 42–48.

Horne, J. H., and Lupton, T. "The Work Activities of Middle Managers." *Journal of Management Studies,* 1, No. 1, 1965, pp. 14–33.

Lawrence, Paul R., and Lorsch, Jay W. *Organization and Environment.* Homewood, Ill.: Richard D. Irwin, 1969.

Likert, Rensis. *New Patterns of Management.* New York: McGraw-Hill, 1961.

Likert, Rensis. *The Human Organization.* New York: McGraw-Hill, 1967.

Litwin, George H. and Stringer, Robert A., Jr. *Motivation and Organizational Climate.* Boston: Division of Research Graduate School of Business Administration, Harvard University, 1968.

McConnell, John J., and Parker, Treadway C. "An Assessment Center Program for Multi-Organizational Use." *Training and Development Journal,* 26, No. 3, March 1972, pp. 6–15.

McLarney, William J., and Berliner, William M. *Management Training: Cases and Principles.* Instructor's Manual and Conference Leaders' Guide. Homewood, Ill.: Richard D. Irwin, 1970.

Mager, Robert F. *Preparing Instructional Objectives.* Palo Alto, Calif.: Pearson Publishers, 1962.

Payne, Roy L. and Pheysey, D. C. "G. G. Stern's Organizational Climate Index: A Reconceptualization and Application to Business Organizations." *Organizational Behavior and Human Performance,* 6, No. 1, January 1971, pp. 77–98.

Reddin, William J. *Managerial Effectiveness.* New York: McGraw-Hill, 1970.

Stern, George G. *People in Context: Measuring Person Environment Congruence in Education and Industry.* New York: Wiley, 1970.

Terry, George R. *Principles of Management.* Homewood, Ill.: Richard D. Irwin, 7th Ed. 1977.

This, Leslie. "Results Oriented Training Design." *Training and Development Journal,* 25, No. 4, April 1971, pp. 8–14.

4

Planning the Strategies
and Programs
to Reach
Management Training and
Development Objectives

Well-thought-out plans help channel human efforts and the expenditure of resources to accomplish specific purposes efficiently and economically. Plans are an important prerequisite to almost every pursuit, and the training and development of managers is no exception. Planning is a mental exercise, being largely conceptual in nature, which demands a great deal of clairvoyant and creative powers.

Essentially, a plan is a comprehensive statement of the events that must occur to cause the attainment of the desired end results. The several steps involved in formulating a plan typically include the following:

1. A comprehensive description of the desired end results is formulated. This is a statement of purpose explaining what is to be accomplished.

2. A comprehensive description is made up of the relevant features of present conditions. This step includes an assessment of the organization's strengths, weaknesses, capabilities, and resources, and findings often signal a need to modify the goals formulated in step one.

3. An analysis is made of the situation involved. The relevant planning premises are identified, which involves an identification and statement of significant assumptions, constraints, and parameters.

4. A forecast is made of factors and events that might help or hinder the attainment of the desired end results. Estimates are made as to the probability of the occurrence of these events and their possible impact.

5.   Alternative approaches (plans) are developed. These plans specify the events and their sequence that must occur to cause the desired end results. This is the creative phase of the planning process because it essentially involves developing novel and varied solutions to specific problems.

6.   The best plan of the alternatives generated in step five is selected in light of information gathered in steps two and three, estimated cost of implementation, and probability of its success.

ESTABLISHING TRAINING AND DEVELOPMENT PLANS

The steps involved in establishing training and development plans, which essentially correspond to the general planning steps given above, are as follows:

1.   The desired managerial behaviors are specified.

2.   The present managerial behaviors are observed and identified.

3.   The knowledge, skills and personal characteristics necessary to cause the desired managerial behaviors to occur are specified.

4.   The present kinds and levels of knowledge, skill, and personal characteristics are studied and identified.

5.   Information gathered in steps one and two and in steps three and four is studied to determine the behavioral changes that are needed and the changes in knowledge, skill, and personal characteristics that are necessary to cause these behavioral changes to occur.

6.   An assessment and analysis is made of the organization's climate, constraints that exist, key parameters, and other significant factors that exist or are predicted to occur, which will help or hinder the planned behavioral changes and the training necessary to cause these changes.

7.   Alternative approaches to cause the desired changes are formulated. These alternative approaches (plans) involve a detailed delineation of the steps necessary to cause the desired behavior.

8.   The best plan is chosen from among those developed in step seven.

There are, however, several differences and important difficulties associated with each step that are worth discussing.

PROBLEMS ASSOCIATED WITH THE STEPS

Step 1—Desired Managerial Behaviors are Specified

This step is difficult to accomplish for a number of reasons. Basically, it is extremely difficult to pinpoint specific managerial behaviors that cause effective performance.

One reason for this is that in some situations managers are effective in spite of their ineptness and inappropriate managerial practices. This occurs when factors beyond their control cause their success. In other situations, the reverse is true. Another reason is that the same managerial behaviors do not always yield success in terms of effective performance, just as other managerial behaviors do not always lead to ineffective performance. Here again, external factors are the determinants of effectiveness.

Another reason is that there are a myriad of sometimes-contradictory theories about what constitutes good management and most of these theories have some degree of merit. To believe that there is a definable formula for the best way to manage would be extremely naive. Management is largely an art as opposed to a definite science that must be practiced in a precise and systematic way.

These problems are not totally insurmountable, but they cannot be completely solved or avoided either, as we will see in the following descriptions of ways in which desired managerial behaviors are identified in practice.

One approach used in identifying desirable managerial behaviors might be labeled *patterning after an ideal model*. This approach rests on the notion that training efforts should be aimed at making those who undergo training more like what "successful managers" are like. When using this approach, data are first collected from management literature that describe the predominant traits, attitudes, and behavior of successful managers. These findings, plus the perceptions and beliefs of those who collect and interpret this information, are then organized in such a way as to create a model of the "ideal manager." All training efforts are then directed at developing and changing people so that they will become more like this ideal manager. For example, those who identified the ideal manager as one who subscribes to theory Y, or is heavily employee centered, or typically practices participative management, have as their goal the training of all managers so that they will subscribe to theory Y, or will be employee centered, or will practice participative management, etc., without regard for what the managers' positions, organizations, or managerial assignments may be.

This approach appears to be logical and can produce some valuable improvements in managerial ability. However, it rests on several faulty assumptions and, therefore, can lead to ill-directed training efforts. The most glaringly inaccurate assumption underlying this approach has been mentioned many times—namely, that there is one best way to manage.

The assumption that all managers should subscribe to a particular management style should be seriously questioned. Should all managers manage in the same way? Is it worth the cost of trying to change all of them to be like the ideal manager? Is it even possible to affect such a change? Not all managerial positions require the same traits, attitudes, and behaviors. Moreover, all managers do not do the same things. Some do more planning; others do more communicating by writing; still others do more motivating, and so on. Managers perform their roles differently and are successful for various reasons, depending upon their assignments, organizations, employees, technologies, and themselves.

Another, although less well known, defect of this approach is that it usually ignores behaviors that are often critical to success. These behaviors are ignored because they lie outside the traditional conceptual frameworks that define and describe the work of the manager. Some of the research findings of Leonard Sayles (1964) and Henry Mintzberg (1975) have led to the conclusion that the work of managers and, hence, the behaviors required of them involve behaviors and activities other than simply planning, organizing, motivating, communicating, and controlling. For example, Mintzberg concluded from his research that managers perform in such roles as figureheads, liaisons, disturbance handlers, resource allocators, negotiators, disseminators of information, and spokesmen. Many of the things that Mintzberg observed managers doing he claimed were only obliquely related to traditional concepts of managers' jobs.

One study of first-line supervisors' jobs concluded that supervisors spend a considerable portion of their time observing. Yet, it would be unusual to find a supervisory-management-training program with one of its major goals being the improvement of the observational powers and skills of trainees.

Another approach used in identifying desirable managerial behaviors involves determining what those who are to receive the training actually do. Information regarding what these managers do is gathered by first-hand observation of them at their work. Learning experiences are then designed to teach these managers how to do these things.

This approach aids in avoiding the mistake of trying to make all managers more like some ideal manager model, which may not always be appropriate to particular situations. For example, this approach will call for considerable training in face-to-face communications, problem solving and work planning and scheduling for first-line supervisors who are required to do a lot of these things in their work. The approach avoids the inclusion of inappropriate subjects (such as long-range planning, organizational design, policy making, and labor negotiations) in management programs for first-line supervisors. In essence, this approach is aimed at helping managers to learn to do their jobs better. However, this too is not without problems.

For one thing, this approach more or less assumes that the managerial behaviors observed are, in fact, appropriate. For example, if the people in the training population are observed to spend only a very small portion of their time planning, then, by this approach, one would conclude that planning is a relatively unimportant topic or skill for these people to master, when in fact, these managers should be devoting considerably more of their time to planning and are not as effective as they could be. This approach, therefore, can lead to the reinforcement of dysfunctional behaviors and the nonreinforcement of—or even failure to teach—desirable behaviors. Also, by limiting the training content to only what managers already do, the training fails to broaden the trainees' perspectives and to prepare them for higher-level positions that they may occupy in the future.

Still another approach used in identifying desirable managerial behaviors involves combining the positive aspects of the two preceding approaches and avoiding their negative aspects. This approach begins with a study of what managers do. Next it attempts to determine the relative value and appropriateness of the behaviors or omission of behaviors observed. And finally, based upon expert analysis and judgment, it specifies the desired behaviors.

In practice, the specification of desired managerial behaviors is usually not precise or detailed. There are two important reasons for this. First, it is nearly impossible to describe all of the desired managerial behaviors. To attempt to do so would involve a great deal of work. And second, it would be extremely naive to think that one could define and describe all the ideal managerial behaviors for all situations.

Therefore, when faced with these constraints and the limitations of time, it makes good sense to specify and describe only a few of the managerial behaviors desired and then design learning experiences to bring them about. It is also important that these behaviors be described so that an observer could determine whether they occur and, if so, to what extent. In other words, desired behaviors should be described in *measurable* terms. Moreover, it is also helpful if these behaviors are described to show the desired end result. For example, instead of saying, "Managers should communicate important news to subordinates," it would be better to say, "Managers should keep their subordinates informed about current and future conditions and changes relating to the work environment so that they know and understand this information." Or, instead of saying, "Managers should plan," it would be better to say, "Managers should have well-defined courses of action formulated to achieve their goals so that unnecessary and wasteful actions are avoided."

It is evident that even these suggestions for sharpening the meaning and improving the clarity of the desired managerial behaviors so that they are measurable are, at best, abstract and wanting in clarity and meaning themselves. Thus it is sometimes wise to specify particular behaviors that should not exist, such as those that are dysfunctional or obviously detrimental to the organization.

Beyond these difficulties lies an even larger problem: statements of desired managerial behavior are nearly always superficial. For example, the description of desired managerial behavior relating to planning, mentioned earlier, is not an in-depth description and, hence, ignores important behaviors that lead to effective planning. It does not treat such issues as: Were adequate and creative alternatives generated? Was the one best plan chosen on the basis of logical criteria? How logical were the steps in the plan? While managerial behaviors can be specified, it is nearly impossible to do an adequate job of specifying the quality of thinking which must precede the behaviors. In other words, it is possible to state that managers should plan, but it is nearly impossible to specify the mental processes and procedures that lead to the plan, which is why the specification of desired managerial behaviors is, at best, superficial.

Step 2—Present Managerial Behaviors are Observed and Identified

This step seeks to identify the critical managerial behaviors of the training population. Behaviors (and nonbehaviors) that are particularly effective or ineffective are noted. While this sounds simple enough, there are difficulties involved.

It is difficult for an outsider to observe managers first-hand for prolonged periods. Under the best of conditions, observation is usually for short periods of time—e.g., one day. Those being observed are usually suspicious of outsiders. Moreover, the mere act of being observed will cause most people to behave in ways other than they normally do. Even when observers are known and trusted, their presence is often somewhat of a nuisance to the people being observed. First-hand observations also require a considerable amount of time, which is often not available.

The sources of managerial success and failure are frequently identified incorrectly. For example, it is common to hear someone say that a particular problem was due to poor communications. Upon further investigation, however, it is often found that the problem was not caused by a communications failure, but by some other factor, such as organizational design, the lack of objectives, or a political maneuver for power.

These are only a few of the important reasons why this step needs to be performed by well-trained, perceptive people. Those who perform this step should be quite knowledgeable in the areas of management, organizational behavior, and action-research techniques. They should also be observant and have unobtrusive and inoffensive personalities.

In practice, most of the information regarding actual behaviors comes from secondary sources (e.g., observations made by superiors, subordinates, and peers) and is subject to perceptual distortions.

To some extent, assessment centers are used to identify managerial behaviors first-hand. The drawbacks to assessment centers are that they are limited in scope to observing only a limited number of predetermined behaviors and that the setting is artificial and can cause unnatural reactions.

Paper-and-pencil survey instruments are sometimes used in this step. These, too, are subject to perceptual distortions and are limited in scope.

Step 3—Knowledge, Skills, and Personal Characteristics
Necessary to Cause the Desired Managerial Behaviors are Specified

People who are trained in and knowledgeable of the various areas of management (especially organizational behavior) and action research can usually do a reasonable job of specification. Committees should be used to perform this step so as to take advantage of various perspectives and to obtain insights that might not be generated by one person working alone.

There is a great temptation to assume that the knowledge, skills, and personal characteristics of successful managers should be acquired by those who will receive training. This conclusion may or may not be valid. For one thing, it is essentially the same mistake that was discussed in step one. For another thing, it fails to conclusively justify why particular areas of knowledge, or attitudes, or skills, or abilities, or personal characteristics will cause or help cause the behaviors desired. This requirement should always be met.

There are no shortcuts to doing a competent job in this step. It is a laborious process involving a great amount of thoughtful analysis and judgment. But putting forth the time and effort required will yield a first-rate learning plan and not some haphazard hodgepodge, which would be comparatively ineffective. In order to do a thorough and adequate job of this, it is suggested that each of the desired managerial behaviors be considered individually. Then, for each, the knowledge, the skills, and the personal characteristics that trainees need in order to behave in the ways identified are, in turn, specified. In doing this, it may be helpful to construct a table consisting of four columns: (1) desired managerial behaviors; (2) knowledge; (3) skills; and (4) personal characteristics. This will serve as a helpful device to assure that this procedure is carried out thoroughly and systematically. Figure 4–1 illustrates how this might be done for one managerial behavior.

Step 4—Present Kinds and Levels of Knowledge, Skills, and Personal Characteristics are Studied and Identified

Knowledge, skills, and personal characteristics may be identified through two approaches—direct measurement and inferences based upon observed behaviors as described in Chapter 3. *Direct measurement* should be used and interpreted cautiously as it is imprecise and subject to a certain (although tolerable) amount of error. *Inferences* based upon observed behaviors are even more suspect. An adequate sampling of behaviors is necessary before one should ever attempt to ascertain people's knowledge, skills, and personal characteristics.

Step 5—Desired Behavioral Changes and the Changes in Knowledge, Skill, and Personal Characteristics Necessary to Cause these are Identified

This step is accomplished through completing Steps 1 through 4. It identifies the differences between the present and the desired state of affairs.

There is a tendency to be overly optimistic about how much change can be produced by a training program and to neglect the contributions of other types of developmental experiences such as special assignments, job rotation, and on-the-job coaching. Moreover, training specialists often feel overwhelmed by the amount and magnitude of things that should be changed. They may respond to this feeling by attempting to accomplish too many things

Desired managerial behaviors	Knowledge	Skills: Diagnostic and application	Personal characteristics to diagnose and to apply
(Example) Manager plans all important projects and functions	1. Knows what planning is and what a plan involves 2. Knows the steps in planning 3. Knows the qualities of a good plan 4. Knows the value of planning 5. Knows planning techniques	1. Has the ability to perform "causative thinking." Can visualize cause-and-effect relationships 2. Can creatively design courses of action to cause desired end results 3. Able to perceive and understand the significance of important events. Can sense "helps" and "hinderances" 4. Able to estimate accurately the time required for various events and functions (can schedule) 5. Able to criticize a plan 6. Able to commit plan to writing	1. Believes that planning is worthwhile. 2. Is deliberate in action. Thinks things through before acting. Not averse to mental activity 3. Watches self to guard against being a "reactor"; strives to be a "pro-actor" 4. Is creative. Inclined to develop alternative courses of action and not just one 5. Inclined to criticize own plans. Tendency to raise questions about the feasibility and practicality of various courses of action and to understand their significance 6. Not averse to putting plans in writing

Fig. 4-1. Knowledge, skills, and personal characteristics necessary to cause specific, desired managerial behaviors.

in one training program and may end up doing nothing very well as a result. It is more important to concentrate on a few of the most important areas in need of change and do a thorough and competent job than to do a poor job in many areas. Of course, the selection of the most important areas rests heavily on seasoned judgment and is not an easy task.

In formulating alternative training and development plans, one should keep the various methods and their respective advantages and drawbacks in mind (Fig. 4–2).

Step 6—Constraints and Parameters are Identified

Neglect of important factors that help or hinder training efforts will create problems. A thorough analysis and assessment of important parameters and constraints (such as time and resources available for training; reading abilities of participants; attitudes toward training, and an understanding of the organization's climate) are absolutely necessary. Unfortunately, far too few training specialists do an adequate job of this and, as a result, their efforts do not produce the level and quality of results that are possible. The main reason why these factors are neglected lies in the fact that some people view management training as the most important aspect of the management-development process. Training is an important aspect, but it is not the only building block in the management-development process. Moreover, the organizational climate must be understood and seen as a principal determinant of the developmental process.

A. On-the-job methods
  1. Regular managerial assignments
  2. Special assignments
  3. Job rotation
  4. On-the-job coaching and counseling
  5. Periodic performance appraisals

B. Off-the-job methods
  1. For individuals:
     a) Self-study training packages, such as programed instruction and video cassette training modules
     b) Reading selected articles, books, and materials
     c) Selected courses and seminars sponsored by outside organizations that do the training, such as universities and the A.M.A.
  2. For groups of managers or all supervisory and managerial personnel within an organization:
     a) Reading programs—groups read particular material and meet to discuss it
     b) In-house seminars

Fig. 4–2. Management-development methods.

Step 7—Alternative Approaches are Formulated

The inability to visualize alternative ways of reaching an objective is one of the major barriers to doing an adequate job of this step. Another major barrier is the attachment some training-program planners may have to a particular subject, concept, or classroom exercise. This attachment can exist for any number of reasons: a strong belief that all managers should know and practice the particular concept; the excitement the program planner may have about a recently learned idea or training exercise; or the lack of breadth of knowledge of the training specialist—for example, the specialist knows only a limited number of approaches or exercises. Thus a great deal of creativity is required to come up with several suitable alternatives.

Step 8—The Optimal Plan is Selected

The biggest problem here is in developing a rational approach to identify the plan with the greatest probability of success in view of the constraints imposed and the objectives set forth. Unfortunately, no simple procedure or rule exists for performing this type of evaluation. As a practical matter, it is probably best to list the key objectives and the principle constraints and parameters and then examine each alternative plan with regard to this information. Committees are useful for assessing plans because a group can see more aspects and issues than an individual can.

CONSTRAINTS

Every organization's training needs and particular circumstances are to some extent unique and should therefore be analyzed and understood before planning is completed. It is a good idea to have a clear understanding of the constraints described here so that realistic plans which are likely to be successful can be formulated.

Time Constraints

For reasons of efficiency and profitability most organizations strive to allocate their personnel to tasks and endeavors which are most critical to maintaining the organizations' existence and advancing performance and profitability. This can prove to be very discouraging to training personnel since training and development do not typically occupy as high a level of priority with managements as do other factors. Moreover, operational problems of the day will always receive top priority because they are real and immediate and because the consequences of no action or incorrect action are readily apparent. Problems associated with a lack of management training are not usually perceived to be as pressing and in need of immediate action as operating problems are. Thus, time available for training is often a major constraint for essentially two reasons. First, the need for training is not perceived to be as pressing and in need of attention as operating problems, which are continually cropping up. And second, most managers see doing the work that needs to be performed as being far more critical to their own and their organizations' success than the maintenance and improvement of the skills and abilities which enable them to perform effectively. These are formidable obstacles for training personnel to overcome. They come down to a few key questions, for which training personnel must find answers. Namely, "How can we get top management to appreciate and support training?" and "How can we get top management to release managers from their normal duties so that they can participate in training and development programs?

Training personnel should understand and appreciate top management's priorities so that they will not say or do things that top management will perceive as being contrary to the best interests of the organization. Training personnel should also work continuously at building up management's confidence in and enthusiasm for the value of management training and development.

They should seize every opportunity to promote and implement training, but never at the expense of the long-range profitability of the organization. If top management feels that a four-week (or two-week or one-week) management seminar is too long, the training specialists should find or design a shorter one. The important thing to remember is to have training and to allow its value to become appreciated through experience. Especially when the idea of management training is relatively new to an organization, it is an excellent idea to assure that the materials taught are practical and can be applied on the job. Doing this helps to make the benefits of training more obvious than they might otherwise be if the training did not cover easily applicable concepts.

In-house training programs frequently face the major obstacle of scheduling time-off for managers to attend. In very large-scale operations some strain and disruption occurs when management personnel are away from their normal duties, but it is usually not any more serious than it is when these people are away on vacations. It might be pointed out that these periods of absences permit opportunities for assistants to assume increased responsibilities as they fill-in for absent superiors. This too is a benefit that training personnel can use as a selling point and as a counter argument to the perceived problem of having managers away from their work.

In small-scale operations, it is generally close to impossible to free up enough management personnel during normal working hours to conduct training. This problem can be solved by conducting a series of short (1 to 3 hour), in-house sessions after working hours or by sending one or two people at a time to outside programs. Another possibility is for several smaller firms with similar training needs to collectively hire an outside consultant or specialist to plan and present the management training program for their managers and supervisors. Alone, these smaller companies would not have enough managers in need of training to warrant the expense of having their own programs; by joining forces, several firms can form an adequate size group of managers for profitable training at a minimum cost.

Budget Constraints

As every training director knows, when times are bad, a training program will be one of the first items to be cut from the budget; and, when times are very good, people are too busy to attend training programs. It would seem to make sense for companies to set aside money for training programs during their prosperous periods when personnel are extremely busy, and to spend it on training during bad times when personnel are not so busy.

Since budget constraints are often such an enormous problem, it seems odd that training directors and their staffs do not spend some of their time studying and keeping track of the economy and their company's and its industry's economic picture and projections for the future. Training specialists could work with their firm's economists and profit-planning departments to learn when times will be good or bad for training. By so doing, training departments could base a substantial part of their long-range plans on economic conditions and thus be ready with more realistic and helpful training plans than they might have if they simply spent their time reacting to the fluctuations in business activity, as many do today. Thus, when times are bad and the firm's budget does not allow for training, a substantial amount of the training department's efforts could be spent on program planning and development, which is not costly. Then, when times are good, the training department would be ready with well-planned programs and able to concentrate its efforts on conducting these training activities.

Attitude Constraints

Formal training and development planning frequently neglects many of the more significant attitudes held by members of the organizations. Obviously training activities do not occur in a vacuum. Training will be welcomed and accepted and its teachings implemented on the job only to the extent that prevailing attitudes permit. Attitudes toward training, the training department and its personnel, the subject matter and concepts taught, and the changes in behavior sought should be examined and included with the other factors and constraints that planners must know about if they are to formulate realistic plans.

Attitudes regarding the reactions toward past training programs should be studied and understood. In particular, participants' evaluations of past programs should be examined closely. Appropriate actions should be taken to make future programs more acceptable and profitable to participants, and these efforts should be made known.

Indifference to training is a commonly found constraint. It exists primarily because most people have had no experience with training and do not understand what it involves or what it can do. Quite often, this indifference can be changed to enthusiasm through first-hand experience with first-rate training.

Another attitude constraint is the unwillingness to practice new, untried, sometimes even radically different management practices. Past experience with older approaches frequently acts as reinforcement that they are correct and proper. The utility of untried methods may appear to be minimal, perhaps even negative. If these attitudes exist, it is wise to move slowly in causing change. Attitudes are usually fixed and will persist over long periods of time. Even by following the best of plans, they are difficult to change.

By the same token positive attitudes toward training and the value of new concepts can and should be used to further the cause and purposes of training. One way in which this might be implemented is to include, in the first group of managers to receive training in a company, only those people who are receptive to training and trying out the ideas to be taught. This will help to assure that the first training efforts will be successful and highly acceptable. Moreover, positive feelings toward training will have a chance to spread throughout the organization as this first group of managers return to their jobs and tell their peers about their training experience.

One of the most crucial determinants of the attitude an organization's management holds toward training and development is the attitude and commitment to training displayed by the organization's "number-one" person. Training directors should attempt to earn the confidence and support of the firm's chief executive officer.

CHARACTERISTICS OF THOSE WHO WILL RECEIVE TRAINING

Every good salesman knows the importance of understanding the customer. The same thinking applies to training: understand the trainees. If training is to be helpful and impactful, it must be designed and presented in a manner appropriate to the trainees. Among the participant characteristics that should be considered when planning a training program are the trainees' responsibilities and levels in their organizations, educational backgrounds, work experiences, reading ability, openness to new ideas, and perceived need for self-improvement. Answers to the kinds of questions shown in Table 4.1 will supply program planners with valuable guidance.

TRAINING-PROGRAM INPUTS

After objectives are formulated and the important parameters and constraints have been identified, those who plan training programs need to specify the input resources and how they will be combined. Input resources include program content or subject matter, instructors, teaching aids and materials, and physical facilities. A plan may be thought of in terms of selected resources and how they are combined.

Table 4-1. Guidelines for understanding the characteristics of trainees and tailoring the training experience to match.

A. Levels within the organization

1. Is the program's content appropriate for the levels of management represented?

2. Are the teaching methods and aids (lectures, readings, case studies, role plays, management games, exercises, and simulations) appropriate for the levels of management represented?

3. Do the faculty discussion leaders have the reputation and abilities to teach the levels of management represented?

B. Educational backgrounds

1. To what extent are participants able to conceptualize? Can they think abstractly and in terms of concepts, or must the training focus only on specific examples and concrete prescriptions?

2. Have the participants already learned the contingent principles and concepts to be taught? Do they feel that they already know all they need to about the subjects that are to be covered? Do they really know as much as they should know or think they know?

3. Will they be slow or unable to comprehend the concepts and techniques to be taught because their previous educational experiences have not prepared them well enough to understand or accept these concepts? (For example, they may not have adequate foundations in psychology or mathematics to understand some advanced concepts and techniques of management.) Must the instructor be an experienced practitioner in order to command the attention and respect of the participants? Or, can a scholarly professor, who may be short on first-hand experience, be acceptable and effective in causing learning?

C. Work experiences

1. How can the work experiences of the participants be drawn upon as a resource to aid the learning process? (The case-study method is well suited to groups of trainees who have vast amounts of work experience.)

2. Are the illustrations, examples, problem assignments, and case studies appropriate for those attending the program? (For example, if the learners come predominantly from line positions in manufacturing companies, it would be most logical to select examples and case studies involving line positions in manufacturing.)

D. Reading ability

1. At what level of sophistication should the reading materials be?

2. How much reading can the participants realistically be expected to do?

3. How lengthy and complex should the case studies be?

Table 4-1. *cont'd.*

E. Openness to new ideas

1. What are the prevailing value systems and attitudes of the participants relative to new ideas? How rigid are these people in their thinking? What kinds of new concepts are participants likely to be most receptive to? Which ones are they likely to be least receptive to?

2. How open are participants to ideas and concepts that will help improve their managerial ability as opposed to concepts and practices which are immediately applicable only to specific problems they have at work?

F. Perceived need for self-improvement

1. Do the participants perceive a need for self-improvement? If so, in which areas?

2. Do participants have some knowledge of their own developmental needs? Do they know where they are strong and weak? How accurate are these perceptions of themselves?

PROGRAM CONTENT

The content of a training program is specified during the fifth step in the planning process which was discussed earlier. In practice, program content decisions include the following:

1. Identifying the topic areas that should be covered to reach the stated objectives

2. Specifying key points and specific concepts and thinking processes that should be learned

3. Determining the emphasis that should be given to each topic and the specifics within each topic.

4. Sequencing the topics so that they fit together in a logical progression and build on one another to form a systematic whole

5. Establishing a learning pace that is stimulating and impactful

Identifying Topics and Specifying Key Points

By grouping into topical areas related concepts and techniques that must be learned to reach a stated training objective, the learning process is made easier because it helps trainees to focus their attention on a specific and limited subject area and allows them to digest closely interrelated ideas at one time. A useful technique for grouping concepts and techniques into topic areas is to prepare a table such as the one shown in Fig. 4-3.

Training objective	Concepts and techniques	Topic
Manager is able to establish clear, measurable goals	Values of objectives and typical results that occur, when they exist and are known. What a well-written goal is—its qualities	Goal setting

Fig. 4-3. Format for grouping concepts and techniques into topical areas.

In preparing this table, first list the training objectives. Next specify the concepts, techniques, skills, and personal characteristics that must be learned and mastered to reach the associated objectives. Third, group the related concepts and techniques according to logical topical units. Figure 4-3 illustrates how this might be done for one topic area.

There is often a great temptation to go through this process in reverse order—that is, to establish topic areas first and then identify the concepts and techniques to be taught within it. Finally, specify the end results that should occur as a consequence. The danger here is under-emphasizing or even totally ignoring some training objectives that might otherwise be addressed or addressed more completely. Moreover, it often leads to the neglect of what may be the most crucial training needs because it confines training to just the traditional functions.

Planners who follow the approach recommended here will find that it is difficult to implement at first because it requires them to carefully think through and specify what must be learned to reach the stated objective. There is also a great temptation to use only traditional management functions as the topic headings (e.g., leadership, planning, organizing, controlling, etc.). One should not feel restricted to use only these. The advantage of the approach suggested here is that it can lead to the designation of novel, but relevant, topics to be covered in a program, such as: organizing to secure and foster interdepartmental coordination and cooperation; counseling those who are upset, hostile, emotional, or completely irrational; and challenges faced by firms doing business in the inner city of a major metropolis, to name a few.

Determining the Emphasis to be Given to Each Topic

The emphasis given in terms of the time allotted to each topic or each specific aspect of a topic should be determined with regard to its relative importance, difficulty and complexity, attitudes, and opinions held that are either contrary to or in agreement with it, and the total amount of time available for training. As a rule, it is better to do a thorough job of teaching only a few topics, giving them the time and emphasis necessary, than it is to cover many topics in a superficial way.

Very often, training-program planners find that there is not adequate time to reach all of the objectives they originally set. When this occurs, this guideline will help eliminate wasted efforts.

Sequencing the Topics

Ideally, topics should be presented in a logical order. Practically, this is not always the case because of time constraints and instructor availability. Nonetheless, the logical sequence of topics is an important aim. For example, goal setting should be taught before planning; the fundamentals of planning should be taught before special planning methods and techniques; and the fundamentals of human behavior should be taught before topics such as discipline or implementing change.

The careful sequencing of topics can serve purposes beyond assuring the logical presentation of concepts. Careful sequencing can also be used to overcome resistance to particular concepts and adherence to dysfunctional approaches to managing. For example, some of the more advanced concepts and techniques, especially those of the behavioral sciences, are especially prone to rejection if some of the more basic and fundamental concepts are not understood and accepted first. As an illustration, participative management and job enrichment are concepts and techniques that require an initial understanding and acceptance of ideas (such as Theory X and Theory Y, or Maslow's hierarchy of needs and human motivation) before they can be appreciated and accepted. Many of the concepts and approaches used in management are subtle and require reflection on the part of trainees before they can be fully accepted. Thus it is wise to spread out the teaching of some topics (such as motivation, communications and leadership) over several, separated periods to allow initial resistances to subside and the values and benefits of basic concepts to "sink-in" and become accepted.

By carefully sequencing topics to be learned, the trainees' interest will be held and boredom will be prevented. Trainees can absorb only so much of the structural aspects of management, for instance, at one time, just as they can absorb only so much organizational behavior or topics relating to the business environment at any one time. A certain amount of variety is needed to maintain interest and attention. Moreover, some of the content in a typical management training program is more abstract and less relevant to concrete problems than other content. Both types, however, are very important and need to be stressed. Often, those attending training programs are very eager to find concrete answers to specific problems that they are experiencing on their jobs. Naturally, these people will be very interested in anything that they perceive as being directly helpful to them. They will be very much less interested in content that is intended to expand their thinking and enlarge their perspectives. In fact, if they are given an "overdose" of abstract, conceptual material, they may become "turned off" and "tune out." It is a good idea, therefore, to sequence topics in such a fashion so as to avoid too much concentration on either abstract or immediately applicable content.

Still another benefit of sequencing can be the establishment of a desired tone and nature of the program. If, for example, the program is one which aims to cause considerable self-awareness and calls for self-introspection, then the subject areas that require this type of behavior should come early in the program so that this pattern will become established and accepted. If the first three or four days of a course consist totally of lectures and there is no discussion or student involvement, it is doubtful that self-assessment will occur; and that which does occur will likely be only very superficial.

A Consistent Theme

The impact of a program will be deeper and longer lasting when its content "hangs together" and is consistent, thus forming a theme or philosophy. An underlying theme serves to tie together the various topics covered to form an integrated whole. This helps participants develop their own philosophies for managing. So, instead of returning to their jobs with a handful of methods and procedures that would otherwise be applied mechanically, participants will return with a philosophy and underlying attitudes and personal characteristics that will greatly influence how they handle whatever unique situations they may encounter.

A consistent theme also helps to prevent having contradictory points of view covered in a program. There are different opinions regarding the question of the desirability of having contradictory points of view or philosophies covered in a program. Those in favor of this claim that it is broadening and that it discourages the "one-best-way" approach. Those who are against it claim that contradictions cause unnecessary confusion and only encourage trainees to become more entrenched in the ways in which they already manage. As a result, they will not change. Moreover, the opponents to having contradictory philosophies and points of view taught on a program claim that it leads the less intellectually sophisticated trainees to reject almost everything that is taught. The reactions these people have to a program filled with contradictions is, "These egghead instructors can't agree on anything. They don't have consistent answers. Therefore, the management they teach us must be a lot of nonsense. There must not be much to it."

INSTRUCTORS

Certainly, the caliber of instructors in a program is a major determinant of its success. Even if the program has excellent and appropriate content, materials, facilities, and coordination, if its teachers are poor, its overall impact will be minimal. The impact may even be dysfunctional because of the negative attitudes generated. Therefore, the necessity for having high-caliber instructors should cause program directors and planners to find answers to the following questions:

1.   What should one look for when selecting instructors?

2.   What kinds of backgrounds and abilities should instructors have?

3.   Where can good instructors be found?

4.   How can one learn who the good instructors are?

How to Identify High-Caliber Instructors

The surest way to determine whether an instructor is a good teacher is to observe that person in action, teaching. This assumes, of course, that the observer knows how learning occurs, knows the difference between something that is simply entertaining and superficial versus something that is educational and penetrating, and knows enough about the subject being taught to render a valid assessment as to whether the instructor has covered the important and appropriate aspects of the subject for the audience being addressed. As a word of caution, the average person does not have this level of understanding of either management or the process of management education.

If the people who are responsible for planning a program and selecting instructors to teach on it are weak in the areas mentioned above, or if they have not observed prospective teachers in action, it would be wise to obtain evaluations of the prospective instructors from someone who has this knowledge and has observed the prospective instructor in action.

Participant evaluation of an instructor's teaching is one useful source of information, but it should not be accepted outright as being a complete or even competent evaluation. When selecting instructors, it is necessary to know when and where they have previously taught, the subjects they taught, and what their performance ratings have been. The greater the instructors' experience and the higher their evaluations, the more likely it is that they will do a competent job.

The participants' evaluations of instructors must be interpreted with caution, however. Instructors, even very competent ones, will not perform as well as they normally do when they teach a new topic for the first time, for example. It usually takes a half-dozen or so sessions of teaching a topic before the instructors can perfect their presentation to a point where it is excellent. So one of the first things to ask when reviewing the evaluations of instructors is, "How many times have they taught this subject?"

Another important thing to consider when reviewing a professor's evaluations is the age differential between the trainees and instructors. If, for example, participants in a program are middle-aged or older or they are in senior-level management positions, they will not, as a rule, respond favorably to young instructors, no matter how much they know or how well they present it. Planty and Freeston (1954, p. 17) have made a similar observation:

Only highly able and successful men can influence the behavior of major executives. This means men of reputation and acknowledged ability in their fields who also have professional skill in presenting their subjects to others. Executives are justifiably critical of mediocrity in teaching.

In one sense, learning involves the act of trainees permitting the instructor to open their minds to new ideas and approaches. The middle-aged trainee will generally not permit the young instructor to do this and thinks, "Only an older person with years of experience equivalent to mine can know enough to teach me something new." There are a few exceptions to this generalization. Younger instructors can be highly effective with older trainees or higher level groups if their subject is technical, matter-of-fact, and mechanical in nature and not subjective or philosophical. In other words, younger instructors can effectively teach such things as new techniques and procedures when they are perceived as being relevant to real problems and situations. And they can teach things that involve the dissemination of specific, factual information, such as a summary of current legislation and court rulings on particular business matters. They are not, however, as effective as older, seasoned teachers in trying to convince older trainees or higher level managers to adopt new management styles and approaches.

Another difficulty with participant evaluations is that participants often have a tendency to highly rate instructors who are colorful and entertaining or who reinforce what they already believe, regardless of how educational or noneducational the message may be. While evaluations might indicate that instructors performed either well or poorly, one should always ask why instructors were rated as they were. Were the instructors rated poorly because they were dull, or ill-prepared, or off-target with the materials presented, or because of their age and experience? Or, did the instructors receive high ratings because they were entertaining or because they told their audiences what they wanted to hear and thus reinforced what they already believed. Instructors who are highly authoritarian and strongly supportive of Theory-X management, for example, can be very popular among groups of people who hold similar beliefs. But they will not be much help in assisting them to learn and use other management approaches and techniques that have a great deal of utility. Or, were the instructors rated highly because they presented deep, stimulating, and penetrating messages and were inspiring and convincing?

Qualities and Characteristics

Past studies of teaching ability suggest that general intellectual ability (including knowledge of subject and teaching techniques) is the most important characteristic of a good instructor. Personality factors are considered to be important, but slightly less so. The *Handbook of Human Engineering Data* (1952) states, as reported by Bass and Vaughn (1966, p. 136), that good instructors have the following characteristics:

1. In terms of scholarship, they should
   a) have knowledge of the subject.
   b) have a good command of the language.
   c) contribute to their field of knowledge.
   d) keep current.
   e) be interested in teaching.

2. In terms of academic skills, they should
   a) organize course materials clearly around definite objectives.
   b) always be prepared.
   c) arouse interest and stimulate curiosity.
   d) present information skillfully and with suitable illustrations.
   e) use a variety of methods.
   f) adapt methods to the level of the class.
   g) be alert to individual needs.
   h) analyze errors.
   i) correct specific difficulties.

3. In terms of personality, they should
   a) be patient, sympathetic, and friendly with students.
   b) be at ease in social situations.
   c) have a sense of humor.
   d) be tactful and enthusiastic.
   e) be cooperative, mature, self-reliant, and confident.

These statements of qualities and characteristics are general and vague, and they do not pinpoint specific qualities or behaviors. Moreover, they neglect the need for instructors to have an appreciation and understanding of the practical dimensions of their subject—that is, the application of the concepts they teach, which is particularly important in the management training.

One can generally be assured of securing top-notch management instructors when he or she insists that whomever is selected possess three important characteristics.

1. Knows the subject to be taught from both theoretical and practical standpoints.

2. Knows and understands the processes of learning. Knows how to bring the trainees to each of the four stages of learning mentioned in Chapter 2, by using appropriate and impactful methods.

3. Has the ability to work with people. Can establish a rapport with trainees that is conducive to learning. Can earn trainees' attention, acceptance, and trust quickly. Is genuinely interested in people and in helping them to learn and develop their knowledge, skills, and personal characteristics.

Effective instructors of management can also be identified by specific behaviors, which include the following.

1. They know what managers do and, because of this, they focus on and emphasize those aspects of the subjects they teach that are most useful to those whom they teach.

2. They answer trainees' questions clearly and directly.

3. They illustrate the concepts and ideas they teach by means of practical examples so that they will be understood, accepted, and remembered.

4. They present their subject clearly and present the major points in a logical and orderly manner. They make the difficult and complex points easy to understand and accept.

5. They show how and where to apply the concepts they teach.

6. They stimulate the trainees' interest and enthusiasm for the subject. They capture the trainees' attention and interest.

7. They encourage and stimulate participants to think creatively about the subject taught and its application on the job.

8. They respect and welcome other points of view. They encourage questions and, at the same time, they are not fearful of questioning and gently criticize other points of view expressed.

9. They treat trainees as mature individuals.

10. They use a variety of teaching methods, but rely most heavily on those which involve active participation because these methods are most effective for developing the skills and personal characteristics discussed in Chapter 2.

In addition to ascertaining the degree to which prospective teachers possess certain qualities and abilities, a cost-benefit analysis can also be used for selecting instructors. The basic idea behind this approach is to select instructors who are adequate, but not overly competent and expensive, for the group to receive the training. It would not be economical to hire someone who has an international reputation in management training to instruct beginning managers or first-line supervisors when other very able instructors could do the job competently for much less the cost. However, it would be unwise to employ mediocre instructors to lead a discussion for senior-level executives, who are skillful and sophisticated managers.

The following questions will help planners select appropriately qualified instructors.

1. Will this instructor produce an adequate (acceptable) amount of learning for the cost of her or his services?

2. Could some other, less costly, instructor provide a suitable level of learning?

Sources of Teachers

Planty and Freeston (1954, p. 344) have identified six good sources for locating potential instructors.

1. The trainee's boss, on a continuous day-to-day basis through coaching, counseling, and guided experience.

2. Employees of the organization—people at executive and supervisory levels who teach formal classes upon the request of the director of training.

3. Full-time, internal training people or instructors who may or may not be professionally trained.

4. Instructors from schools, colleges, and universities.

5. Outside specialists and highly qualified experts in various fields, drawn from government and other businesses.

6. Training consultants who are professionally prepared as educators.

It is wise to consider all of these sources in light of the particular program and audience. There are, of course, advantages and disadvantages to using instructors from each of these sources. (See Table 4-2.)

How Many Instructors Should a Program Have?

There seems to be a great temptation, especially for novice training directors, to have a large number of instructors and subjects in the programs they plan. This is an understandable urge, since most beginners in the field have unusually high expectations of how much learning and change training programs can bring about. Forceful arguments are also frequently voiced in support of having a large variety of subjects and instructors in a program. These include thinking such as, "It is our objective to expose participants to as many viewpoints as possible," and "The variety of having many different subjects prevents boredom."

If the objective of a program is the improvement of management ability, none of these arguments is very sound. Having a wide variety of instructors and topics on a program, which are intended to acquaint the trainees with a wide range of information or give them an overview of a subject, has some appeal; but these kinds of programs do not make lasting changes in on-the-job behavior since they take the trainees only to the first stage of the learning process—knowing about. Surprisingly, many people are unaware of this fact and are committed to what could be called *information overkill*—that is, the *bombardment approach*, which uses a wide variety of topics and employs many instructors. A few major and well-known universities use this approach and have a large number of different instructors teaching on their executive-development programs. For example, one university's five-week executive program

Table 4–2. Typical pros and cons of using instructors from six sources.

Trainee's boss

Pros		**Cons**	
1.	Knows trainee well—strengths and weaknesses	1.	May not be good teacher; unrealistic to expect all superiors to be top-notch instructors
2.	Daily contact permits closer observation of the results of the training and a greater chance to encourage the application of specific concepts and practices	2.	May not have a solid theoretical background. May even be backwards in knowledge of management
3.	On-the-job counseling permits a greater opportunity to overcome specific problems and difficulties found at work	3.	May be afraid to level with the boss
4.	Good source for teaching company policies and practices	4.	Usually has only a shallow knowledge of reading materials cases and learning devices
		5.	Does not have time to fully prepare and teach the subject and learn about specific needs

Employees of the organization—people at executive levels

Pros		**Cons**	
1.	Know trainees in some cases	1.	May not be trained instructors or experts on the subject
2.	Know problems and other situations the company faces	2.	Usually have only a shallow knowledge of reading materials cases and learning devices
3.	Can work with learners on an on-going basis	3.	Do not have time to fully prepare and teach the subject and learn about specific needs
4.	Senior-level executives give credibility and support to concepts taught	4.	Trainees may not level with them
5.	Good for teaching company policies and procedures	5.	May find it difficult to avoid shop-talk
		6.	Usually presents the subject along the lines of, "The way I handle things is . . ." or "The way I came to be successful was . . . ," which suggests that there is one best way

Full-time internal training specialists

Pros		**Cons**	
1.	Are usually well qualified in the subject and training methods	1.	Credibility and novelty can wear thin over time as they become regarded as just another member of the corporation; this is especially true when results are only minimal or come slowly
2.	Have time to make an extensive study of training needs and know problems in depth		

Table 4–2. *cont'd.*

3. Are in a position to obtain feedback on results and impact of training 4. Can work with trainees on the job after the formal training session	2. Difficult (but not impossible) for training directors to have much of an impact on senior executives who earn from twice to ten times as much 3. Tend to regard themselves as their company's "savior," which causes negative feelings toward training

Instructors from schools, colleges, and universities

Pros	Cons
1. Are professionally trained in their subject and teaching 2. Have a thorough theoretical understanding of the subject and very often a similar knowledge of the practical application 3. Have a wide range knowledge of training methods and materials 4. Have a reputation and an image of being an expert that gives them credibility	1. May not be too familiar with training needs of the organization 2. May be too theoretical for group 3. May have a tendency to talk down to the group. May have difficulty getting out of the role of professor and getting into the role of discussion leader 4. Have a tendency to give canned talks 5. Are not available for day-to-day guidance on the job

Outside specialists

Pros	Cons
1. Are experts in the field and have advanced technical knowledge 2. Have a high degree of credibility	1. May not be good instructors 2. Sometimes give "canned" presentations 3. Usually are lecture oriented 4. Have little lasting effect on day-to-day practices because they cannot monitor the application of what was taught

Training consultant

Pros	Cons
1. Knowledge of subject 2. Professionally trained instructor; professional consultant 3. Usually knows practical aspects of the subject 4. Has credibility because of expertise and experience	1. Usually gives a canned presentation because of busy schedule 2. May not be entirely familiar with organization or its problems and needs 3. Little or no chance to follow through to help trainees apply what was taught

employs thirty-seven professors. Another prestigious university has a four-week program which has sixty-three professors presenting subjects plus thirty-one guest speakers. In-house, company programs often use this approach. One major company had twelve different topics and twelve instructors during the first three days of its four-and-one-half-day program for executives.

If management training is to be impactful and long lasting, there must be continuity in the subjects covered, and these subjects must be covered in depth, which takes time. A single one-hour or two-hour session is not enough. Moreover, change will not come about as a result of a program that has instructors who advocate contradictory and conflicting philosophies and practices. The typical reactions to these programs are confusion, frustration, and the persistence of old forms of behavior and management practices. Participants react by saying, "Those eggheads don't know what management is all about. They can't even agree among themselves. Therefore, I'll stick to what I already believe to be true and will continue to do things pretty much as I have all along."

The argument that a great number of different topics and instructors is refreshing and prevents boredom is fallacious. Instead of being refreshing, it actually puts a greater strain on participants, who have to continually "shift gears" mentally and readjust to each speaker. Moreover, if subjects are treated in depth and appropriate detail and if they are worthwhile and well presented, they will not be boring, but instead stimulating and interesting. Actually, it would probably be more boring to listen to a series of superficial presentations on a variety of topics than one in-depth presentation.

Another factor that should be considered is how well the instructor is known and accepted by the group. The group's acceptance of the instructor will usually influence its acceptance of what he or she teaches. Acceptance is earned slowly. Even for the best instructors, it takes at least a half a day and, in most cases, a full day before acceptance is earned. Thus, because of the need for instructor acceptance and the need for continuity of thought, it is far better to have one professor cover several closely related topics than to have the same topics covered by several instructors.

If a program has only a few instructors, participants have a greater inclination and opportunity to interact on a more personal basis, because barriers are reduced and participants become more likely to seek assistance on problems they face at work than would be the case if there was a large number of instructors. Moreover, this closeness builds greater group cohesiveness and openness to self-reflection and self-understanding which are the first steps toward personal growth and development.

As a rule of thumb, programs should have a minimum of two and a maximum of five instructors per week. This assumes a five-day week consisting of two sessions per day. One of the nation's most successful university programs, Pennsylvania State University's four-week Executive Management Program, has been run following the format of having two professors per week with an additional guest speaker on one evening during the week. In this program, an instructor will conduct sessions all day Monday and Tuesday and until noon on Wednesday. Wednesday afternoon is free for recreation and relaxation. Then a second instructor will conduct sessions all day Thursday and Friday and until noon Saturday.

In cases where instructors teach for a full day at a time, it is essential that they be excellent teachers so as to hold the trainees' attention and enthusiasm. The successful programs which have instructors teach for whole days at a time schedule part of the day to include case-study preparation and presentation or other activities such as games or role-plays that involve participants. This breaks up the day so that it has variety and is not six or eight straight hours of listening to lectures and participating in general discussions.

Other programs schedule their instructors to teach for only half days at a time. Under this system, one instructor may teach on the mornings of Monday, Tuesday, and Wednesday and another on the afternoons of Monday, Tuesday, and Wednesday. Generally speaking, the programs that follow this format have participants prepare their case-study assignments on the evening before the class. This format is more demanding on the trainees in terms of the work required. However, it permits the coverage of more cases and allows participants to interact more closely as a group during the off-hours than they would if they were free to socialize during the evenings.

THE PHYSICAL FACILITIES

The physical atmosphere and set-up in which a training program is conducted will have a strong impact on the learning that occurs and, hence, its overall success. Thus the location, setting, and layout of the training site and the physical facilities used are extremely important aspects which must receive attention in the planning phase of any program. This section will consider the location and setting of a training site, the facilities necessary for programs, the arrangement and layout of training facilities, and training equipment and hardware.

Location

The training site should be situated in a location that is convenient to as many participants as possible for two basic reasons. First, the cost of travel should be held to a minimum. Second, traveling time for participants and faculty should be held to a mimimum. A location that is well serviced by air transportation is most desirable. The local airport should be within a few minutes driving time from the training site. There should be several incoming and outgoing flights conveniently scheduled throughout the day and evening, with connecting flights to other major cities. This will prove to be a welcome convenience to busy participants and faculty alike.

If participants must commute daily by automobile to and from the training site, it should be located so as to minimize the driving time of the most people. As a rule of thumb, the site should be situated so as not to require more than an hour's driving time in each direction.

The amount of difficulty and inconvenience participants encounter in traveling to and from the training site will, to some extent, affect their attitude toward the training. The more inconvenient the location of the training site, the worse their attitudes. Therefore, the location should be easy to get to and from. It will affect not only the trainees' attitudes, but also their ability to concentrate and become totally involved in the learning experience.

Unwanted interruptions can become an annoying problem if the training site is located too near participants' places of work. If their offices are nearby, there is always the temptation of "sneaking out for just a few minutes to handle *just one* urgent problem or attend *just one* important meeting." These absences frequently stretch into hours and days and involve many more important matters. Also, there is the temptation for participants to stop by their offices before and after the training sessions to catch up on or complete important work. Doing this will tax their energy and power of concentration, and will divert them from learning as much as they possibly can.

The work that needs to be done *is* important, but training is also important. Serious study and learning are severely hampered when the participants cannot and do not give their full and uninterrupted attention to the training program and its demands.

Climate is another important factor to consider when selecting a training site. Winter snow and ice storms can snarl traffic and halt air and ground travel. Many programs are held in warmer sections of the country during the winter months and in cooler locations during the summer months. There is always the possibility, however, that participants from the northern and eastern states will perceive a program held in warm climates during January and February to be more of a vacation than a serious learning experience. The quality and nature of the program and the way in which it is run can quickly overcome these very natural temptations.

Setting

The physical setting and layout of the training site or conference center will affect the outcome of the training. The training facility should be located in a setting which is free from the pressures, annoyances, and distractions that are typically encountered in the course of a busy workday. It should provide an atmosphere conducive to serious study and reflection. For programs of a week of more in length, a retreat type setting is most desirable. In such a setting, trainees can escape from the everyday pressures and worries that tax their attention and energy so that they can devote themselves to examining their own values, philosophies, and management practices in light of other methods or newer approaches, which they study and learn about from others.

It is possible to have a setting that is too isolated. While the setting ought to be conducive to study, there should be some sources readily available for entertainment and recreation during the evenings and days off when rest and relaxation is scheduled. Large resorts and universities typically have adequate recreational facilities for swimming, tennis, golf, bowling, and the like, which provide needed diversion, relaxation, and relief from the strain of days of learning.

Settings that are too isolated can sometimes invite unwanted types of escapes from the pressures of learning, such as heavy drinking and rowdiness. A training center located on a ship, or in a desolate place, or worse yet on a small island tends to add to the pressures which accompany self-reflection. Such locations cause participants to feel trapped with little else to do but drink heavily and play cards as the only means of escape and relaxation.

The Meeting Room

Since in most management training programs the participants spend approximately six hours each day in the meeting room, it should be obvious that this room must meet specific conditions to assure a good and comfortable learning environment. Many will be tempted either to under-value or ignore one or more of the features listed here, which have been found, through experience, to be absolutely necessary. To neglect any one of these features invites trouble and discomfort to participants.

Size

The size of the room depends on the nature of the meeting, the seating arrangements, and the number of participants attending. If the participants are to listen to an address, then theatre-style seating, which can accommodate large groups in a relatively small space, is appropriate. If the nature of the meeting is lecture-discussion, as is the case with most good management development programs, then the usual horseshoe or U-shaped table arrangement is appropriate. In this arrangement, participants can face the center and front of the room.

People should never be crowded too closely together or around table configurations that are too spread out or bunched too tightly together. When seated at a table, the average person needs a minimum of thirty inches of table space. Three feet (36 inches) will be more appropriate, especially for large people. Frequently, people are seated around tables as closely as the chair space permits, which invites discomfort, sore muscles, and irritable participants. It is a good idea to decide on the appropriate seating arrangement before choosing a room that will accommodate it.

The meeting room should be large enough to hold audio-visual aids and equipment, such as chalk boards and easels located at the front of the room, and for visitor seating in the rear of the room.

Layout

Since most management-training programs call for horseshoe table arrangement, it is helpful to point out several mistakes most commonly made in the selection of meeting rooms and the arrangement of tables into the horseshoe or U-shaped mode. (See Fig. 4-4.)

Guidelines for selecting

Several additional guidelines should be followed to assure an adequately sized room.

1.   There should be at least three feet between the outside edge of the tables and the wall. This will give the participants enough room to get to and from

---

1.   *Room too small.* Participants crowded too closely together. Not ample space between outside edge of U-shaped table arrangement and walls of room. Not enough space in front of room for chalk boards and easels. No room for visitors. Participants feel cramped.

2.   *Room too large*—60 ft by 80 ft and larger. Auditoriums, ballrooms, and recreation areas are frequently too large to be used as meeting rooms. These rooms usually have 18 to 22 ft ceilings. Large rooms have acoustic problems; it is difficult to hear speakers and other participants in these rooms.

3.   *Room too wide.* Makes U-shaped table arrangement into a short, very wide U, which makes it impossible for those seated at the base of the U to see others at the base or to interact with them during discussions.

4.   *Room too long and narrow.* Makes it difficult for those at the base of the long, skinny U to see and hear others at the top of the U and the front of the room, where the speaker-discussion leader is located. It also causes the tables that compose the two sides of the U to be too close together (10 ft or less).

5.   *L-shaped room.* Makes it difficult if not impossible to arrange tables into U-shaped configuration. May block the vision of some participants.

6.   *Room with supporting columns.* Such rooms are frequently found in basements. The columns obstruct the participants' vision and make it difficult to arrange tables in the most desirable configuration.

Fig. 4-4. Most commonly made mistakes in selecting meeting rooms.

and in and out of their chairs. Four to five feet is better and will keep the participants from feeling cramped. More than fifteen feet is too much space.

2.   It is desirable to have space available in the rear or along the side of the meeting room for visitors. The room should be arranged so that visitors can come and go without disturbing the meeting. Exits should be at the side or rear of the room.

3.   Allow ten to fifteen feet in the front of the room (at the top of the U) for the professor and any audio-visual equipment to be used. There should be room to place chalk boards and easels so that they can be easily seen by all participants.

4.   Consider ceiling height as a critical dimension of the meeting room. Seven to eight foot high ceilings are too low and cause ventilation problems and the feeling of being cramped. Twelve foot high ceilings are ideal. Ceilings higher than 15 feet cause acoustic problems, making it difficult for people to hear the unamplified voice.

5.   As a rule of thumb, select meeting rooms approximately 25 feet wide by 35 feet long for groups of 15 to 25 participants. For groups of 26 to 45 participants, the meeting room should be approximately 45 feet wide by 50 feet long.

6.   The U-shaped table arrangement is not appropriate for groups of more than 45 participants because the size of the U required becomes too large. When the group contains more than 40 to 45 people, a series of concentric semicircles in tiers makes a better seating arrangement. Some would argue that more than 40 to 45 people is too many for an effective program, while others would disagree with this generalization, pointing to the Harvard, Cornell, and Columbia University Executive Programs that have from 60 to 75 participants.

Eliminating unnecessary noise

The meeting room should be free of outside distractions, especially noise. Many hotels have moveable room dividers to partition larger rooms into smaller meeting rooms. However, these walls are not effective noise barriers and such arrangements should be avoided if at all possible. There is an exception to this generalization—that is, the moveable room divider which consists of two panels with dead air space between. It is secured to the floor and ceiling, and works well in eliminating noise between rooms. All other partitions are unacceptable as they fail to eliminate the noise of clanking dishes, noisy busboys, other groups, P.A. systems, etc., which can be disastrous. (Note: P.A. systems and telephones in the hallways that adjoin the meeting room should be avoided.)

Light

The meeting room must be well lighted. A few 100 or 250 watt incandescent light bulbs are inadequate. Adequate fluorescent lighting is needed to illuminate a meeting room properly.

There are some honest differences of opinion among training professionals regarding the desirability of natural lighting from the out of doors. Some argue that meeting rooms should not have windows opening to the outside, as this invites distractions. Others claim that windows in the training room are desirable because they offset the feeling of being imprisoned. In this case, it is suggested that windows be located above eye level and where there will be no distractions taking place outside.

Men and women attending an intensive training program face many pressures: their ideas and beliefs are challenged; they are struggling to grasp many new ideas and concepts; they are interacting closely with people whom they do not know well; and they are working very hard for 8 to 12 hours each day. These pressures can be intensified by the physical environment, which includes the meeting room and its arrangement and setting of the training site. Many experienced training professionals are sensitive to these pressures and work to minimize or provide outlets for them; they avoid meeting rooms and settings that cause feelings of being entrapped or imprisoned.

Acoustics

The acoustics of the meeting room should be such that people seated in the rear of the room can hear the speaker in the front of the room speaking without shouting. Floor covering and acoustical ceiling tiles will help to absorb extraneous noise, such as the rustling of papers or the shuffling of feet. Very large rooms are usually not suitable because they usually require a P.A. system.

Ventilation, air conditioning, and temperature

The meeting room should have heating and air conditioning facilities for year-round comfort. It should also have adequate ventilation to extract smoke and keep a flow of fresh air circulating. Air-conditioning systems in buildings are designed to be operated with all windows and doors closed, otherwise the system will not be able to provide the cooling and air-circulation functions it was designed to perform.

Electrical outlets

Electrical outlets should be available for the audio visual equipment. Most well-designed conference centers have several outlets set into the floors of the meeting rooms, as well as along the walls.

Exits

Building codes require adequate exits for quick evacuation of buildings. Doors should be located near the rear of the room so that the participants can leave and reenter the meeting room without distracting others. Fire exits should be kept unlocked at all times. It is advisable to point out the fire exits out at the outset of the meeting.

Seating Arrangements

The seating arrangement should be appropriate to the nature and purpose of the meeting. Several types of seating arrangements are shown in Figs. 4-5, 4-6, 4-7, 4-8 and 4-9.

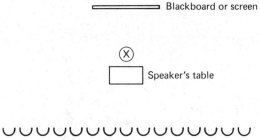

Appropriate for:

1. Formal information transmission presentations such as lectures or movies
2. Short programs of up to a few hours in length
3. Large groups that observe and listen

Not appropriate for:

1. Programs of more than a day in length
2. Participant interaction and discussion
3. Sessions where it is desired that participants get to know one another and learn from each other

Fig. 4-5. Traditional classroom (or theatre-style) layout.

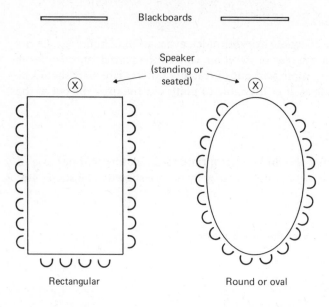

Fig. 4–6. Conference table seating.

Appropriate for:

1. Small groups (usually a maximum of 20 people)
2. Programs or meetings that require discussion and interaction
3. Sessions where the leader serves as formal chairman or chairwomen or plays a less directive role
4. Sessions of up to a few hours in length

Not appropriate for:

1. Large groups
2. Programs of more than a few hours in length
3. Sessions that require a variety of activities
4. In the rectangular arrangement, discussion among all participants. In the rectangular table arrangement, discussion frequently breaks into smaller subgroups because people on same side of table cannot face each other and interact

The Buzz-group Room for Case-study Preparation

Case studies are prepared by small groups of participants, frequently referred to as *buzz groups*. These groups are composed of from 5 to 8 people. It is desirable to have separate rooms set up for buzz groups so that they can discuss and prepare case-study assignments. These rooms should be free of noise and distractions and should have temperature controls and adequate lighting. The rooms should be large enough to accommodate the group. Since smoking is objectionable to many people, buzz-group meetings should not be held in one

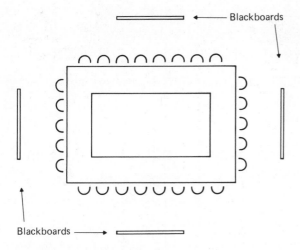

Appropriate for:
1. Large groups of 20 to 30 people
2. Conferences of several days in length
3. Open discussion, although it will be difficult for those on the same side of the table to see each other
4. Programs or meetings where there either is or is not a formal leader

Not appropriate for:
1. Small groups of less than 8 people

Fig. 4-7. Conference discussion.

of the members' hotel room. The buzz-group meeting room should be approximately 120–220 square feet in size and it should contain a large table for participants to sit around so that they can face one another as they discuss the cases.

Lounge and Dining Facilities

The areas adjoining the meeting room should provide a pleasant and quiet atmosphere. There should be ample restroom facilities nearby for men and women. There should be a smoking area, where participants can congregate, relax, and chat. Telephones should be available, as well as message boards near the meeting room where announcements and messages for participants can be posted. A coat rack should be located just outside (or inside, provided there is space) the meeting room.

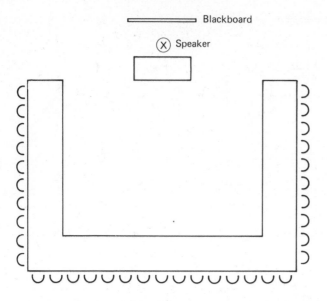

Appropriate for:

　1. Conferences of any length
　2. Sessions where there is a formal discussion leader and where
　　participant discussion and interaction is desired

Not appropriate for:

　1. Large groups of more than 45 people
　2. Very small groups (5 people or less) because
　　participants become too spread out

Fig. 4–8. Horseshoe or U-shaped layout.

Dining facilities should be located a convenient distance from the meeting room. If the dining area is too near the meeting room, noise may be a problem. Sometimes well-meaning but unknowing hotel managers will try to sell prospective customers on the idea of having meals served in the meeting room. This always spells inconvenience and disruptions.

Chairs

So important is the comfort of the meeting room chair that it deserves its own section in a discussion of conference facilities. As the saying goes, "The mind can absorb only so long as the seat can endure." Comfortable chairs are a must for successful meetings and programs. In many situations, program attendees

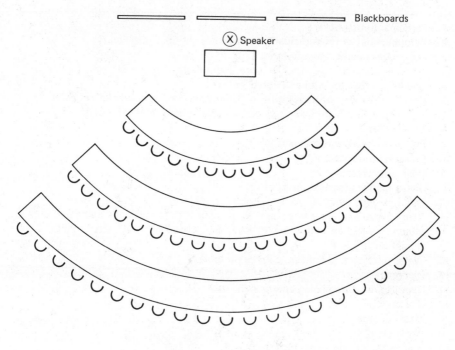

Blackboards

Appropriate for:

   1. Lectures and movies—some discussion
   2. Large groups of more than 45 people
   3. Some participant interaction and discussion

Not appropriate for:

   1. Small groups

Fig. 4–9. Concentric-semicircle layout.

will be seated for 4 to 6 hours a day. The chairs should be large and adequately padded for comfort. The ideal chair has 2½ to 3 inches of padding on the seat, one inch of padding on the back, and an 18 inch by 18 inch seat. Chairs that have arm rests and that swivel and tilt back are even more desirable.

    Metal folding chairs can usually be tolerated for only a half an hour. Hard wooden chairs can be tolerated for a maximum of 70 to 80 minutes. If you cannot have comfortable chairs, you should not have the program.

Conference-room Checklist

The checklist (shown in Fig. 4-10) will help to assure a properly equipped conference room.

1. Participant notebooks
2. Reference books for participants (sometimes set up a mini-library)
3. Large chalkboards—two or more 4' × 7'
4. Flip charts and stands—four or more. Extra pads of paper 22" × 27"
5. Overhead projector with extra bulb
6. Special transparency marking pens. Transparencies for overhead projector
7. 16 mm projector with take-up spool, extension cord, and extra bulb
8. Large screen
9. Podiums—table and standing types
10. Chalkboard pointer
11. Chalk and erasers
12. Magic markers (several, each color)
13. Large crayons (several, black and red)
14. Name plates and holders for each participant with participant's name and organization printed on both sides. Printing should be 2½" to 3" letters. Plates should be 18" × 6"
15. Water pitchers and drinking glasses on table
16. Dictionary
17. Heavy metal, three-hole paper punch
18. Scotch tape
19. Masking tape
20. Paper clips
21. Sharpened pencils—two per participant
22. Pencil sharpener
23. Rubber erasers
24. Rubber bands
25. Extra notebook paper—lined and plain
26. Tape recorder and recording tape
27. Ash trays on table—matches
28. Chairs for visitors
29. Table in rear or just outside of room for coffee and refreshment service
30. Breast badges with participant name

Fig. 4–10. Conference-room checklist.

TEACHING MATERIALS

Training materials, such as case studies, readings exercises, role-plays, films, texts, etc., should be selected in light of two key considerations: (1) the training objectives of the session for which the material is to be used, and (2) the audience who will be receiving the training. Frequently, instructors are tempted to use only materials with which they are familiar. These instructors neglect to perform a careful search of the plethora of available material, largely because they do not know where to look, which often results in the use of inappropriate materials.

A few questions will guide program planners in their selections of training materials.

1. Will the training exercise or material be accepted by the group? Shop supervisors, for example, are typically pragmatic and are more inclined to respond to exercises or reading material that will assist them in developing skills. They are less inclined to respond to exercises or readings that are heavily conceptual and abstract.

2. Will the exercise or material directly aid in the attainment of the training objectives?

3. Are the case studies written about industries and work settings that the participants can relate to easily? It is a good idea to have shop-supervisor-type cases for groups of shop supervisors, middle-management-type cases for middle-management managers, and executive-type cases for executives. If those receiving the training are library or hospital administrators, then case studies should be from library or hospital settings.

4. How much can the participants be expected to read? Do not exceed the following limits. Usually, groups will read between 15 and 50 pages of material per day depending on the content and the participants' reading habits. Higher-level managers and better-educated participants tend to read more than lower-level managers and less formally educated participants.

5. Are the readings pertinent to the participants' work and training needs?

The Notebook

Practically every management and supervisory training program has notebooks for participants. They are generally three-ring binders, which make it convenient to add or remove items when desired. Notebooks should contain the following.

1. Daily schedule of classes and activities

2. Information about conference center and facilities, including maps when necessary

3. Short resumes of biographies of instructors and participants to assist group members in becoming acquainted with each other quickly

4. Outline and assignment sheet for each session (see Fig. 4-11)

5. Case studies

6. Other materials for class exercises, such as in-basket games, role-playing exercises and instructions, management-game guidelines and materials, etc.

ADVANCED MANAGEMENT SEMINAR

MAY 22-27, 1977

Wednesday, May 25	Morning Session

8:30 a.m. − 12:00 Noon

Subject: Planning and Organizing for Results

Discussion
Leader: John F. Mee

Case: Suburban Bank and Trust Company

Readings: 1. The Nature of Planning and Plans
2. Changing Concepts of Management
3. Dashman Company

Wednesday, May 25	Afternoon Session

1:15 p.m. − 4:30 p.m.

Subject: Introducing and Implementing Change

Discussion
Leader: Eari G. Planty

Case: The Dashman Company

Readings: 1. Resistance to Change
2. Principles for Change
3. Listening

Fig. 4–11. Schedule and assignment sheet.

7.   Readings

8.   Lined notebook paper for taking notes

9.   Bibliographies

10.   Notebook dividers

The notebook should be attractive and neat. This goes a long way in conveying a favorable image of the program to participants. A first-rate notebook conveys to participants the image of a first-rate program. All reproduced material should be clear and clean. Offset printing and multilith copies are most attractive. Xeroxed ® copies can usually meet this appearance requirement, but great care is needed to assure it.

Many universities and organizations have attractively printed or embossed notebooks designating their school or organization and the program. The additional cost of this is usually minimal and a justifiable expense.

The notebooks used should be three-ringed binders with a ring size that is one-half-inch thicker in diameter than the thickness of the stack of materials and papers that the notebook will hold.

Notebook dividers will help participants to locate appropriate materials quickly as they are needed. In some programs notebooks are divided by day, and in other programs notebooks are divided by instructor name. Program directors will have to decide which method will be most useful for their program.

The materials for each session should be grouped together for easy reference. A schedule and assignment sheet should precede them. Figure 4–11 illustrates how this sheet should appear.

Sources of Materials

An increase in the quantity and quality of training materials, which continue to expand and change, has been associated with the management-training explosion. There are too many sources for one to catalog, classify, or evaluate adequately. However, a partial listing of excellent sources of good training materials is given here.

Organizations Providing Training Materials and Resources

1. American Management Association
   135 W. 50th Street
   New York, NY   10020
   Publications, films, cases

2. American Society for Training and Development
   P.O. Box 5307
   Madison, WI   53705
   Training Resources: A buyer's guide to training services and materials

3. Bob Richards Attainment Institute
   100 N. 6th Street, Butler Square
   Minneapolis, MN   55403
   Motivational films

4. BNA Communications, Inc.
   9401 Decoverly Hill Road
   Rockville, MD   20850
   Films and audio cassettes on most aspects of management and supervision

5. Clearinghouse for Experiential Exercises
   Bureau of Business Research
   Indiana State University

Terre Haute, IN   47809
Sourcebook of Experiential Exercises by Samuel C. Certo (Ed.)

6. Columbia Pictures Cassettes
711 Fifth Avenue
New York, NY   10022
Video cassette series in management

7. CRM/McGraw-Hill Films
110 15th Street
Del Mar, CA   92014
Films on management

8. Dartnell
4660 Ravenswood Avenue
Chicago, IL   60640
Reference materials, readings, films on management and supervison

9. Development Digest
A publication of CREDR Corp.
3347 Motor Avenue
Los Angeles, CA   90034
Mailing address: P.O. Box 49938
Los Angeles, CA 90049
Audio cassette library on management, personnel, OD, human relations

10. Development Dimensions, Inc.
P.O. Box 13069
767 Colony Circle
Pittsburgh, PA   15243
Assessment and development exercises

11. Document Associates, Inc.
211 E. 43rd Street
New York, NY   10017
Films and video cassettes in organizational behavior

12. Education Research
P.O. Box 4205
Warren, NJ   07060
Business games in management and supervision

13. Experiential Learning Methods
39819 Plymouth Road
Plymouth, MI   48170
Training exercises and diagnostic instruments

14. Intercollegiate Case Clearinghouse
Soldiers Field Post Office

Boston, MA   02163
Case studies in all phases of business and administration

15. Lansford Publishing Co.
P.O. Box 8711
1088 Lincoln Avenue
San Jose, CA   95155
Transparencies, lecture notes, articles, audio cassettes

16. Leadership Resources, Inc.
One First Virginia Plaza
Suite 344
6400 Arlington Boulevard
Falls Church, VA   22042
Monographs in supervision and management

17. Masterco Press
P.O. Box 382
Ann Arbor, MI   48107
Distributors of diagnostic tests, books, and articles

18. National Educational Media, Inc.
15760 Ventura Boulevard
Encino, CA   91436
Films and video cassettes in management and supervison

19. NTL/Learning Resources Corp.
7594 Eads Avenue
La Jolla, CA   92037
Distributors of books in applied behavioral sciences

20. Organizational Tests, Ltd.
P.O. Box 324
Fredricton, New Brunswick, Canada
Diagnostic tests in management and supervisory knowledge and skills

21. The Psychological Corp.
757 Third Avenue
New York, NY   10017
Psychological tests and services for clinical, counseling and industrial use

22. Roundtable Films, Inc.
113 North San Vincente Boulevard
Beverly Hills, CA   90211
Management and sales training films

23. Science Research Associates, Inc.
259 East Erie Street
Chicago, IL   60611
Industrial Psychological tests

24. Teleometrics International
    P.O. Box 314
    The Woodlands, TX   77380
    Learning instruments, self-scored diagnostic instruments

25. Training Magazine
    Ziff-Davis Publishing Co.
    One Park Avenue
    New York, NY   10016
    Training Action Postcards: A catalog of training materials, equipment and services

26. Training, the magazine of human-resources development
    (formerly Training in Business and Industry)
    Lakewood Publications, Inc.
    731 Hennepin Avenue
    Minneapolis, MN   55403
    Information on training practices and products, yellow pages of training software

27. University Associates, Inc.
    7596 Eads Avenue
    La Jolla, CA   92037
    Films, experiential learning exercises, books in human relations and organizational development

Sources of Readings in Management

I. Periodicals

1. Advanced Management Journal
   Society for Advancement of Management
   135 W. 50th Street
   New York, NY   10020

2. Business Horizons
   Graduate School of Business Administration
   Indiana University
   Bloomington, IN   47401

3. California Management Review
   Graduate School of Business Administration
   University of California
   Berkeley, CA   94720

4. Fortune
   Time Life Building
   New York, NY   10020

5. Harvard Business Review
   Graduate School of Business Administration

Harvard University
Boston, MA   02163

6. Management Review
   AMACOM
   American Management Associations
   135 W. 50th Street
   New York, NY   10020

7. Michigan Business Review
   Graduate School of Business Administration
   University of Michigan
   Ann Arbor, MI   48104

8. MSU Business Topics
   Graduate School of Business Administration
   Michigan State University
   East Lansing, MI   48824

9. Organizational Dynamics
   AMACOM
   American Management Association
   135 W. 50th Street
   New York, NY   10020

10. Nation's Business
    Chamber of Commerce of the United States
    1615 H Street, N.W.
    Washington, D.C.   20062

11. Personnel
    AMACOM
    American Management Association
    135 W. 50th Street
    New York, NY   10020

12. Personnel Journal
    100 Park Avenue
    Swarthmore, PA   19081

13. Research Management
    Industrial Research Institute
    100 Park Avenue
    New York, NY   10017

14. Supervisory Management
    AMACOM
    American Management Association
    135 W. 50th Street
    New York, NY   10020

15. Training and Development Journal
    ASTD
    P.O. Box 5307
    Madison, WI   53705

II. Books of Readings

 1. *Behavior in Organizations, An Experiential Approach.* James B. Lau. Homewood, Ill.: Richard D. Irwin, 1975.

 2. *Behavioral Decisions in Organizations.* Alvar O. Elbing. Glenview, Ill.: Scott Foresman, 1970.

 3. *Business Policy and Strategy: Concepts and Readings.* Joseph R. Curran; Daniel J. McCarthy; and Robert J. Minichiello. Homewood Ill.: Richard D. Irwin, 1975.

 4. *Dimensions in Modern Management.* Patrick E. Connor. Boston: Houghton Mifflin, 1974.

 5. *Interpersonal Communications, Basic Text and Readings.* Kim Giffin and Bobby R. Patton. New York: Harper & Row, 1974.

 6. *Leadership and Organization: A Behavioral Science Approach.* Fred Massarik; Robert Tannenbaum; and Irving R. Weschler. New York: McGraw-Hill, 1961.

 7. *Management: A Book of Readings.* Harold Koontz and Cyril O'Donnell. New York: McGraw-Hill, 1972.

 8. *Management, Organizations, and Human Resources, Selected Readings.* Herbert G. Hicks. New York: McGraw-Hill, 1972.

 9. *The Management Process, Cases and Readings.* Stephen J. Carroll, Jr.; John B. Miner; and Frank T. Paine. New York: Macmillan, 1977.

10. *Management: Selected Readings.* George R. Terry. Homewood, Ill.: Richard D. Irwin, 1973.

11. *The Nature and Scope of Management.* Maneck S. Wadia. Glenview, Ill.: Scott Foresman, 1966.

12. *Organization and People, Readings, Cases, and Exercises in Organizational Behavior.* J. B. Ritchie and Paul Thompson. St. Paul, Minn.: West Publishing, 1976.

13. *Organizational Behavior: A Book of Readings.* Keith Davis. New York: McGraw-Hill, 1974.

14. *Organizational Behavior and The Practice of Management.* David R. Hampton; Charles E. Summer; and Ross A. Webber. Glenview, Ill.: Scott Foresman, 1968.

15. *Organizational Behavior and Administration.* Louis B. Barnes; Paul R. Lawrence; and Jay W. Lorsch, eds. Homewood, Ill.: Richard D. Irwin, 1976.

16. *Organizations: Structure and Behavior.* Joseph A. Litterer. New York: Wiley, 1963.

17. *The Progress of Management, Process and Behavior in a Changing Environment.* Harold Lazarus; Jerome E. Schnee; and E. Kirby Warren. Englewood Cliffs, N.J.: Prentice-Hall, 1977.

18. *Readings on Behavior in Organizations.* James L. Bowditch; Dalmar Fisher; and Edgar F. Huse, eds. Reading, Mass.: Addison-Wesley, 1975.

19. *Readings in Interpersonal and Organizational Communication.* Dwight L. Freshley; Richard C. Huseman; and Cal M. Logue. Boston, Mass.: Holbrook Press, 1973.

20. *Readings in Management.* William A. Nielander; and Max D. Richards. Cincinnati, Ohio: South-Western, 1974.

21. *Readings in Organizational Behavior and Human Performance.* L. L. Cummings and W. E. Scott, Jr., eds. Homewood, Ill.: Richard D. Irwin and Dorsey Press, 1969.

22. *Readings in Organizational Behavior, Concepts and Applications.* Jerry L. Gray and Frederick A. Starke, eds. Wooster, Ohio: Bell & Howell, 1977.

23. *Readings in Organizations, Structure, Processes, Behavior.* James H. Donnelly, Jr.; James L. Gibson; and John M. Ivancevich, eds. Austin, Tex.: Business Publications, 1973.

24. *Systems, Organizations, Analysis, Management: A Book of Readings.* David I. Cleland and William R. King. New York: McGraw-Hill, 1969.

25. *Tomorrow's Organizations: Challenges and Strategies.* Jong S. Jun and William B. Storm. Glenview, Ill.: Scott Foresman, 1973.

III. Books Containing Cases

1. *The Administrator, Cases on Human Aspects of Management.* John Desmond Glover; Ralph M. Hower; Renato Tagiuri. Homewood, Ill.: Richard D. Irwin, 1973.

2. *Behavior in Organizations, An Experiential Approach.* James B. Lau. Homewood, Ill.: Richard D. Irwin, 1975.

3. *Behavioral Decisions in Organizations.* Alvar O. Elbing. Glenview, Ill.: Scott Foresman, 1970.

4. *Business Policy: Strategy Formation and Management Action.* William F. Glueck. New York: McGraw-Hill, 1972.

5. *Communication and Organizational Behavior, Text and Cases.* William V. Haney. Homewood, Ill.: Richard D. Irwin, 1973.

6. *Critical Incidents in Management.* John M. Champion and John H. James. Homewood, Ill.: Richard D. Irwin, 1975.

7. *First-Line Management, Approaching Supervision Effectively.* Lawrence L. Steinmetz and H. Ralph Todd, Jr. Austin, Tex.: Business Publications, 1975.

8. *Human Behavior at Work, Organizational Behavior.* Keith Davis. New York: McGraw-Hill, 1977.

9. *Interpersonal Behavior and Administration.* George F. F. Lombard and Arthur N. Turner. New York: Free Press, 1969.

10. *Management: A Behavioral Approach.* Edwin B. Flippo. Boston, Mass.: Allyn and Bacon, 1970.

11. *Management: An Experiential Approach.* Cecil H. Bell; Harry R. Knudson; and Robert T. Woodworth. New York: McGraw-Hill, 1973.

12. *Management, Functions and Modern Concepts.* Clayton Reeser. Glenview, Ill.: Scott Foresman, 1973.

13. *Management and Organization.* Henry L. Sisk. Cincinnati, Ohio: South-Western, 1973.

14. *The Management Process, Cases and Readings.* Stephen J. Carroll, Jr.; John B. Miner; and Frank T. Paine. New York: Macmillan, 1977.

15. *Management: Theory and Practice.* Ernest Dale. New York: McGraw-Hill, 1969.

16. *The Managerial Experience: Cases, Exercises, and Readings.* Hinsdale, Ill.: Dryden Press, 1977.

17. *Managing: A Comtemporary Introduction.* John Douglas and Joseph L. Massie. Englewood Cliffs, N.J.: Prentice-Hall, 1977.

18. *Organization and People, Readings, Cases, and Exercises in Organizational Behavior.* J. B. Ritchie and Paul Thompson. St. Paul, Minn.: West Publishing, 1976.

19. *Organizational Behavior and Administration, Cases, Concepts, and Research Findings.* Joseph C. Bailey; Louis B. Barnes; James V. Clark; Robert L. Katz; Paul R. Lawrence; Charles D. Orth, Ill; John A. Seiler; and Arthur N. Turner. Homewood, Ill.: Richard D. Irwin, 1961.

20. *Organizational Behavior and Administration, Cases and Readings.* Louis B. Barnes; Paul R. Lawrence; and Jay W. Lorsch, eds. Homewood, Ill.: Richard B. Irwin, 1976.

21. *Organizational Behavior: Cases and Situations.* B. J. Hodge; Herbert J. Johnson; and Raymond L. Read. New York: Intext, Inc., 1974.

22. *Personnel: A Behavioral Approach to Administration.* Leon C. Megginson. Homewood, Ill.: Richard D. Irwin, 1967.

23. *Policy Formulation and Administration.* Norman A. Berg; C. Roland Christensen; and Malcolm S. Salter. Homewood, Ill.: Richard D. Irwin, 1976.

24. *Policy Making and Executive Action.* Thomas J. McNichols. New York: McGraw-Hill, 1972.

25. *Principles of Human Relations.* Norman R. F. Maier. New York: Wiley, 1952.

26. *Principles of Management.* George R. Terry. Homewood, Ill.: Richard D. Irwin, 1977.

27. *The Process of Management, Concepts, Behavior, and Practice.* William H. Newman and E. Kirby Warren; Study Guide and Casebook, Jerome E. Schnee. Englewood Cliffs, N.J.: Prentice-Hall, 1977.

28. *Strategy, Policy, and Central Management.* James P. Logan and William H. Newman. Cincinnati, Ohio: South-Western, 1976.

29. *Supervision: Concepts and Practices of Management.* Theo Haimann and Raymond L. Hilgert. Cincinnati, Ohio: South-Western, 1972.

30. *Supervisory Management.* George R. Terry. Homewood, Ill.: Richard D. Irwin, 1974.

IV. Books in Supervisory Management

1. *Dynamics of Managerial Leadership.* George T. Vardaman. Princeton, N.J.: Auerbach, 1973.

2. *First-Line Management, Approaching Supervision Effectively.* Lawrence L. Steinmetz and H. Ralph Todd, Jr. Austin, Tex.: Business Publications, 1975.

3. *Front-Line Leadership.* Robert W. Kleemeier; Beyer V. Parker; and Willard E. Parker. New York: McGraw-Hill, 1969.

4. *How to Supervise People.* Alfred M. Cooper. New York: McGraw-Hill, 1958.

5. *Management-Minded Supervision.* Bradford B. Boyd. New York: McGraw-Hill, 1968.

6. *Principles of Supervision.* Donald A. Rudkin, and Fred D. Veal, Jr. Princeton, N.J.: Auerbach, 1973.

7. *Programmed Learning Aid for Supervision.* Roger H. Hermanson and George R. Terry. Homewood, Ill.: Richard D. Irwin, 1975.

8. *Supervision in Action, The Art of Managing Others.* Claude S. George, Jr. Reston, Va.: Reston Publishing Co., 1977.

9. *Supervision: Concepts and Practices of Management.* Theo Haimann and Raymond L. Hilgert. Cincinnati, Ohio: South-Western, 1972.

10. *Supervisory Management.* George R. Terry. Homewood, Ill.: Richard D. Irwin, 1974.

11. *Techniques of Leadership.* Auren Uris. New York: McGraw-Hill, 1953.

REFERENCES

Bass, Bernard M. and Vaughn, James A. *Training in Industry: The Management of Learning*. Belmont, Calif.: Wadsworth, 1966.

Cone, William F. "Guidelines for Training Specialists." *Training and Development Journal* 28, No. 1, January 1974, pp. 44–45.

Handbook of Human Engineering Data. Medford, Mass.: Institute of Applied Experimental Psychology, Tufts College, 1952.

Mintzberg, Henry. "The Manager's Job: Folklore and Fact." *Harvard Business Review* 53, No. 4, July–August 1975, pp. 49–61.

Planty, Earl G., and Freeston, J. Thomas. *Developing Managerial Ability*. New York: Ronald Press, 1954.

Sayles, Leonard R. *Managerial Behavior*. New York: McGraw-Hill, 1964.

5

Training Methods

There are many training methods, each of which is uniquely effective in producing specific results under particular circumstances. The selection of the most appropriate methods for the various segments of a training program is an important determinant of its overall effectiveness. This chapter will examine the most commonly used methods of instruction for supervisory and management training.

One assumption underlying this discussion must be stated at the outset—namely, that the strengths and weaknesses of the methods considered here are due to the methods themselves and not to the effectiveness of the individuals who use the methods. For example, if it is concluded that the case-study method is more effective than the lecture method for changing attitudes, it is because of the nature of the method, and not because the instructor using the case-study method is competent and the instructor using the lecture method is incompetent. In comparing the various methods, it is assumed that they will be used by competent teachers.

THE LECTURE

This is the oldest, and it seems most often used, method of instruction. It involves the direct transmission of information in one direction, from speaker to listeners who remain passive.

Advantages

Although the lecture method has been subjected to more attack than any of the other methods, it is not without several unique advantages.

1.   It is economical. Considerable amounts of information can be conveyed to large numbers of people by one lecture. Quite often it is a time saver too. In the same amount of time it takes to teach a few ideas using the participative methods, the lecture can cover many more facts, concepts, and principles. Moreover, the transmission of information by the lecture method to millions of listeners can be achieved through the use of radio and television.

2.   It is a good way to present principles and background information, facts and theoretical information.

3.   It is useful for quickly acquainting people with new concepts and facts that will enlarge their general knowledge.

4.   Many people learn more from lectures than they do from reading.

5.   The lecture method does not require time for advance preparation on the part of the listeners.

6.   It can be organized and presented in a special way to convey materials that will meet the specific needs of the audience. This may be very important when reading materials, films, and cases are not available.

7.   The learning situation can be controlled by the lecturer to assure that specific information is conveyed.

Disadvantages

Anyone who has studied the subject of communication knows that what is spoken and what is understood are often very different. Learning and listening are not the same; and, basically for this reason, the lecture method has several important disadvantages.

1.   The lecture method often ignores the fact that, among the members of the audience, there may be important differences such as general knowledge, knowledge of the particular subject matter, interest in the lecture material, and experience with the lecture content. For this reason, lecturers and listeners may not always be on the same "wavelength." Also, lecturers may not be able to deliver their materials at a rate that all in the audience can comfortably following or comprehend.

2.   Individual questions from the audience may not be permitted and thus go unanswered.

3.   The lecture is not effective for changing attitudes or altering behavior. While the lecture is useful for helping trainees reach the first two stages of learning (knowledge about and understanding), it is not effective for causing acceptance or teaching application (Watson 1975).

4.   The learning which results from listening to a lecture is superficial. The lecture method ignores the social dimension of learning—that is, learning from one's peers and by doing or experiencing lessons and reflecting on the experience.

5.   The audience remains passive. People tend to remember longer and are effected by things that they learn through their own efforts. The lecture method does not actively involve trainees. All too often we find instructors using the lecture method with the assumption that what they say will have an impact on their students. Planty, McCord, and Efferson (1948, p. 139) put it this way, "Some teachers seem to regard themselves as fountains of knowledge which they pour out to the trainee, expecting him to absorb it, carry it away, and let it influence his behavior for the rest of his life, without any activity on his part."

6.   Lecturing can continue uninterrupted for only short periods of time. One writer claims that the maximum time a lecture should run is 45 minutes, others say an hour. Very dynamic speakers may be able to hold a group's interest for as much as an hour and a half. The exact length of time a lecture can run and remain effective will, of course, vary with the speaker, the group, and the subject matter. The important point to remember is that, even under the best of circumstances, the lecture method is effective for only an hour and a half to two hours at most. Beyond this, the audience's interest quickly wanes and the lecture's effectiveness deteriorates rapidly to the point of restlessness and boredom.

When is the Lecture Appropriate?

The lecture can be effective in providing large numbers of people with straightforward, factual information. Trainees are generally more attentive when they are motivated to learn; when they want to know answers to specific questions and expect the lecture to contain them; and when the lecturer's knowledge of the subject is considerably more substantial than his audience's. Lecturing is not considered an appropriate method for altering attitudes and behavior or when training objectives involve the application of skills or information on the job. It is thought that the lecture method is more appropriate for higher levels of management, where the level of intelligence is generally higher and the audience is more accustomed to verbal presentations of concepts and facts (Planty 1948, p. 181). It is believed not to be appropriate in cases where the intelligence level of the audience is below average.

Preparing the Lecture

Lectures can be made interesting and worthwhile if those preparing and delivering them follow several basic guidelines. The following are a number of suggestions from several authorities on the lecture method.

1.   Analyze the group of people to be addressed. What is their knowledge of the subject? What are their specific needs and interests regarding the subject?

What are their expectations? What illustrations, stories, or jokes will the audience relate to or enjoy? How will the audience use the information presented in the lecture? It is advisable to write out the answers to these questions and others like them which describe fully the audience to be addressed.

2.   Determine and formulate the exact purposes of the lecture. Why is the lecture being given? What should it accomplish? What specifically should the listeners know, understand, value, feel, and be motivated to do as a result of it? Are the exact purposes achievable? If they are not, they must be reformulated. If the lecture is to serve several purposes, what are their priorities? Which is the most important purpose? Which purposes must be reached?

3.   Based on the information gained from suggestions 1 and 2 above and on the amount of time available, determine the main points to be contained in the lecture. Key points should not be excessive; allow a maximum of three or four key points for an hour-long lecture. As a general rule, it is better to have too few key points rather than too many.

4.   It is wise to have a theme which holds the major points together. Thus the audience will have a useful conceptual framework and will be more likely to remember the information presented and better able to use it.

5.   Organize the lecture so that it will be clear and logical to the audience. There should be logical transitions from one point to the next in order to avoid comments from the audience such as the following: "I don't understand how the speaker got from point C to point D. I did not get the connection between the two," or, "One minute the speaker was talking about X, and the next minute about Z. I couldn't follow the logic."

6.   Thoroughly research the subject. Master the material to be conveyed. Collect data, facts, research findings, illustrations, anecdotes, and stories to support, clarify, or make the points being made impactful. Be careful in choosing materials used to illustrate or support the points to be made; be sure they will be understood and appreciated by the audience. Prepare charts, tables, graphs, and illustrations beforehand.

7.   The material should be meaningful to the audience. Prepare and present it so that the audience can relate to it readily. Provide suggestions as to how the audience might use the concepts presented or benefit from their knowledge of the information and ideas presented.

8.   Gear the grammatical composition to be used to the audience. What is the vocabulary of the audience? Will they understand all of the words used? Can long, complex sentences be used or should short, simple sentences be used? Should technical terms be defined or explained? Will the group feel comfortable if four-letter words are or are not used? Be careful not to "talk-down" to the audience, but do not talk over their heads either.

9.   Plan the delivery to meet the needs of the audience. Spend more time on complex areas. Spend less time on familiar areas.

10.   Practice, practice, practice! Become comfortable with the lecture. Become so familiar with it that notes are not needed. If it is a lecture from which you may be quoted, then you may want to read it; even then, practice reading the lecture so that it will flow smoothly.

Delivering the Lecture

1.   Be confident and positive (not cocky). Be self-assured in the knowledge that you are well acquainted with the material to be covered and are prepared to deliver it well. If you are confident, you will most likely be relaxed and, as a result, will relate well to the audience and deliver the lecture smoothly.

2.   Begin the lecture on time. It is discourteous to keep an audience waiting. Time is valuable. By starting on time, you will communicate the fact that what you have to say is important and you are prepared. You will also communicate your respect for the group.

3.   Posture and bearing are important because they communicate your self-confidence. Do not "worm" around, rock, sway, lean, or slouch in front of an audience as it is irritating and distracting, and it indicates that you feel meek and uncomfortable. Stand solidly on both feet and project yourself as you talk to the group.

4.   "Break the ice" with the audience before you get started on the lecture. Show them that you are relaxed. Make them feel comfortable with you. There are many ways to do this and you will have to find the method best suited to you. Some speakers tell jokes or stories; others level with the audience or tell something about themselves; others indicate their pleasure at being present; others modestly indicate their mastery and expertise of the subject.

5.   Establish a rapport with the group. Indicate through your actions that you respect them as individuals and that you are eager to communicate with them. Look directly into the eyes of the listeners. Remember, you are talking to them and not just verbalizing to hear yourself talk. You are not speaking to impress them with your knowledge; if this is your attitude, your audience will sense it and quickly tune you out.

6.   Be enthusiastic. You want your audience to know and understand and accept what you have to say. Your enthusiasm will make the material seem more interesting and worthwhile. If you are not enthusiastic, an audience will usually lose interest in what you have to say.

7.   Present the lecture so that it motivates the audience to want to know what you have to say. "Any instructor who assumes that his learning group is eager

to receive his material may be courting disaster" (Zelko 1952, p. 144). Make what you are going to say and why you are going to say it clear. Explain to the audience what you intend to cover and where you will be taking them.

8. Pace the lecture appropriately to the audience. Deviate from your initial plan if necessary. Realize that you may have to condense or eliminate material from your presentation.

9. Never apologize to the audience for being ill-prepared or for having poor illustrations, or for your inexperience or discomfort. Doing so will create a barrier between you and the audience and will make the audience uncomfortable. People can sense areas where you are ill-at-ease or ill-prepared. Apologies will only make these areas more evident and will cause the audience to discount your presentation, including its good points.

10. At the conclusion of the talk, summarize the main points. Provide perspective to what you have said.

11. Answer questions clearly and directly. If you do not know a particular answer, say so. Doing so will not discredit you. (Unless, of course, it is an elementary question, in which case you should not have been so presumptuous as to have lectured to the group in the first place.)

12. Finish the lecture on time. Never go beyond the designated stopping time; it is highly discourteous to do so. Stop for designated breaks or lunches.

THE CONFERENCE METHOD

Training does not always involve the presentation of new information and concepts. Sometimes its objectives may be (1) to share ideas and experiences and pool information among participants, (2) to solve problems common to a group, (3) to get acceptance to new ideas or policies, or (4) to increase tolerance and understanding. In these and many other situations, the conference method may be appropriate.

Lerda (1967, p. 155) describes the conference method as involving

> . . . a group of people who pool ideas, examine and share facts, ideas, and data, test assumptions, and draw conclusions, all of which contribute to the improvement of job performance. It should involve a group of people who have all had experience related to the problem, or be among people who are capable of analyzing the problem from information provided by the conference leader.

Conference Board Reports (1960) have defined a conference as involving the pooling of information for solving a problem. Lerda (1967) and Planty, McCord, and Efferson (1948) do not see it necessarily as having to involve problem solving. In fact, problem solving is not always desirable. For example, a group of people who confer on a subject with which they are partially or totally ignorant are not likely to arrive at sound conclusions or solutions to related problems. Instead they will pool their ignorance and become further committed to their faulty beliefs and incorrect assumptions because they have had their thinking supported by others who share similar opinions. For this reason, conferences are usually most beneficial when definite conclusions by consensus (or, worse yet, by majority vote) are not made.

There are exceptions to this generalization, however. The conference method is typically used by small groups (buzz groups) composed of 5 to 8 people who discuss and prepare case studies. In this situation it is desirable for groups to reach conclusions that will be presented to a larger group, where other buzz-group teams will also present their reports and conclusions on the same case. The discussion leader, or instructor, will then react to the group reports by giving his or her own views and conclusions.

The training conference must be conducted only with individuals who have backgrounds of knowledge and experience that will permit them to contribute to the discussion, understand it and profit from it. Moreover, the conference should be well planned, not a free-wheeling discussion, that turns into "a conversational boatride on uncharted seas to an unknown port" (Planty 1948, p. 182).

A planned conference involves the following.

Preconference

1. The subject to be discussed is identified.

2. Specific objectives of the conference are formulated.

3. An outline for the discussion is prepared, and the cases, articles, issues, etc. are selected.

4. Participants are carefully selected.

5. Conference purposes, schedules, and procedures to be followed are communicated to participants.

6. Participants receive conference materials (cases studies, articles, questions) to be discussed so that they can study and prepare themselves before the conference begins.

7. Meeting rooms and materials are arranged.

Conducting the conference

8. Participants are welcomed, reoriented to the purposes and methods, and put at ease.

9. The topic is introduced and discussed according to the general plan.

10. The conference ends on schedule with a summarization of its highlights.

Advantages

The principle advantage of the conference method is that it involves the active participation of everyone present. It is also useful for teaching interpersonal skills such as understanding and communication. More specifically, the advantages of the conference method are as follows:

1. It appeals to practical people, especially those with considerable experience and the desire to talk about it.

2. It is a good way to share ideas and exchange information and to learn from others. It encourages people to learn from each other and it permits people to extend their practical knowledge by learning about the experiences of others.

3. It provides people with a better understanding of others' experiences, opinions, and feelings.

4. It is a fairly good way for getting new ideas, policies, plans, etc. accepted, sometimes by clearing up incorrect assumptions and unnecessary fears.

5. It is more effective than the lecture method for changing attitudes.

6. It serves to correct misinformation and misunderstanding.

7. It encourages new thinking and creative solutions to problems.

8. It provides an opportunity for people to improve their ability to verbalize.

9. It can teach people to work effectively together as a group. It encourages tolerance and understanding.

10. It can sometimes produce useful solutions to real problems.

11. It can provide opportunities for expressing fears so they can be seen for what they are.

Disadvantages

1. It requires considerable time to plan and organize.

2. It is not for the novice or untrained instructor. It requires skill in group processes and a solid knowledge of the subject to be discussed.

3. Discussions can easily be dominated by the most outspoken person, or the person in the highest level position in an organization, or the person possessing the highest perceived status.

4. Participants must be fairly well informed about the conference before it starts. They must be knowledgeable of the subject and interested in discussing it.

5. Discussions can easily get off the planned path. The group leadership skill necessary to get back on course is rare.

6. Groups sometimes gloss-over important areas; in-depth lecturing may be more appropriate.

7. Some individuals may be unwilling to listen and learn from others, especially those whom they perceive as having low status.

Suggestions for Leading a Conference

In addition to the ten suggestions on planning and conducting a conference, competent leadership is a critical element necessary for conducting a successful conference.

1. The conference leader should have training experience and be interested in both training and the subject to be discussed.

2. The conference leader should be adept at leading discussions, keeping group discussions "on the beam," keeping "talkers" and "wise-guys" from monopolizing the discussion, asking thought-provoking questions, keeping the discussion lively but not too fast for the group to follow, and making sure everyone has an opportunity to be heard.

3. Conference leaders should not set themselves up as authorities. They should refrain from imposing their own thinking on others.

4. They should not ridicule, belittle, argue, clown, take sides, or lecture. They should practice democratic group leadership and should view themselve as "catalysts."

5. They should be good at restating others' statements to their satisfaction and should not twist them around to what they want them to say. Conference leaders should be able to summarize the group's thinking regularly and frequently.

6. They should make a good ending, on time, that summarizes what took place or identifies the key conclusion or highlight or both.

THE CASE-STUDY METHOD

The case-study method of instruction is by no means a recent approach to education. Aesop (620–560 B.C.) illustrated important truths in his fables. Jesus taught many important lessons through the use of parables. And Plutarch used examples in his writings.

Perhaps the earliest formal introduction of the case-study method of instruction to American education was made by Christopher Langdell of the Harvard Law School in 1871. Langdell, wanting more realism and practicality in the law school, initiated the use of the case-study method as a revolt against the lecture method. Using this method, students studied court records (cases) using the courts' decisions as precedents for understanding the law and interpreting it in new cases.

When the Harvard Business School was founded in 1908, many of the very successful businessmen of the country had received their academic preparation for business from law schools. Realizing that the law school was the most serious competitor for good students and status that the newly established business school had to face, the Dean, Edwin F. Gay, took steps to implement his decision to have instruction, as far as practicable, take the form of classroom discussion of specific problems and cases. Supposedly it was Dean Gay's belief that if students were educated to think for themselves and handle business problems and situations, they would more likely have successful careers then they would if they were educated by means of traditional methods. And, if the students were successful, their success would reflect well upon the school. From the outset, the business school's commercial law courses were taught by using case studies.

Four years later, in 1912, two further steps were taken to advance Dean Gay's philosophy of education and, as a consequence, the development and usage of the case-study method. The first step was an outgrowth of an idea of A. W. Shaw, a friend of Dean Gay. Shaw was a Chicago businessman who published *System*, a magazine for managers, and several business books. It was Shaw's belief that students could learn a great deal about business from those who were actively engaged in it. To implement this idea, a new course, required of all second-year students, was established. Its aim was to teach students to integrate the subjects they had learned in their first year to solve top-management problems. Today this would probably be called a course in business policy. Fifteen business executives participated in this first course, which had the following format:

1. During one class period, a visiting business executive would present a real problem. The problem would be described as much as possible and questions would be answered for the students for further clarification.

2. At the following class meeting, the students would present their written analyses and recommendations. The visiting business executive would listen to their reports and perhaps ask a few questions and make comments.

3. During the third class meeting, the reports would be criticized and discussed by the business executive, who would also then present a solution and reasoning. Questions from the students and discussion followed.

The second step, which moved the development of the case-study method forward, was an unplanned comment made by Dean Gay to one of the school's faculty members. The statement captured succinctly the philosophy underlying the case-study method. And, as anyone who has worked in organizations knows, comments and suggestions from the top rarely go unheeded.

The faculty member in this situation was Melvin T. Copeland, who was assigned to teach a section of a course in commercial organization (marketing) for the first time. In his own words, Copeland (1954, p. 27) recounts that incident:

> . . . I was coming from a meeting of the class, I met Dean Gay on the steps of the Harvard Yard, where he had his office. He asked me how things were going, and since at the moment I was feeling optimistic, I told him that I had found enough to talk about so far. "Humph," was Dean Gay's rejoinder, "that isn't the question. Have you found enough to keep the students talking?"

That question captured the difference between lecturing and case discussion and perhaps even the difference between talking and teaching.

Upon the resignation of Dean Gay in 1919, Wallace B. Donham was appointed the second dean of Harvard Business School. A graduate of the Harvard Law School and a man of considerable business experience, Donham was also a strong advocate of the case-study method. At Dean Donham's request, Melvin Copeland wrote a case-book on marketing, which he completed in 1920. This is believed to be the first case-book written in the field of business administration.

What Is a Case Study?

A *case study* is a description or history of a real, or imaginary yet realistic, situation. Most case studies are quite readable as they are written in story form. Case studies may deal with the total organization or specific units within it, such as personnel, finance, marketing, or manufacturing. Or, the case may deal with general problems or issues common to all departments, such as planning, decision making, motivation, or change. Case studies may be written from the viewpoint of a neutral observer or from the viewpoint of one or more individuals in the case. Case studies should be objective and free of editorialization. If they are presented from a third party's perspective, they should be free of judgments. However, if written from the perspective of several of the key characters in the case, the case is enriched because it contains the emotions and perception of the characters.

Some case studies are written at an elementary level so that problems and their causes are easily discernible. Case studies are more realistic and challenging when they represent comprehensive descriptions of situations and when they present both good and bad management practices intermingled and unidentified as such. Case studies may vary in length from one to forty or fifty pages or more; however, length alone should not be taken as a definite indication of the scope and complexity of the case study. For example, one of the most popular case studies ever written (The Dashman Co.) is only one and a half pages long. Yet it contains many of the knottiest problems managers face.

It is felt by many that case studies must describe actual situations. These people argue that fictitious cases are often filled with inconsistencies that tend to confuse students and cause them to become discouraged. Thus students may lack a strong interest in working on a case that they feel is unbelievable or not challenging. Even with cases that depict unusual, yet true, situations, students who are not inclined to face up to the challenge of difficult questions or ambiguity will often try to escape by saying, "It isn't real, it couldn't really happen where I work so why bother."

Using Case Studies

There are two distinct approaches for using case studies, each one being strongly advocated by very able educators. One of these is the *deductive method*, by which students first acquire a knowledge and understanding of certain concepts and principles. Then they are given a case to study and analyze, and on which to practice the application of theory recently learned. They start with management principles (premises), study a situation (case), and arrive at conclusions (solutions to the case-study problem).

The other approach, the *inductive method*, is considerably more demanding of the students and the instructor. In this method, students are given a case to study, along with readings and references to theoretical materials containing the concepts and principles being taught. Unlike the deductive approach, which simply asks the students to apply the concepts learned, this method requires the students to discover the principles and concepts for themselves. Using this method, the students start by studying a situation (case), formulating conclusions (solutions to the case), and discovering the management principles (premises) for themselves. This is the Harvard method and, of the two approaches, is generally thought to be the better approach for teaching students how to identify, analyze, and solve problems, how to formulate creative solutions to problems, and how to become more able to search beyond their own immediate knowledge for answers.

Sometimes cases are used merely to illustrate principles and concepts; this is called the *case problem method*. Cases used for this purpose are usually short, only a paragraph or two in length. The instructor leads the students through the case problem, pointing out what is taking place and illustrating the principles and concepts being taught. This method is thought to be a good way for reinforcing ideas or illustrating points that need further clarification.

How the Case-Study Method Works

Because of its superiority, only the Harvard or inductive method will be discussed. The basic aim of this approach is not only to teach concepts and principles (knowledge), but also to increase one's abilities in problem identification, analysis, judgment, decision making, and problem solving (diagnostic skills), as well as attitudes of tolerance of others and other points of view, openness to novel, untried approaches to problems, tolerance of ambiguity, and nondogmatic thinking (personal characteristics).

This method places the burden of learning on the student. It is nondirective. The student must become self-motivated and deeply involved in learning the many subtle, complex lessons which, when combined, are generally referred to as "wisdom." The use of this method is based on the supposition that wisdom cannot be taught, but must be learned from experience. It is believed that the materials and lessons learned by this method will be remembered better and longer and will be more likely to guide students in their future decisions and actions (Gragg 1940).

In the case-study method, the entire class of participants is divided into several study groups of five to eight people (buzz groups). The case is given to participants sometime prior to the buzz-group meeting so that they can study it and read pertinent theoretical material, such as chapters in textbooks and articles, and form their own judgments individually. The more thorough and conscientious participants are in making their preliminary preparations, the more fruitful the buzz-group discussion becomes. Each group analyzes, discusses, and consolidates the thinking and opinions of their members to formulate a group report on the case. In the buzz-group case-preparation meeting, participants may discuss anything that they feel is pertinent and significant. The buzz-group leader will usually try to keep the discussion "on track." However, through free-wheeling discussion the group's thinking often becomes both broader and deeper and, as a result, students delve into elusive, complex subtleties that might otherwise go unexamined. Through these open, give-and-take case discussions participants frequently learn to realize that their own individual approach is not the only "good" one and that there are often many other ways to solve problems. Moreover, they learn to sense weaknesses in their own approaches and thinking and come to respect the thinking of others. But, perhaps most importantly, they learn to identify and analyze problems for themselves and then to arrive at creative solutions to these problems on their own, without having to rely on the instructor to identify the problem for them and give them the correct solution to it.

Some time after the buzz groups have prepared their reports, the entire class is reassembled. Representatives from the various buzz groups present their group's report to the entire class and the instructor. All are free to raise questions and comment on the reports presented. Additional discussion usually follows and this typically is directed at further explorations into concepts brought out by the reports and comments made about them. The instructor will then summarize what she or he has observed from the group reports, make additional comments on the case analyses and reports, and finally give her or his own thinking and conclusions. The instructor may even go further and lecture to the class, providing insights and conclusions, adding support through research evidences, and include illustrations of the principles being taught from personal experience or from the experiences of others.

The Buzz Groups

Buzz groups work to study, analyze, discuss, and solve case-study problems. They delve deeply into the complexities of the case being studied with the aims of understanding what took place, the reasons for it, the significance of it, and perhaps how the problems could have been avoided or might be avoided in the future, or solved now that they exist. Buzz groups should steer clear of simplistic, "black-and-white" thinking, such as the manager is bad or incompetent, which is equivalent to saying, "The problem would not have occurred if people were perfect." This kind of thinking is entirely unrealistic and does not teach participants other kinds of managerial interventions that might work.

Buzz groups should work to develop a variety of approaches to problems before selecting a course of action. They should also realize that there are perhaps other approaches that they may not have uncovered and that their solution is not necessarily "the best one."

Buzz-group activities provide experiential learning for their members. When conducted properly, this experience teaches cooperation, active participation, respect and tolerance for other people's viewpoints, and teamwork. Scott Nicholson (1956, p. 118) has observed,

> None of the customary methods of instruction have proven (as) successful (as the case method) in developing two critical management skills: the ability to think logically and concisely and the ability to work with other people.

Planty, an ardent advocate of using the buzz-group approach to case-study preparation, has spelled out the roles and responsibilities of the buzz-group members. According to Planty (1967, p. 2),

> All participants in a work-study discussion group have responsibilities for all the necessary functions in the group. These include leading, observing, understanding, recording, questioning, summarizing, serving as a resource person, contributing to the flow of thinking, getting agreement, learning and helping others to learn, and assisting in the problem solving process.

> Each group member:

1. Helps decide on specific problems, actions, or attitudes to be considered.

2. Helps decide upon ways of working as a group.

3. Contributes ideas and suggestions related to the problems or questions being considered.

4. Listens to what other members say and seeks helpful ideas and insights from them.

5. Requests clarification when needed. Summarizes. Questions. Answers. Illustrates. Plays back what he hears. Reacts to feelings expressed as well as to facts.

6. Observes the group process and makes suggestions about its effectiveness or its improvement.

7. From time to time observes his own behavior in the group, judges its effectiveness, adapts and improves his performance.

The leader:

1. Organizes the group for time, place, etc.

2. Helps decide and periodically redecides the rules for conduct of the group.

3. Helps new group members get acquainted.

4. Develops an atmosphere that is free and permissive. Encourages all to contribute.

5. Develops in the group members an attitude of willing critical objectivity which encourages high quality, careful thought.

6. Analyzes the latent resources within the group members and devises ways of releasing and using these resources when needed. Gets people to think, talk, and advance group goals.

7. Develops ways of continuous evaluation of both group productivity and group processes. What did we get done? How effectively did we work at it? Gets group to take this responsibility habitually.

8. Frequently calls on group members to clarify, express, and analyze feelings, values, problems, or assumptions in the cases, role plays, or readings.

9. Draws out the "timid soul" and keeps the dominant person from monopolizing.

10. Arranges the best possible physical conditions. Proper heat, light, and ventilation. Seats his group so that members face each other. Preferably in a circle or a near circle.

The recorder:

1. Keeps a record of the main problems, issues, ideas, facts, and decisions as they develop in the discussions.

2. Summarizes points and plays them back to the group from time to time as needed.

3. Consults with group about the kind of report they would like made.

4. Prepares final group report and is responsible for getting it ready for presentation (art work, charts, etc.). Gives the report of his group to the reassembled members. Defines or explains it in the discussion period.

The Instructor's Role

The instructor who uses the case-study method of instruction faces a formidable and challenging task. Those not acquainted with the case-study method's philosophy and methodology sometimes think that the instructors who uses it "are taking it easy" or "are not really teaching and earning their keep." Not so. The case-study method requires considerable subject knowledge, understanding of people and group behavior, and the ability to think on one's feet, communicate, and above all, to relate well to the trainees.

Following are several suggestions for instructors (discussion leaders) for successfully using the case-study method of teaching.

1.   Meet with the students prior to their buzz group sessions. Get to know them and let them get to know you. Cases are usually prepared in the evening before the session in which they are presented and discussed in class.

2.   Introduce the case they will be studying and preparing for the next day's class. Point out things to pay particular attention to and identify the more important segments of their reading assignment. Answer questions they might have.

3.   Visit the groups as they are preparing the case for your session. Listen to what they say and how they feel. This does two things: (a) It shows them you are interested in them and their learning and it shows them that what they are doing is important. (b) It can give you an idea of what to expect in class the next day. Thus you will be more aware of the difficulties students are facing, what new materials you can present (going further than planned if they are a particularly advanced group), and how to handle various aspects of the presentation you make.

4.   When visiting the buzz groups as they prepare their cases, refrain from lecturing or from giving them the answer to the case or from pointing them in the direction in which they will discover the answers you expect. This is their time and their learning experience. Directive leadership from the instructor is counterproductive to the goals of individual learning and self-discovery.

5.   In class the next day, present your objectives and methodology. Let the students know what you expect to accomplish and what they will be doing in class. You may wish to provide an introduction to your session by lecturing, but this should be minimized.

6.   Spend the first half of your class time listening to the buzz-group reports. Listen to what the groups concluded and to what led them to their conclusions. Bring out the groups' assumptions, logic, feelings, and evidence. Invite questions, comments, discussion, and ideas from those listening to the reports. You may highlight particular aspects through short lectures of about three to ten minutes in length, provided they are timely and appropriate. Compare reports showing how they differ and what led them to become different.

7.   Create a climate of in-depth inquiry. Ask probing questions such as, "What led you to this conclusion?" "What attitudes, values, beliefs, or feelings

do you think caused your report to be shaped as it is?" "Why do you suppose the other groups answered the question differently?" "Can you explain this answer further?" There is a distinct difference between serious, honest, probing inquiry and cutting, belittling or heckling comments. The latter should never be permitted. Honest, sincere, in-depth inquiry will tend to create a oneness between trainee and instructor in search of knowledge. When this condition exists, trainees are ready for competently delivered, scholarly, and informative lectures.

8.   When the time is right, lecture. Use illustrations, research evidence, stories, and the case-study reports. Provide your professional knowledge to amplify, clarify, deepen, enrich, and broaden students' knowledge, understanding, and acceptance of the concepts and principles you are teaching.

9.   The trainees will consider you to be an expert in the field you teach. They will want to hear your ideas, analysis, and conclusions regarding the case. Give them the benefit of your thinking. They can decide for themselves whether they want to accept or reject it. But at least they will have something with which to compare their thinking.

10.   Evaluate the case reports, but do so quickly, carefully, and gently with a visible attitude of genuine helpfulness. Identify what you see as good, well done, carefully thought out. Suggest what some may have omitted or covered too superficially. Show what your expectations were and where trainees did or did not meet them. According to Planty (1968),

> Men work well where there are standards of performance and where the standards are made explicit. More and more, executives in training courses are asking for feedback on their performance. Research proves that knowledge of how well one is doing is a requirement of effective learning. Experience repeatedly shows that such feedback from instructors sharply and quickly improves group analysis, written reports, their presentation in class, and, most importantly, involvement and responsibility for their own and other men's insight and growth.

11.   Comment on what you saw during the evening buzz-group sessions that led to effective case analysis. Without identifying individuals, comment on what they did or refrained from doing that led to effective or ineffective case analysis. Get participants to think further as to how they can work together more effectively in their buzz groups.

Selecting Case Studies

Case studies should be selected with care. This is often difficult because, while there are many, cases that are appropriate for teaching a particular subject to a particular group may not be readily available. They must be searched for, and this usually requires the expenditure of a considerable amount of time and voluminous reading.

Following are several useful questions which, if answered, will quite likely direct the instructor to good case selection.

1.   What are the overall aims of the course? What are the aims of the session to be taught?

2.   Will the trainees identify with and respond favorably to the case, its setting, the levels of management involved, and the types of problems uncovered? (For example, a group of steel-mill supervisors will be quickly turned off by a case involving high-level decisions made in a library case-study setting, and conversely.)

3.   Will the trainees be familiar with the technical language used in the case? Will they be able to understand the issues presented?

4.   Does the case involve work problems with which participants are familiar and with the levels of management and settings in which they work?

5.   Is the case at the appropriate level of complexity and difficulty for the group?

6.   Is the case one which participants can read without too much difficulty? Is it too long? Can it be understood by the trainees?

7.   Will trainees have enough time to prepare the case before class? Is there enough class time to discuss the case properly and thoroughly?

8.   Does the case contain appropriate content? Does it bring out the points and principles you intend to teach?

Advantages of the Case-Study Method

1.   The case-study method brings realism to the classroom, which appeals to practical-minded manager. Case studies involve reality, they are not just a lot of theory.

2.   Cases are challenging and invite active participation. They encourage students to learn for themselves. The case-study method encourages self-learning.

3.   The method provides trainees with an opportunity to test their thinking against that of others and what the research findings suggest. Through taking stands, making decisions, and arriving at conclusions in their buzz-groups, trainees have an opportunity to learn through trial-and-error experiences.

4.   The buzz-group experience teaches students how to learn from each other.

5.   The experience of case-study discussion teaches students that there are many viewpoints. Managers from one department of a company learn from

the viewpoints of managers from another department—e.g., marketing people can learn the production view, etc.

6.   When conducted properly, case-study analysis and discussion discourages "black-and-white," simplistic, and dogmatic thinking.

7.   Trainees discover and establish principles in their own frame of reference for themselves.

8.   Case-study preparation teaches people to work with others in groups. It helps students tolerate, understand, and cooperate with others of different opinions, viewpoints, values, and beliefs.

9.   The case-study method not only teaches generalizations and contingent principles, but, most importantly, it teaches people how to inquire and search for meaning in complex situations and discover truths and generalizations for themselves.

Disadvantages of the Case-Study Method

1.   The case-study method is a slow way of teaching. Case selection, preparation, analysis, and discussion take time. One case can easily take an hour of buzz-group-preparation time, two to three hours of buzz-group discussion, and one or two hours of presentation and discussion time in class. Also students can learn just a few key ideas.

2.   Case selection is difficult and time consuming. It requires considerable competency to select cases that are appropriate for particular groups. Moreover, an instructor often needs to spend considerable time searching for the right case, which may involve screening as many as one hundred cases and reading as many as ten to twenty-five cases just to select one that is appropriate.

3.   The case-study method is sometimes ambiguous and frustrating. People accustomed to being given the "correct" answer frequently become uncomfortable when the answers are not set forth or when the instructor does not give them the answer straight out.

4.   In many cases there is no "one correct answer." This ambiguity is frustrating, especially to dogmatic students who cannot live with uncertainty.

5.   The nondirective, conference-type method of teaching cases requires competent and highly trained instructors who are patient, can think on their feet, and are not threatened by questions that they may not be able to answer.

6.   Trainees must be willing to express their thoughts and feelings and hold them up for others to question and react to. Unless the trainees are managers with some measure of experience, case-study analyses and discussion may be superficial and boring to uninterested minds.

THE INCIDENT PROCESS

This is a variant of the case-study method which involves instructors who are thoroughly knowledgeable of case situations. They begin the process by introducing to the entire class a "bare-bones" description of a critical incident from the case situation. The instructors then invite questions from class members who seek more information as they think it is needed for case analysis and solution. Instructors answer only these questions and do not elaborate on additional details. They make the class work to uncover the situation, its problems, and causes. They supply only the information requested. The principal aims of the incident process are twofold:

1. to teach management concepts and contingent principles;

2. to teach problem-analysis and problem-solving skills.

Unlike the case-study method, which also aims for the same objectives, the incident process concludes with an intensive analysis of the problem-identification and problem-solving methods followed by the group. This aspect is often the focal point of the entire exercise.

Professor Paul Pigors of the Massachusetts Institute of Technology (who is credited with the development of the incident process), with the cooperation of Faith Pigors, began using the incident process in 1950 in seminars on personnel administration. Dissatisfied because of the shortcoming of the traditional case-study method, which did not teach students how to handle everyday incidents in practical and thorough ways while at the same time adhering to principles of good human relations, Pigors developed the incident process to bridge the gap between verbalizing and doing. Pigors' approach to the use of the incident process was in dealing with human-relations problems and their solution. His first incident-process exercises therefore dealt with human-behavior problems that students were asked to solve, placing themselves in the position of one of the characters depicted in the incident. Since that time, the incident process has been adapted for the purpose of teaching analytical skills and problem solving by requiring students to ask pertinent and appropriate questions to gather the information needed for incident problem analysis and solution. It appears from the literature available today that there are three distinct approaches to the incident process.

1. The Pigors approach, which emphasizes the solving of human relations problems from the perspective of a character depicted in the case incident.

2. The analytical skills/problem-solving ability improvement approach, which emphasizes the development of analytical and problem-solving skills.

3. The three-step approach to having students solve an actual case study. This was described earlier in the section on the history of the case-study method.

The Pigors Approach

Pigors' approach to the incident process combines elements of case analysis, problem solving, and role playing. However, it does not involve actual role playing in that students intellectualize and explain how they would handle a situation rather than play acting the role. This has a dual emphasis of (1) teaching trainees how to handle human-relations problems and (2) teaching the trainees how to make critical analyses using fact-finding, clear thinking, and decision-making techniques through questioning from other trainees.

The aims of the incident process, according to Pigors (1967, p. 180) are to develop the following abilities.

1. *Intellectual ability:* The capacity to think clearly, incisively, and reasonably about specific facts and abstractions.

2. *Practical judgment:* The capacity to modify conclusions arrived at intellectually to meet the test of common sense, including organization sense.

3. *Social awareness:* The capacity to appreciate the force of other people's feelings and to adjust or implement a decision so that it can be more acceptable to persons who are affected by it.

There are five steps to the Pigors incident-process method (Gambatese 1955):

1.   Students begin with an incident which is a short description of some behavior, usually only a paragraph or two in length, but sometimes are as long as a page and a half. The incident usually calls for some action or decision. Thus the group starts out with initial questions of "What is going on here?" and "What should be done?" This is not altogether clear since it is purposely written containing none of the pertinent facts necessary to answer these questions. Interest is further heightened as students are asked to take the role of a "responsible insider," that is, some key character depicted in the incident. Thus they are in a position of trying to work out a decision from the role of an insider.

2.   Next, students engage in fact finding. They interview the discussion leader or instructor, who knows the incident thoroughly, to obtain information necessary to assess what went on and what should be done. This phase involves asking what, where, when, who, and how questions. It does not permit asking, "What is the problem?" Sometimes incident leaders require students to ask questions that can be answered by a simple yes or no. The mass of facts gathered must be organized, condensed, and assembled to make a bridge between fact and issue. This is usually done by small groups or by some appointed member.

3.   The group next decides what the central issues are, what needs to be decided, and what the pertinent factors are.

4.   Each person writes out his or her decision and the reasons for it. Next, these are shared and discussed after which the various solutions are debated. Sometimes the solutions are even put to the test of role playing to follow through to see what would happen. Finally, the discussion leader tells the group what actually took place, what was said and done, how the situation was handled, and what happened as a result.

5.   An analysis of the fact-finding process is made. Someone who has observed the fact-finding questioning will critically evaluate the strengths, weaknesses, and appropriateness of the questions. She or he may even point out where the group wandered at times. Next, both the content of the case and the approaches taken in analyzing and solving it are discussed. The aims of this phase are twofold: (1) to determine what can be learned from the content portion of the exercise and thus formulate useful generalizations, and (2) to evaluate the appropriateness of the problem-solving methods used with the aim of determining which ones were or might be most useful.

Analytical Skills—Problem-Solving Ability Improvement Approach

This approach to the incident process emphasizes the development of questioning abilities, information assimilation, and judgment. In this method, the students read a critical incident or hear one described to them by the discussion leader. They are then asked, "What took place? What should be done? How should the situation be handled?" and "What is needed to solve the problem?" or other similar questions. They are free to ask the instructor questions so as to gather the information needed to make sound conclusions or answer the questions logically. They may only ask for facts and are not permitted to seek the instructor's opinions or conclusions as to what the real problem is or what should be done. All questions and responses are carefully recorded by the instructor or someone appointed by the instructor. When the students feel that they have derived enough information for a conclusion, the questioning ceases and they present their conclusions and supporting logic and arguments. These too are carefully recorded for later analysis.

When these steps are concluded, the instructor reveals what really occurred, including the pertinent data that has a bearing on the incident, and then explains what happened afterward or how the problem was actually solved.

Finally, the discussion turns to the central issue of the lesson to be learned—namely, questioning ability, assimilation, and judgment.

Questioning ability

The instructor critiques the questioning that occurred by addressing such questions as the following:

1. How relevant were the questions?

2. Did trainees get at the pertinent issues or did they wander off course?

3. What was the utility of each question? Which were useful? Which were not?

4. What did trainees assume as evidenced by their questions? Were these assumptions sound, logical, and warranted? Why were they made?

5. How carefully did students listen to the questions of other students and the answers that were given? Is there evidence that questions were redundant? That is, did they ask for information that was already given?

6. Did questions build on one another? Was there any logical pattern to them?

Assimilation

The instructor assesses the problem definition step in terms of both the content and process. Some of the things he looks at are:

1. Did students make incorrect or unwarranted inferences from the data available?

2. Did they try to solve the problem as it became clearly defined or did they try to use some pet method or approach which they already knew as the solution to the problem? In other words, did they go about the problem-solving process creatively by identifying the problem first, regardless of what they had in the way of remedies, and then work out a solution to match it?

3. Did students combine information logically? Did they build a logical and consistent line of reasoning as they defined the problem? Did they spot any inconsistencies in the data provided and were these cleared up?

Judgment

Finally, the students' decisions are analyzed.

1. Were their conclusions logical? Did they have necessary and sufficient evidence to support their point of view?

2. Did they exhibit simplistic thinking; that is, did they see situations only in terms of black or white, right or wrong, good or bad, or were they more sophisticated?

3. Were students aware of their inferences?

4. Did students contemplate and understand the consequences of their discussions? Were they aware of the significance and probable impact of these?

wol

These are only a few of the many considerations that can and should be made with regard to these three areas. Moreover, it would be incorrect to believe that these three areas cover the total spectrum open to critique. Indeed not. They merely represent some of the key areas for post-exercise analysis. In total, the analysis part of this type of incident-process exercise should consume from one and a half to two hours of study.

In summary, it should be stated that both the Pigors and the analytical-skills/problem-solving ability improvement methods are somewhat similar in content, differing only in emphasis. Both have unique advantages. Training people will have to determine their specific objectives and select one or the other or some combination of the two as they feel necessary.

ROLE PLAYING

The role-playing method is a relatively recent training innovation. It was developed by Jacob L. Moreno, a Viennese psychologist who immigrated to the United States in 1925. The method was an outgrowth of psychodrama, which Moreno introduced to the field of counseling in 1911. Through his work with psychodrama (focus on the individual in a group setting) and with sociodrama (focus on the group), Moreno introduced role playing as one of several means for illiciting non-directed behavior that could be analyzed and studied. The first recorded use of role playing was in the early 1930s when Moreno used it in a program to rehabilitate inmates at the Hudson School for Girls in New York. In 1933, Moreno introduced the technique to business training for a program he conducted for the Macy Company. Others, seeing that the method had possibilities in human relations training, soon adapted it to this purpose.

Role playing is a laboratory method—that is, it is a technique carried out by the guidance of a trained leader and is presented before observers. It involves the spontaneous acting out of a prescribed role in a given realistic situation by two or more "actors." The dialogue and actions of the trainees (actors) grow out of the situation as it develops in the ways and directions the individuals lead it. It is not play acting. The instructor and the other students in the class serve as observers and critics.

Role playing is a form of experiential learning but is usually more impactful than everyday experience because it also involves observation, discussion, and analysis—that is, systematic reflection on the experience with the aim of learning something from it. Maier (1957) says role playing is a technique of creating a life situation involving conflicts between people and then having them play the parts of specific personalities. Corsini, Shaw, and Blake (1961) describe role playing as a method of human interaction that involves realistic behavior in imaginary situations.

Through role playing, trainees can discover from their own experience and from the reactions of observers the relative effectiveness of various behaviors in a given situation. Whereas in normal, everyday experience a person has only one chance to handle a situation, in role playing he or she often has an opportunity to test out the appropriateness of several approaches. It is one form of "hands-on" experience that does not just talk about how to solve problems, but actually involves solving them. It incorporates learning by doing, feedback to the trainee from his or her own observations of self and from those of the observers, and analysis and conceptualization of what took place and why.

Role playing makes evident what a person has the ability to do, thus illustrating dramatically the gap between knowledge and ability to apply it, or the gap between thinking and doing. It also teaches the interrelationship between intellectual solutions to problems and the emotional aspects of implementing these solutions. Perhaps the greatest value of role playing is its capacity for teaching the emotional dimensions of interpersonal relations because

1.   it often shows trainees that others do not always interpret their actions, statements, and attitudes as they intended them;

2.   it illustrates dramatically the reactions people have to others' behavior and allows them to see this for themselves; and

3.   it helps a person to increase her or his sensitivity to others and to realize the feelings that underlie their behavior and statements.

Typical Problems for Role Playing

There are a great many ways in which role playing can be useful. One of the ways in which it is used is to teach the application of concepts and techniques. For example, it may be used to teach people how to conduct a performance appraisal interview or how to counsel people in a nondirective fashion. When its purpose is to teach the application of concepts and techniques, trainees have first acquired a knowledge and understanding of the particular concept or technique. Role playing then provides trainees with a guided experience which is aimed at helping them perfect their ability to apply it. In the case of teaching people how to conduct a performance appraisal, this might involve groups of three, with one person taking the part of the interviewer, another the interviewee, and the third being an observer. The first two would be given roles describing their respective parts and the situation. The observer might be given a guide to assist her or him in looking for particular attitudes, and behavior. The mock interview would proceed for some designated length of time, after which the three people would analyze and discuss the experience. If time permitted, the trainees could switch roles a few times so that each person could play each role.

A second way in which role playing can be used is to teach students something about themselves. All people have values and attitudes which affect their behavior without their full awareness. Through role playing and feedback, this can be brought out for the trainees to see. For example, a trainee might be given a role of a supervisor who encountered an employee who was not performing as he or she should. The role play would involve how to handle this situation. Does the person who is playing the role become aggressive? or passive? Does she or he confront the problem head on or tend to avoid it? How does he or she respond to the other role player's actions and statements? Through reflection upon the role player's actions, the role player and those who observed him or her in the situation might arrive at some understanding of his or her values, attitudes, and beliefs.

A third way role playing is useful is for making trainees aware of whether or how well they apply contingent principles and management concepts. In this use of role playing, the enactment is used to dramatize what a person knows or does not know. Role playing precedes the actual teaching of the concept or contingent principle. It is used as a device to call attention to the importance of what is to be taught and the need for students to learn it. For example, most managers would agree that it is important and logical for one to know what her or his objectives are before making a decision. Or, stated as a generalization, decisions should be made with regard to stated objectives, and objectives essentially serve as criteria for decision making. A role-play could be developed placing trainees in situations requiring decisions. Through their handling of the problem, observers could quickly discover whether they applied this concept. Then, through the observers' feedback to trainees, they would become aware of whether or how well they applied the idea, the consequences of their behavior, and the importance of the generalization itself. Thus, it is likely that they would become motivated to learn and even apply this knowledge in their work.

Role playing can be used to teach interpersonal skills. This might involve having students play conflicting roles that involve totally different perceptions of a given situation. Through the role-play enactment, trainees become aware that the others involved in the role-play have different perceptions and feelings than they do about the same situation. Through their handling of the conflict, trainees can gain insights and appreciation for the adequacy of their behavior.

Maier has developed many role-playing exercises along the lines of conflict situations. One of these involves two participants—one in the role of supervisor, the other in the role of subordinate. The players are given instructions about their parts; they know who the other player is and know her or his role, but they do not know any background information on the other person. In this particular situation, the supervisor is told that she or he has a rush project to complete and is somewhat behind schedule, but if everyone works hard, it can be completed on time. The supervisor has just observed one of her or his better workers arriving an hour late and then becoming involved in a small scuffle with another employee.

The subordinate knows that he or she was kept awake on the previous night until 3:30 a.m. by the noise from a neighborhood party and that this morning he or she overslept, missed breakfast, and almost had a fight with the neighbor after finding a new hedge ruined by one of the party-goers. Upon arriving at work late, the subordinate found another employee doing something he or she should not have been doing and yelled at him or her.

The person playing the role of supervisor has observed the subordinate's late arrival and the problem with the other employee. The supervisor does not know about the party the night before, the ruined hedge, etc. The role play that follows affords the person playing the part of the supervisor a good opportunity to learn how well he or she listens and handles an emotional subordinate.

Sometimes role playing can be used in a fifth way—i.e., to illustrate the emotional dimensions of a case study. For example, it might be useful to have students become aware of how characters in a case felt or why they behaved as they did. Through role playing, these things can be brought out. This technique might be particularly useful for providing students with insights to the appropriateness or practicality of their solutions to case-study problems.

Role playing enactments need not be performed only by trainees. Sometimes the instructor or professional actors and actresses are employed to play parts opposite the trainees. This brings added realism and drama to the learning situation. The city of Philadelphia uses role playing to train its police officers how to handle situations that are commonly encountered and historically have been handled poorly by inexperienced officers. For example, two actors might play the roles of husband and wife or father and daughter, having a loud and ugly argument. The police are called by a complaining neighbor to quiet things down. The two trainees, playing the roles of police officers, arrive on the scene and the role playing begins.

The Sun Oil Company uses actors and actresses in role-playing exercises to teach their managers how to counsel employees who are having problems at work. The company's managers play the parts of the supervisors who are called upon to counsel employees who are played by the professional actors and actresses.

Comparison with the Case-Study Method

Building upon the work of Solem, Lowell developed an extensive list of similarities and differences between case studies and role-playing cases. According to Lowell (1968, pp. 32–34), both methods are similar in that they:

1. are project or laboratory methods providing active learning experience which involves participants both intellectually and emotionally;

2. stimulate participants to think purposefully and creatively in relating theory to action;

3. require the participants to define and analyze the problem, to determine available alternative solutions and the possible consequences of those alternatives, and to make decisions;

4. include discussion which affords not only opportunities to develop communication skills but also to acquire new insights through the interchange of ideas and points of view;

5. describe actual, real-life problems which are disguised to prevent embarrassment of the real persons who were involved in the situation;

6. create a spontaneous history of common experience and dialogue which serves as a basis for initiating, maintaining, and evaluating natural inquiry;

7. do not give solutions because there are no right and wrong "answers" (necessarily);

8. develop new insights and skills in dealing with others;

9. provide vicarious experience through projection into the case to try out new ideas without running the risks that experimenting on the job entails;

10. illustrate how the same situation can be perceived differently by different persons and may have several solutions;

11. offer a constructive method or frame of reference for approaching the analysis and solution of any human problem in the future; and

12. provide a basis for repeated reinforcement of learning when participants refer back to case experiences when related situations are discussed later.

Some of the differences between role playing and other types of cases include:

1. Subject matter: Management role playing cases are usually centered in the area of human and interpersonal relations; other types of case studies include all phases of the management process—planning, organizing, motivating, and controlling.

2. Length: Role-playing cases are normally quite short, cover a limited time span, include just one incident, and have few characters. Some case studies, noticeably case reports and case histories, may be quite long, cover a period of years, include a number of incidents, and have many characters.

3. Participant involvement: In role-playing cases, participants tend to be emotional because they identify with the characters and the problems and hence require insight into the needs and feelings of others; other types of cases tend to be more logical and intellectual and include more managerial principles. (Role playing involves the learner directly.)

4. Content: Role-playing cases usually emphasize the human element in everyday work situation, whereas other types of cases are likely to emphasize facts, organizational structure, plans, policies, controls, and other administrative problems. (Role plays typically emphasize the emotional and attitudinal dimensions.)

5. Feedback: Interaction between the participants in role playing provides immediate and continuous feedback during the enactment, indicating the effect of one person's behavior on others. In other types of cases no feedback comes

from the solution arrived at because there are no characters to react to the decision; however, participants do get feedback to their ideas from their own discussion group.

6.   Action: Role-playing cases differ from other types of case studies in that they carry the decision into action. For example, in other types of case studies, the decision might be to dismiss an employee, but the participants do not have to follow through and tell the employee. In a role-playing case, the player must face the employee and inform him of the decision. (Lowell 1968)

Advantages of Role-Playing

1.   It is an effective process for developing sensitivity and insights into interpersonal relationships, attitudes held by oneself and others, and feelings and the emotional dimensions of problems.

2.   It provides practical experience in human relations.

3.   It helps to increase perception of self and others.

4.   It is an effective means for changing attitudes.

5.   It provides trainees with an opportunity to see for themselves their interpersonal skills and the appropriateness of their behavior in given situations.

6.   It brings theory to life. It brings reality to the classroom and it does so dramatically and convincingly.

7.   It teaches that one's perception of a situation is not always like others'.

Disadvantages of Role Playing

1.   It takes considerable time just to teach one point.

2.   It requires the direction of a highly competent and understanding instructor.

3.   If not introduced and handled properly it can degenerate into silliness as some trainees try to "ham it up."

4.   Some, not understanding the technique, may regard it as childish play-acting.

5.   It can degenerate into belittlement and become hurtful to sensitive people.

6.   It is sometimes difficult to get involvement especially if people do not feel comfortable and feel threatened by being in front of others. It should not be used in training programs until a climate of mutual trust between participants has developed, which usually takes several days.

7.   It takes a considerable amount of time to prepare the role players and the observers for what they are to do.

Conducting Role-Playing Exercises

Role playing can be exceedingly impactful in teaching complex concepts and bringing about their acceptance. It can be deep and penetrating, or it can be a boring, childish exercise of superficial content. The tone of the class and the ways in which the exercise is introduced and conducted depend on the instructor. The following suggestions will help to make role-playing exercises worthwhile learning experiences.

Before introducing role playing

1.   Establish a serious and demanding learning climate. The learning may be enjoyable to the group, but nonetheless it is serious business.

2.   Develop a climate of mutual respect and trust among the trainees. Trainees should exhibit definite signs of leveling with and learning from each other.

3.   Pinpoint the "clowns" in the group and avoid involving them in role-playing situations until their learning pursuits become serious.

4.   Establish a definite purpose for role playing. It should fit into an overall training plan to accomplish specific objectives. Never have a role-playing session just to have one.

5.   Find out what experience the trainees have previously had with role playing. Talk to those who have had experience with it before introducing it to the group.

Introducing role playing

6.   Provide the trainees with a full explanation of what role playing is and is not and what can be expected to be gained from it.

7.   Put the role players and observers at ease before the role play starts. Create a pleasant but serious climate.

8.   Assure the trainees that they will not be embarrassed, hurt, or belittled by anyone. It is usually wise to get those who will be playing roles prepared for their parts; if this can be done, sit down with them, and explain their parts the evening before. Answer their questions. Be sensitive to their feelings and apprehensions. Reassure them.

9.   Provide definite directions for the observers. An observer's guide is very helpful. Have observers watch for the attitudes expressed and the emotional dimensions of what occurred.

10.   Make certain that the situation to be role-played is meaningful and realistic.

11.   Maintain the seriousness of the role play. Make sure that no one is embarrassed.

12. Follow through and complete the role play as planned. Do not change course in midstream. Make sure the trainees stick to their roles.

13. If appropriate stop the role play at particular times to interview the players. This technique is known as *soliloquy* and it is done to bring out on-the-spot feelings and reactions, which observers or other role players or both may be unaware of. It also permits trainees to evaluate the effectiveness of their behavior immediately, thus allowing them to learn from their own mistakes. Have players reverse roles. That is, have players change roles so they can develop greater insights into the situation and their previous behavior.

14. Do not permit trainees to consult their roles while playing a part, as this tends to make an attitude a static condition, not subject to alteration. Real attitudes are dynamic forces and are subject to change in direction as well as intensity.

15. Role players should not behave in the way a person in the position described in the role should behave. This ability to play the part of another person is perhaps a requirement for acting in a play, but it is a distinct disadvantage in successful role playing. (In other words, play the role as you would if you *were* in the other person's shoes, not as you *think* he or she would behave.)

Analysis and feedback

16. After the role playing enactment has been concluded, interview the players first. Obtain their reactions and feelings about what took place.

17. Obtain observers' feedback. Spend as much time on drawing out from the actors and observers as necessary. Do not leave the trainees with bottled-up feelings and reactions. In this discussion, bring out all the views and feelings that exist. Do not evaluate or judge what each person says, just try to understand it, clarify it, or get them to clarify what they say. Ask for supporting evidence for their claims or at least ask them to tell the class what it was that led them to their conclusions.

18. Avoid "expertising," but try to arrive at what can be concluded from the role play. Better yet, get the students to formulate a group analysis of what occurred in the role play and what can be learned from it.

19. Summarize the points made. Tie together what took place and the significance of it. Relate it to the overall training plan and objectives.

The In-Basket Method

The in-basket method, which is a combination of case study and role playing, is a simulation, paper-and-pencil exercise. It involves having a trainee assume the role of a manager in an organization confronted with a stack of memos, notes, letters, problems, etc. in her or his "in-basket" that require action. After reading and studying the background information on the organization and the role that she or he is to assume, the trainee starts looking through the "in-basket" for the first time. The amount of information contained in the background description and the "in-basket" items is typically quite limited. So is the time available for making decisions.

The in-basket exercise is usually used to teach such topics as policy making, decision making, use of time, establishment of priorities, delegation, and coordination. In handling the role, some trainees tend to spend time on trivial, unimportant problems; others arrange the work to be done and the decisions to be made in terms of priorities and spend most of their limited time on crucial matters. Some trainees make decisions quite rapidly without considering all the ramifications; others are more cautious and deliberate. Some try to do everything themselves; others delegate the work.

The trainee is observed by the instructor and a group of observers (usually other trainees). After the exercise is completed, they critique the trainee's handling of the role and managerial performance.

The "in-basket" exercise involves only one role-playing person. It involves no interpersonal interaction. Therefore, the areas of learning involve the administrative aspects rather than the human-relations aspects of management. It is similar to role playing in that

1. it involves hands-on activities that are realistic and life-like;

2. it permits trainees to learn from their own behavior;

3. it allows trainees to learn about themselves and the consequences of their behavior; and

4. it can bring self-realization which will prompt or motivate trainees to want to change.

MANAGEMENT GAMES

Management games have enjoyed enormous acceptance since their introduction to the field of management training and business education twenty years ago. The concept of learning through simulation exercises is not new. War games have been played for centuries. Simulation apparatus and exercises have long been used to train people in all kinds of skills, ranging from flying airplanes to maintaining quality control.

With the advent of the high-speed electronic computer, it became possible to construct simulations of complex business environments, involving multitudes of interacting variables, for the purpose of training people in general management. The first such game on record was developed by the American Management Association in 1956, and was first used at a training program held at the AMA Academy at Saranac Lake, New York. It was known as the AMA General Management Simulation and employed an IBM 650 computer.

Within a few months, the *Harvard Business Review* published an article by G. R. Andlinger (1958) entitled "Business Games—Play One!" Andlinger described a noncomputer, top-management game he developed with J. R. Green. Their game soon became widely known and did much to further the usage of games as a respected management-training method.

According to Clifford Craft (1967, p. 267),

> A management game is a dynamic training exercise utilizing a model of a business situation. Executives, grouped into teams representing the management of competing companies, make the same type of operating and policy decisions as they do in real life. Using a set of mathematical relationships built into the model, the decisions are processed so as to produce a series of performance reports. These decisions and reports pertain to a specific time period which, depending on the model, may be a day, a month, or a year. Decisions are then made for the next period; they are processed, reports are returned and the game proceeds. In this manner time is compressed, and many years of operations may be covered in a single day.

Greenlaw, Harron, and Rawdon (1962, p. v) define a business game as:

> . . . a sequential decision-making exercise structured around a model of a business operation, in which participants assume the role of managing the simulated operation.

Some describe games as being real-life, unfolding cases with feedback. Through the successive periods of play (which may represent either days, weeks, months, quarters, or years, depending on the game) conditions change, new problems are encountered, and opportunities arise which call for fresh analysis and decision making. Teams receive timely feedback after each period on their and their competitor's actions and the consequences of both.

Sometimes games contain provisions for the unexpected disasters or windfalls that can occur. Thus, in some games, teams may be plagued with disasters such as strikes, fires, earthquakes, tax investigations, or materials delays, or they may benefit from windfalls such as price rolebacks, increased demand, tax breaks, and so on. These factors, plus the competition between teams, add realism and challenge to the game and provide for stimulating learning and excitement.

Games may be scored manually or by computer. Manually scored games are usually much simpler and less costly to construct and play. However, there are more elaborate, complex versions of manually scored games, which require a cadre of score keepers and judges who feverishly collect team decisions, compute their impact according to the game model and scoring systems by using tables and desk calculators, and give feedback to the participating teams either before or shortly after successive playing periods. Because of the limited time available for scoring, manual games must be limited to a set of simple mathematical relationships between the variables.

Computer-scored games, on the other hand, can involve many more interacting variables having a set of complex interrelationships. Scoring is performed rapidly and accurately and is returned to the participating teams on neatly laid-out computer printout reports. These games are fairly costly to prepare and play, and they can be a nuisance when access to the computer is difficult or when the computer is not operating properly.

Games may or may not involve interaction between competing teams. Games involving team interaction are like football, basketball, tennis, etc., where the actions of one team have an effect upon the others. Games not involving interaction are like golf, target shooting, track and field events, etc., in which performance is measured against some scale or specified standards. Interaction-type games require two or more teams while noninteraction-type games can be played by one or more. Games may represent any imaginable kind of organizational division or unit. Games may simulate large-scale enterprise, where each team represents a large firm. They may simulate a particular industry, which would be very similar to the large-scale enterprise games but written with unique details and interrelationships to the particular industry represented. They may simulate some group of functional areas in which each team represents an individual or group of individuals involved in some functional area, such as labor relations, maintenance, purchasing, marketing, finance, accounting, advertising, etc. Some of the nonbusiness games used in the teaching of urban affairs and civics involve complex simulations with individuals or groups playing various kinds of governmental bodies, business organizations, political groups, and special interest groups frequently found in most communities.

Depending upon the particular game, the types of decisions called for may include such things as type of product produced or sold, level of production, method of production or sales, financing strategies, taxes, manpower, purchasing, customer relations, labor negotiations, and so forth. In short, games may be constructed to involve decision making in a wide variety of areas, and they might involve many different kinds of decisions that are interactive. For example, a decision made in manpower will affect the financial picture of the simulated firm, which in turn can have an effect on the types of products that the firm can produce.

Just as the types of decisions made in games are varied, so too are the areas of learning they can provide. These areas of learning include such things as developing knowledge and skills relating to decision making, working under time limitations, budgeting, forecasting, cash flow analysis, cost accounting, manpower planning procurement, use of models and quantitative tools of operations research and advertising, to name a few. Post mortems on games offer an excellent opportunity for trained observers to feed back to participants another very important set of data—i.e., their behavior while playing the game. Observed interactions between participants can provide valuable insights into their behavior under various conditions including such things as stress, competition, good news, bad news, victory, and defeat. The game-playing experience often provides groups with an opportunity to assess how well they functioned as a team, what type of leadership was provided, who led and when and why, who communicated with whom, how good or how bad the communications were, who helped the group reach its goals, who detracted or caused trouble, and who was innovative. The entire playing of the game can, in effect, be a real-life case study of human behavior, which participants can analyze and discuss and from which, as a result, can learn much about themselves.

Examples of General-Purpose/Total-Enterprise Games

The AMA General Management Simulation

Any number of teams composed of from 5 to 18 members can play this game. Teams manage The Mose Company, which has two manufacturing plants. Teams may choose to manufacture one, two, or three products for either the consumer or industrial market. A central warehouse serves both plants and plant outputs are shipped to two, four, or six sales regions in the East and West.

At the beginning of the game, teams start with a company in tight straits—low profits, low return on investment, and poor utilization of production capacity. Teams are required to make decisions in the following areas: marketing, production, research and development, finance, survey information of competition with regard to price, advertising, and share of market. Emphasis is placed on planning and controlling. Quarterly statements are issued appraising company performance. It is a noninteraction-type game. Scoring is performed by an IBM 650 computer. Specific decisions made by participants involve the following:

1. Raw material purchases

2. Raw material conversion and inventorying

3. Plant equipment and depreciation

4. Labor force, wages

5. Production level

6. Warehousing and shipping

7. Marketing research

8. Advertising

9. Pricing

10. Sales: bookings, back orders, deliveries, lost orders

11. Sales force: level, remuneration

12. Administrative expenses: production, sales, research and development

13. Borrowing, emergency loans

14. Loan repayments, dividends

The game is the property of the AMA.

The Arizona Business Game

This is an interaction-type game, which involves at least two and no more than four competing teams having four members each. The teams simulate domestic, capital goods companies in a competitive market manufacturing the same, single product. The game is constructed with the aim of teaching planning, obtaining market information, making expenditures in advertising research and development, and manufacturing.

The first simulated six months of play is devoted to team organization, the next six months for operating the company. Teams start the game with $800.00. The market is highly competitive. Actions of one company impact upon their competitors. The decisions made by participants include the following:

1. Construction and size of plant

2. Securing and resolving bank loans

3. Product research and cost reduction

4. Determining size of sales force and hiring and firing

5. Product promotion and selling price

6. Administrative expenses

7. Number of shifts per day the plant will operate

Scoring is done by an IBM 1401 computer. The game is copyrighted by the Department of Management, University of Arizona.

Examples of Functional Games

The General Electric Management Game I

This is a manufacturing product scheduling game; it is a noninteraction-type game played by from one to ten teams of three to six players each. Teams attempt to optimize the total variable costs of inventory holding costs and changes in the size of the workforce by producing at the proper levels of quantity. Each team attempts to minimize four costs—payroll, hiring and terminations, overtime, and inventory. Participants are called upon to make decisions on quantity of product to be produced, number of employees, purchase of sales forecasts, and purchase of estimates of competitor's results.

Contract Negotiations

The Contract Negotiations Game is a simulation in which a company and a union are attempting to negotiate a second contract. A number of changes are necessary in key contract clauses since there have been an unreasonable number of grievances and arbitration cases that have occurred during the last contractual period. Two teams play the game. One plays the part of company management, the other the part of the union. The union team has the attainment of union and individual security as well as increased fringe benefits as its primary goals. The company team feels that it must engage in subcontracting and automation in order to remain competitive. The simulation is thus designed to bring to the surface many of the major areas of union-management relations.

Players have at hand the first contract and other labor market statistics. The conduct of the negotiations is such that the players experience all stages of the collective bargaining process including preparation, initial meeting, and actual bargaining.

The game concludes with a post-negotiation audit, which involves a critique of the negotiations strategies and the actions of each team and their significance and effectiveness. The audit also involves a discussion of the bargaining process and in-depth insights about it (Zif and Otlewski 1970).

Example of a Special Simulation Game

Management-in-Action

This is a production game played by two teams of ten people. The two teams are in competition during wartime to produce two items—propellers and bombsights. The team that produces the most, wins.

The items are constructed from sheets of lightweight cardboard cut out with scissors and paper punch and fastened together by staples. The game takes about two hours, which includes time for pregame orientation and post-play discussion and summary.

The competing teams are managed quite differently, and the heart of the learning process involves the comparison of their respective production and team morale. Team one is led by a strict autocratic, theory X manager who has each person work on just what he or she is told to do. Theory X manager refuses to allow communications to flow in any direction other than downward and does not provide overall goals. He or she also introduces change without warning or explanation. Team two is led by a participative, theory Y manager who announces goals and purposes, encourages teamwork, permits communications to flow in all directions, and introduces change with explanation. The game is most impactful when played at the conclusion of a training program, as it does a good job of summarizing the key principle taught. The game is the property of Charles E. Watson.

Using Management Games

Games may be played to achieve any number of purposes, which include the following:

1. Games can be used to get a program started. Used at the beginning of a program, a game can break the ice by having participants become actively involved in the learning process and get to know each other. It can also provide valuable data for further analysis and discussion.

2. Games can be used to discredit ways of thinking and approaches to handling problems. Games permit participants to see dramatically, for themselves, the effectiveness of their approaches. Thus, when one views present methods as being ineffective, she or he will often seek new ones that work, and will become more interested in learning.

3. Games give participants experience in working on management problems of which they have had little or no experience or understanding. Thus accountants can learn about making marketing decisions, production managers can learn about finance, etc.

4. Games can be useful in proving the need for and value of special techniques such as forecasting, the uses of models, quantitative analysis, and other methods from operations research.

5. The behavior that occurs through playing a game may be used as data to study and analyze just as a case study is analyzed. This permits participants to learn more about themselves by analyzing their own behavior and having it analyzed by others.

6. Games can be used for employee testing and selection. Most assessment centers utilize games for the purpose of testing people's behavior to determine their aptitude and readiness to accept management positions.

Games can be misused, and Nanus (1962, p. 468) cites several of the most flagrant abuses of games.

1. Using the game strictly for entertainment or publicity without clearly warning the participants that the training value of a game, which is not part of a larger, carefully planned educational context, will be very small. Much of the criticism levied against games has come from participants who had unhappy experiences in one or two of these carelessly run exercises.

2. Using a game for a course before its parameters have been thoroughly tested. Too many games used today can be "beaten" by unreasonable strategies.

3. Designing a game before its objectives have been clearly defined. This was a particularly common problem in the early days of game design, but even now games are being built by mathematicians and operations research specialists with insufficient guidance by educators. The result is games which are more "sophisticated" than necessary or too difficult to handle administratively.

4. Permitting a game to be used before complete documentation of its model and computed program is available.

Choosing an Appropriate Game

Carefully chosen games can provide valuable and stimulating learning for program participants. Games can add invaluable depth to the materials learned at a program provided they fit the particular needs of the participants and match the other content of the course. To assure that the right game is selected, the following considerations will be helpful.

First, the game should be appropriate for the participants who will play it. It should be challenging, but not too simplistic or too complex. It should be meaningful to them. (It is best to have a game representing their industry.)

Second, the game should be appropriate to the training objective that it is intended to achieve. Instructors should be clear as to the objectives that they intend to fulfill and should choose a game accordingly, not the other way around.

Third, the game should be within the capabilities of those who will administer it. Ample time, finance, computer availability, assistance, and knowledge to run the game should be available. Never start a game until you are absolutely sure the "bugs" have been eliminated and the computer program is well tested and reliable.

Fourth, the participants should have respect for the game seeing it as a serious learning experience, and not just a fun exercise for their amusement. Excitement should not overshadow the seriousness of the learning that the game can provide.

Fifth, the game should be played at a time in the course schedule when it will have a maximum impact. Some believe that general-purpose, complex games should be played at the beginning or the end of a program, while special-purpose games should be played in the middle of a program (Kibbee 1961).

Advantages

1. Perhaps the most often cited advantage of management games is that they are dynamic. They are real-life cases that require decision making that

has real consequences. Participants are able to see the actual consequences of their strategies and decisions.

2. By the very nature of the simulation in which teams make decisions during each time period, time becomes collapsed and, as a result, participants get the experience of making many more major decisions than they would normally make in real life.

3. Feedback to teams on their decision is objective and nonpunitive. Even if the participants perform poorly in playing the game, they will not lose their jobs or receive serious reprimands from their superiors. It is an opportunity to make important life-like decisions without having to live with the consequences.

4. Because it is only a game, learners are encouraged to experiment with new, untried, untested behaviors and strategies. The nonpunitive game environment encourages participants to test and learn new approaches.

5. Games are exciting and motivating to play. They challenge the ingenuity and abilities of the players. They are fun and people enjoy them.

6. They teach the importance and need for both short- and long-range planning. They help develop the dual perspective of looking at short-run problems that must be solved in the immediate time frame, while keeping an eye on long-range goals and taking the necessary actions that will lead to their achievement.

7. They teach problem analysis and decision making. Games provide practical, experiential learning.

8. Total-enterprise and industry-type games teach participants the interrelationships of the various business functions and activities. They teach participants to coordinate these diverse and sometimes incongruous business functions.

9. Games usually teach the usefulness of mathematical models, operations research tools, and the use of computers. Through the experience of actually using these methods, participants tend to lose the fears of them, which perhaps caused them to avoid using them in the past.

10. Games dramatically illustrate concepts and contingent principles. Participants learn such through experience, thus making them real.

Disadvantages

1. Games are costly in terms of time, personnel needed to conduct them, and money. Games take time to develop and perfect, and they take time to play (ranging from a few hours to several days). Most games require the assistance of several people. They involve judges, scorekeepers, data processors, observers, and an instructor or gamemaster. Computer-scored games, which require computer time, are especially costly.

2.   Games that involve a computer can sometimes be a problem, especially when access to the computer is difficult or when computer breakdowns occur.

3.   Sometimes teams hit upon strategies that "beat the game." By following a certain approach, they will constantly get higher production and profit rates and thereby fail to play the game as a game. This can also arise with less complex games.

4.   The excitement generated by playing the game can cause participants to become so caught up in winning that they lose sight of the learning aspects. Winning can become more important than learning.

5.   Sometimes games are played for the sake of playing and not for the sake of learning. Too much time is spent on playing the game and not enough, if any, is spent on post-play critique. Insufficient attention is placed on tying the lessons gained or the potential lessons that could have been gained to the course and its content.

6.   Some feel that games are too quantitatively oriented. They think that games can be won by expertise in operations-research tools and techniques.

7.   Games can sometimes result in the participants reaching incorrect conclusions, such as R & D is not necessary for a firm to survive, or advertising does not pay off.

SENSITIVITY TRAINING

T-groups (T for training), encounter groups, laboratory-training groups, and human-awareness groups are all names usually associated with what is known as sensitivity training. Unlike training methods that serve to teach more or less predetermined content, *sensitivity training* attempts to teach people about themselves and why and how they relate to, interact with, impact on, and are impacted upon by others. Essentially, this is accomplished by having trainees observe and analyze their own, actual, "here-and-now" behavior in T-groups.

It would be impossible to describe precisely all of the ways in which sensitivity training is conducted, since the style, content, and goals of sensitivity training depend so much upon the particular leader who conducts it. This discussion, therefore, will provide only a general description of the nature and process of sensitivity training.

Lewin (1968) along with his principal associates, which included Kenneth D. Benne, Leland P. Bradford, and Ronald Lippitt, can be credited for the discovery of T-group learning.

Sensitivity training emerged by accident in 1946 at a summer workshop designed by Lewin for the Connecticut Interracial Commission to train community leaders to deal with intergroup conflicts. Three ten-member groups discussed the intergroup problems they faced at home. They also play-acted the various roles in an attempt to clarify the problems and test out solutions. In each group a research observer noted the interactions, which she or he would report at an evening staff meeting. A few group members asked if they could attend the staff meetings and hear these reports. Despite staff doubts, Lewin agreed. Soon all the workshop participants were drawn into the staff meetings. The interaction reports, they said, gave them valuable insights into their own behavior and the way their groups were shaping up, and they began offering their own reactions to one another (Ogg 1972).

This experience was tremendously stimulating and exciting to those involved. A number of the staff members began to develop theoretical explanations as to what had occurred. Planning was begun on how similar learning experiences could be conducted for a wider audience. As an outgrowth of this unintentional discovery and the enthusiastic planning that followed, the National Training Laboratory for Group Development, now NTL Institute, conducted the first formal sensitivity training program in Bethel, Maine, in the summer of 1947. Today, sensitivity training has greatly expanded. The NTL Institute is a widely known and well-respected nonprofit organization, headquartered in Arlington, Virginia. Most of its central office staff (approximately twenty full-time professionals) have advanced degrees in the behavioral sciences. The NTL Institute sponsors programs in Bethel and at other locations throughout the United States. The Western Training Laboratory (WTL) at U.C.L.A. and the Intermountain Laboratory for Group Development (ILGD) at the University of Utah have since been established along the same lines as the NTL Institute. They too conduct programs. Many other groups (some reputable, responsible, and competent, some not) have since come into existence and offer programs similar to those of the NTL Institute.

What Is a T-Group?

A T-group consists of interdependent individuals who are committed to a shared examination of the behavior and interrelationships of themselves and others. This occurs in a seemingly unstructured setting which requires people to become more aware of and sensitive to one another's feelings and behavior. The learning situation appears to be unstructured because there is no formal lesson plan and the instructors do not teach in the traditional sense. Instead, they help people learn about themselves. Exactly what is learned is largely determined by the group members themselves, although the instructors provide some guidance. The focus of attention is not on abstractions, but on real, "here-and-now" behavior. Golembiewski and Blumberg (1970, pp. 5–8) identify three distinguishing features of the T-groups, which are as follows:

1.   It is a learning laboratory.

2.   It focuses on learning how to learn.

3.   It does so via a "here-and-now" emphasis on immediate ideas, feelings, and reactions.

A learning laboratory

Not a laboratory in the usual sense, the T-group is a laboratory in that it offers the opportunity for inquiry and exploration of behavior and permits experimentation with new forms of behavior. Characterized by some as a miniature society, the T-group is oriented toward creating a "psychologically safe" atmosphere which is conducive to learning through exploration and experimentation with behavior. That which is learned is largely determined by what takes place among the group members. However, the instructor usually provides guidance. This guidance is usually of a nature that facilitates learning by getting trainees to pursue particular trains of thought which will lead to increased understanding of themselves and others. The goal of the T-group is *not* to make people change. The T-group is a laboratory that aims at creating a group that will provide feedback to its members in a supportive way and will thereby permit them to discover whether new behavior will yield more of what they desire from interpersonal and intergroup relationships.

The so-called *real world* denies this. Most people are only remotely aware of their daily behavior, its effectiveness, and how it is perceived by and impacts on others. The T-group encourages its members to level with each other to discover these things, which the real world largely fails to do. The T-group experience encourages its members to experiment with new forms of behavior. Thus, for example, a person who is meek and timid might try a more aggressive role in a T-group to discover from the eventual feedback how this new behavior affects others and whether he or she is more or less satisfied with it and its consequences.

Learning how to learn

Learning how to learn, according to Golembiewski and Blumberg (1970, p. 7), may at first seem nonsensical. After all, haven't we all been to school for many years? However, Golembiewski and Blumberg say that we have learned to learn in a particular way.

> Primarily, for most of us, that way involves learning those things we have been told from a lecture or a book. In far too many cases, it almost seems that learning was equated with memorizing.

Learning how to learn from a T-group experience means essentially three things. First it means that T-group participants learn that they, and not necessarily some authority figure or teacher, can provide real answers to all kinds of questions. The inductive nature of the experiences encourages participants to search for meaning from their own experiences and arrive at their own conclusions, which can be just as valid and meaningful as conclusions made by some authority.

Second, learning in a T-group setting helps participants to learn to tolerate and live with ambiguity. A T-group situation, for most people, is highly ambiguous. Typical reactions to it are, "What are we doing just sitting here talking aimlessly. Why doesn't the instructor teach us something?" To most people it is not clear what it is they are going to learn in such a setting. Learning how to tolerate ambiguity, to see and examine their own behavior in this kind of a setting, and then finally to make some sense out of what has occurred are some of the ways in which T-groups help people learn how to learn.

Third, T-groups teach their members to learn from one another and to appreciate the potential contributions others can make to their learning. Contrary to traditional education, which holds that the instructor is the only one who can teach, T-groups operate primarily on the basis of lateral learning—that is, learning from one's peers. Thus the instructor's role in a T-group setting is played, from time to time, by whomever provides meaningful information for the group's learning. Thus, in a T-group, trainees help each other learn and also learn to value the help others can provide.

The here-and-now emphasis

The subject matter for discussion in a T-group is not theories or principles or concepts or ideas that have been formulated and written down. Instead, the focus of the T-group discussion is on that which is actually happening in the present.

Seashore (1970, p. 15) provides an example of what an instructor might say as he or she starts a group session. This illustrates the kind of framework in which the here-and-now discussion takes place.

> This group will meet for many hours and serve as a kind of laboratory where each individual can increase his understanding of the forces which influence individual behavior and the performance of groups and organizations. The data for learning will be our own behavior, feelings, and reactions. We begin with no definite structure or organization, no agreed upon procedures, and no specific agenda. It will be up to us to fill the vacuum created by the lack of these familiar elements and to study our group as we evolve. My role will be to help the group to learn from its own experience, but not to act as a traditional chairman nor to suggest how we should organize, what our procedure should be, or exactly what our agenda will include. With these few comments, I think we are ready to begin in whatever way you feel will be most helpful.

In this unstructured situation, some members may try to take charge or monopolize the discussion. Others may remain passive. Others may criticize those who remain passive, challenging them to say something or complaining that they are not contributing or are acting superior. Others may be critical of those who try to dominate the group. Still others may try to get the instructor to take a more commanding role and be more directive. No matter what role a person plays, he or she also observes and reacts to the behavior of others. These perceptions and reactions are given as feedback and become the focus for discussion and further exploration. This is so unlike what most people are accustomed to that some degree of frustration is often experienced. Moreover, the self-examination of one's behavior, or its evaluation by others, is threatening.

Types of Groups

Huse (1975, pp. 252–253) has identified three types of T-groups: (1) the "stranger" laboratory (members have never met and know nothing about each other); (2) the "cousins" laboratory (members may be part of the same organization, but do not work together); and (3) the "family" laboratory (members work together). Huse also classified T-groups as being either structured or unstructured. Structured groups follow a predetermined schedule and rely on specific exercises, role-plays, games, etc., which are designed to elicit behavior that is discussed later. Unstructured groups' only agenda emerges spontaneously from the group members as they interact.

What a T-Group Is Not

Perhaps almost as useful as a description of what sensitivity training *is*, is a statement of what sensitivity training *is not*, which will enhance one's understanding of it. Argyris (1963, pp. 25–30) has identified what T-groups are not, to correct several common misconceptions about goals and processes.

1. Laboratory methods in general, and T-Groups in particular, are not a set of hidden, manipulative processes by which individuals can be "brainwashed" into thinking, believing, and feeling the way someone might want them to without realizing what is happening to them.

2. A laboratory is not an educational process guided by a staff leader who is covertly in control and who by some magic hides this fact from the participants.

3. The objective of laboratory education is not to suppress or induce conflict; and neither is it to get everyone to like one another, nor hate one another. Rather the focus is on understanding whatever does happen.

4. Laboratory education does not attempt to teach people to be callous, disrespectful of society, and to dislike those who live a less open life. Rather the issue is how to make use of all group resources.

5. Laboratory education is neither psychoanalysis nor intensive group therapy.

6. Laboratory education does not have to be dangerous, but it must focus on feelings.

7.   The objective of laboratory education is to develop effective reality-centered leaders.

8.   Change is not guaranteed as a result of attending a T-Group.

Assumptions Underlying Sensitivity Training

A number of assumptions, though rarely formally stated, underlie sensitivity training. To a large degree, therefore, this training method will be able to produce or not to produce the results it seeks depending upon the correctness of its underlying assumptions. Campbell and Dunnett (1968, p. 77) perceive the principal assumptions underlying sensitivity training as being the following:

1.   A substantial number of group members, when confronted with others' behaviors and feelings in an atmosphere of psychological safety, can produce articulate and constructive feedback.

2.   A significant number of the group members can agree on the major aspects of a particular individual's behavior exhibited in the group situation. Certainly a complete consensus is not to be expected, but neither must the feedback go off in all directions. A certain degree of communality is necessary if the feedback is to be helpful for the individual.

3.   Feedback is relatively complete and deals with significant aspects of the individual's behavior.

4.   The behavior emitted in the group is sufficiently representative of behavior outside the group so that learning occurring within the group will carry over or transfer.

5.   Psychological safety can be achieved relatively quickly (in the matter of a few hours) among either complete strangers or among associates who have had varying types and degrees of interpersonal interaction.

6.   Almost everyone initially lacks interpersonal competence; that is, individuals tend to have distorted self-images, faulty perceptions, and poor communication skills.

7.   Anxiety facilitates new learning.

8.   Finally, transfer of training occurs between the cultural island and the "back home" situation.

The validity of these assumptions is not fully known. Very little research exists to substantially support or thoroughly discredit any of them.

Goals of Sensitivity Training

While the emphases, styles and specific goals of the multitude of sensitivity training programs vary, there does seem to be some consensus as to general goals. According to Schein and Bennis (1965, p. 35) these include:

1. Self-insight, or some variation of learning related to increased self knowledge.

2. Understanding the conditions which inhibit or facilitate effective group functioning.

3. Understanding interpersonal operations in groups.

4. Developing skills for diagnosing individual, group, and organizational behavior.

Beyond these are what Schein and Bennis call *meta-goals*, or values, which shape the stated goals. These meta-goals serve to guide the training design and the actions and interventions of the instructors; that is, they influence the laboratory culture, and they help affect the outcomes of the training. Schein and Bennis say that there are two main value systems that influence laboratory training and these are what they call meta-goals. The first are the values of science, which include:

1. A spirit of inquiry which involves (a) the feeling for tentativeness and caution with a respect for probable error, and (b) a willingness to expose ideas to empirical testing "or experimenting with one's behavior."

2. Expanded consciousness and recognition of choice which involves a very complex process, but essentially gets people to become more aware of their behavior and to think about how they choose to behave.

3. Authenticity in Interpersonal Relations. This meta-goal aims to get people to feel free to be themselves, to level, to express their feelings, and to say what they think and feel instead of what they suppose others expect or want them to say.

The second set of meta-goals are those values that embrace democracy. These are:

4. Collaboration: which means the traditional authoritarian student-teacher relationship is minimized insofar as possible and the participation, involvement, self-control of the delegate (participant) are encouraged.

5. Conflict resolution through rational means: which means there is a problem-solving orientation to conflict rather than bargains, power-plays, suppression, or compromise.

Campbell and Dunnette (1968, p. 75) identify six goals which they have found from their surveys of the literature as representative of most T-groups. These include:

1. Increased understanding, insight, and self-awareness about one's own behavior and its impact on others, including the ways in which others interpret one's behavior.

2. Increased understanding and sensitivity about the behavior of others, including better interpretation of both verbal and nonverbal clues, which increases awareness and understanding of what the other person is thinking and feeling.

3. Better understanding and awareness of group and intergroup processes, both those that facilitate and those that inhibit group functioning.

4. Increased diagnostic skills in interpersonal and intergroup situations. For the authors, the accomplishments of the first three objectives provide the basic tools for accomplishing the fourth objective.

5. Increased ability to transform learning into action, so that real-life interventions will be more successful in increasing member effectiveness, satisfaction, output, or effectiveness.

6. Improvement in individuals' ability to analyze their own interpersonal behavior, as well as to learn how to help themselves and others with whom they come in contact to achieve more satisfying, rewarding, and effective interpersonal relationships.

Different sensitivity programs may emphasize one or more of these goals or may neglect some. However, they are goals that are common to most T-groups.

Outcomes

Schein and Bennis (1965, p. 37) have developed a framework to classify training outcomes. The outcomes they depict (self, role, and organization) are only possibilities, and cannot be guaranteed for everyone attending a sensitivity training program. This is because some participants do not learn or learn very little from a T-group experience, others learn some things, and others learn a considerable amount and variety of things and because programs vary so much in terms of their nature and goals. Possible outcomes are as follows:

Self

1. Increased awareness of own feelings and reactions, and own impact on others.

2. Increased awareness of feelings and reactions of others, and their impact on self.

3. Increased awareness of dynamics of group action.

4. Changed attitudes toward self, others, and groups; i.e., more respect for, tolerance for, and faith in self, others, and groups.

5. Increased interpersonal competence; i.e., skill in handling interpersonal and group relationships toward more productive and satisfying relationships.

Role

6. Increased awareness of own organizational role, organizational dynamics, dynamics of larger social systems, and dynamics of the change process in self, small groups, and organizations.

7. Changed attitudes toward own role, role of others, and organizational relationships, i.e., more respect for and willingness to deal with others with whom one

is interdependent, greater willingness to achieve collaborative relationships with others based on mutual trust.

8. Increased interpersonal competence in handling organizational role relationships with superiors, peers, and subordinates.

Organization

9. Increased awareness of, changed attitudes toward, and increased interpersonal competence about organizational problems of interdependent groups or units.

10. Organizational improvement through the training of relationships or groups rather than isolated individuals.

Concerns About Sensitivity Training

Supported and praised by some, denounced as a "bloodbath in a psychological nudist colony" by others, sensitivity training has been and probably will continue to be the subject of considerable controversy. Leaving aside the concerns of professionally involved "insiders" (which resemble those common to most any group of professionals), we will examine the concerns held by those who are not professionally involved: users and potential users.

Difficult to understand

A fair amount of mystery surrounds sensitivity training and, understandably, some fear and suspicion exists about it. For those who have not experienced sensitivity training, communicating about it, let alone understanding an explanation of it, is difficult if not impossible. First of all, it is unlike traditional learning that we have previously experienced. Its major emphasis does not involve a body of subject matter. Instead, it involves emotional and behavioral processes, not cognitive ones. T-groups aim to help people to become more aware of the emotional and attitudinal dimensions of the interpersonal behavior of themselves and others. Second, it employs a unique methodology, open-ended discussion guided (though sometimes imperceptibly) by a leader who does not play a directive or authoritative role. Last, those who have experienced it find it difficult to describe, so complex are its methods. They typically tell others things like, "It's hard to explain. You'd have to experience it to understand it." "I don't know how it worked, but it did." or, "Our leader didn't tell us anything. In fact, most of the time she or he just sat silent, but we sure learned a lot."

And so there develops a common attitude which can be characterized by the statement, "If you can't explain it so that I can understand it, there can't be much to it. It probably is just a bunch of nonsense."

Results are difficult to measure

The specific results achieved by sensitivity training are difficult, if not impossible, to measure. There is no universally accepted statement of the precise

objectives T-group learning is supposed to achieve, let alone a system for measuring them. Moreover, the results achieved by sensitivity training are often
different for different people. Sometimes, for example, that which is learned is
increased tolerance for and patience with others. Sometimes it is the tendency
and ability to listen for feelings in addition to the rational content in communications. Sometimes it is improved abilities in interacting with others when conflict exists. There are all kinds of possible outcomes. Those things which are
learned by one person are not necessarily learned by another. Well-defined
learning results cannot be guaranteed.

The criticism levied against sensitivity training by Odiorne (1963) is
principally for this reason. According to Odiorne, in good training the desired
terminal behavior can be identified before the training begins. He argues that
sensitivity training has not met this condition, at least not to his satisfaction.
(It should be mentioned however, that the other training methods probably
cannot guarantee specific results either. So why should the condition set forth
by Odiorne be accepted as a valid criticism of only sensitivity training? Perhaps it should not.)

The main reason why the measurement of learning resulting from sensitivity training is so difficult is because sensitivity training seeks to produce
emotional learning as opposed to cognitive learning, which is much more
amenable to objective measurement. But even in areas where attempts have
been made to identify the terminal behavior T-group experiences seek to produce, Odiorne and others levy criticism. They argue that statements of
terminal behavior, such as "authenticity in interpersonal relationships,"
"esteem," and "interpersonal competence" are not and cannot be measured.
Proponents of T-group training would take issue with this. Argyris (1967,
p. 221) for example, has advanced what he and others consider to be an
acceptable definition of desired terminal behavior. For example, his definition
of *interpersonal competence* is the ability to cope effectively with interpersonal relationships. According to Argyris, there are three criteria of effective
interpersonal coping:

1. The individual perceives the interpersonal situation accurately. He is able to
   identify the relevant variables plus their interrelationships.

2. The individual is able to solve problems in such a way that they remain
   solved. If, for example, interpersonal trust is low between A and B, they may
   not have been able to solve the problem competently unless and until it no
   longer recurs (assuming the problem is under control).

3. The solution is achieved in such a way that A and B are still able to work with
   each other at least as effectively as when they began to solve their problems.

Odiorne does seem to have a strong argument insofar as those who conduct
sensitivity training frequently fail to define their objectives or do so loosely. It
seems reasonable to think that a person's competence in the area of sensitivity

training can be gauged, to a large degree, by her or his ability and willingness to specify, in well thought-through and measurable terms, the terminal behavior desired.

Negative experiences

The most severe and widespread criticism of T-groups appears to center around negative, even traumatic, experiences participants have had with them. Many people believe that sensitivity training frequently causes people to "crack-up" and that a substantial proportion of all those who take part in T-groups come away from their experience "all screwed up," while some even suffer irreparable psychological damage.

Maliver (1973), a psychotherapist and psychologist (formerly chief psychologist at Harlem Hospital), charges that one out of ten persons who joins an encounter group *is liable to become* a casualty. He defines a *casualty* as someone who later shows a symptom or serious psychiatric problem (such as depression, insomnia, weight loss, a psychotic episode, or even physical injury) that she or he did not have before joining the group. Maliver's claim, however, refers to the entire array of activities carried out under the name of encounter groups and is not restricted to those that are run by accredited professionals.

The data collected on individuals who have attended sensitivity training do not support these observations. Quite the contrary. Conclusive evidence to suggest that participants of T-groups stand even a small risk of suffering severe psychological damage or traumatic reactions does not exist. This is not to say that no one has ever suffered negatively from sensitivity training. A few have. And it is these few who have received considerable notoriety, thus causing a great deal of alarm. Cases of lesser negative psychological reactions to T-group experiences have perhaps been blown out of proportion causing more criticism than is justified. And, in even less troublesome situations, negative experiences with sensitivity training have resulted when people were unhappy and annoyed because they learned very little from their T-group experience.

In a 1963 debate on the issue of psychological damage and traumatic reactions due to T-group experiences, Argyris pointed out that at that time only four breakdowns had occurred among 10,000 who had taken sensitivity training and that each of these four people had a previous psychiatric history. Such is the record of NTL sponsored training. This does not consider problems to people that may have been caused by all the other encounter group activities conducted by everyone from housekeepers and well-meaning clergymen to psychologists and university professors, who may know anywhere from very little to a great deal about sensitivity training.

Responding to the second criticism regarding dissatisfaction because a T-group experience did not produce observable learning for some individuals, it should be pointed out that not everyone can learn in a T-group. This will probably not, of course, remove the annoyance from those who cannot learn from such an experience. Nonetheless, it should be recognized that those people who have high needs for rigid structure and authority generally do not profit from T-group experiences, because the process and content is too ambiguous for them and is at odds with their needs and patterns of thinking. These people are not stupid; it is just that their barriers to this kind of learning are too great for them to profit from it. It is generally from these people that strong criticism of sensitivity training arises. This, of course, should not be accepted as conclusive evidence that sensitivity training is bad or nonproductive. Golembiewski and Blumberg (1970, p. 213) advance a similar argument:

> . . . not everyone can learn algebra or French. I had a miserable time with it; they may explain. Or they may say I guess I lack the aptitude. I just couldn't learn algebra! Or they may question the competence of the teacher. But no learners are likely to say that algebra is bad, or to advise others not to learn algebra. In other words, people easily accept that there are individual differences in capacities and in predispositions to do well in one kind of academic learning or another. . . . But we are less willing to acknowledge individual differences in emotional capacities. On the emotional level, it seems that there is a general feeling that we are all pretty much alike. "People are people." Given this assumption, if one person's experience in a T-group was not productive for him, it follows that the same will be true for his neighbor.

But herein lies the catch. We are all not alike, and as a result there exists a wide range of differences in the amount and kind of learning different people acquire from T-groups.

Although seemingly sound rebuttals are made to those arguments regarding the problems of traumatic experiences and hostile reactions to T-group, much less satisfactory responses can be found to the criticism of the poor selection processes generally used in deciding who may or may not attend sensitivity training.

Reputable T-groups will caution people against using sensitivity training for therapy purposes and will advise those having histories of psychological problems not to attend. But what the vast array of other T-groups do with respect to this is not known. Beyond this caution, even with the so-called reputable groups, very little, if any, screening is done to determine why people want to join a group and to determine whether they can withstand the mental stress. The present situation is that anyone with the registration fee can attend. Beyond this, there seems to be little in the way of presensitivity-training screening.

The possibility of dysfunctional reactions to T-group experiences is a major concern of the well-respected proponents of sensitivity training. It would be irresponsible not to emphasize the fact that they do have this concern. Moreover, these people have promulgated useful advice to those who contemplate attending or running encounter sessions. Rogers (1975, p. 206–207), for example, recommends the following considerations:

1. A qualified trainer (psychiatrist or clinical psychologist) should be used to conduct and control the training.

2. The trainees should be tested prior to training to ensure that they are suitable to this type of training.

3. Participation in unstructured laboratory training should be strictly voluntary with no sanctions imposed against those who refuse to participate.

4. There should be a post-session observation of the participants by the trainer to assure that no dysfunctional psychological consequences arise.

Purposes are often unclear

Dunnette (1970, pp. 44–46, 52–55) has conceptualized the process of sensitivity training as a sequence of essentially six stages:

1. Escaping from loneliness—a being together, around others.

2. Providing warmth and support—where people find a kind of acceptance from belonging to a group.

3. Learning sensory and emotional sensitivity and being able to tolerate anxiety —becoming aware of beauty in one's environment; people attend to one another; nonverbal interaction occurs; anxiety is first observed.

Dunnette regards these first three stages as recreational. He sees stages four through six as learning.

4. Understanding oneself and others—This is the stage where really honest feedback begins. People start to see how they affect and are affected by others. They get an honest glimpse of their own "hang-ups." In this stage group members not only start to understand themselves, but also the others in the groups. They start to deal with others as individuals instead of stereotyped "others."

5. Learning to change interpersonal behavior—In this stage people begin to learn new patterns of interpersonal behavior. Experimentation followed by honest but supportive feedback occurs.

6. Resolving conflicts—A problem-solving attitude prevails in this stage. People take their likes, dislikes, hang-ups, etc. as givens to be accounted for. Reason is brought into the picture in light of the social milieu that is now uncovered.

Dunnette criticizes many T-groups for the lack of clarity on the part of group leaders and participants to the stage toward which the group is headed. Many groups, according to Dunnette, only get through the recreational stages (stages one to three). Sometimes groups try to jump from stage one to stage four or stage five, or they try to move through earlier stages to later ones too quickly and, as a result, never really advance there. Other groups, he observes, get stuck on stage four and fail to move on.

Weekend marathon sessions usually never progress beyond the recreational phases. They fatigue participants, but rarely achieve permanent change.

A two-week session, on the other hand, is likely to get through stages five and six.

Invasion of privacy

Many believe that T-groups force some unwilling members to reveal to others and themselves things about themselves they might not otherwise choose to expose or admit. Thus these critics question the ethics of T-groups. After all, they argue, isn't this nothing more than an invasion of one's privacy? Even if people choose to attend encounter group sessions, do they know beforehand what they are getting into? Are they fully aware of the group pressure that will likely be applied to get them to admit some hang-up or the fact that others may identify "their problem" as they see it?

Many groups implicitly hold the belief that everyone in the T-group has some problem and the group will find it and correct it. A person in a group cannot tell the others that he or she is O.K. and healthy and satisfied with life. Groups will not accept this. So they badger the person into confessing to some sort of hang-up or problem which they can analyze in detail and attempt to "help" him or her. Sometimes people discover problems they have had all along, but were never aware of. Now they are stuck with these problems and perhaps frustrated because they do not know how to live with or solve them.

There should be some safeguard of the individual's right to privacy. What about executives who are essentially forced to attend a sensitivity training session? Shouldn't they be protected too? Is it ethical to force a person to take part in something that is an invasion of privacy as he or she perceives it? There is a fine line between voluntary choice and coercive pressure when someone is "asked" to do something by his or her employer.

Another set of unanswered questions of ethics has to do with the kind and accuracy of feedback one receives about self in a T-group. What guarantees are there to assure that the feedback is accurate, helpful, and given in an atmosphere of acceptance and support? Quite obviously, simple answers to these questions do not yet exist. They are and will likely continue to be the subject of considerable discussion and the source of differences of opinion.

Contrary to commonly held values

A very understandable source of objection to sensitivity training is that its values or meta goals are contrary to many of society's dominant values and beliefs. Consider the following statements, which are fairly characteristic of what our society considers to be correct.

1. An effective person controls emotions and does not reveal feelings, especially negative feelings, openly to others. Opinions may be expressed, but never feelings.

2.   It is inappropriate for a person to openly express feelings. One should stick strictly to business and leave personality and emotional factors out of the work setting.

3.   Purely rational thinking is the most effective way to reach decisions.

4.   A boss is needed if a group is to accomplish anything and be productive.

5.   In any organization authority must flow from the top down. Those in charge should control.

To a large extent these values are at odds with many of the values or meta goals of sensitivity training, which stress much the opposite. For example, sensitivity training stresses consciousness and acceptance of feelings, admitting to and facing up to differences of opinion and perception, leveling and the open expression of feelings and reactions to others, learning from peers, acceptance of suggestions and guidance from peers and subordinates, and a collaborative conception of authority.

An object of ridicule

Whereas the more traditional forms of sensitivity training have received criticism for the reasons mentioned here earlier, the more erotic versions of encounter groups seem to openly defy many of society's mores and, as a result, have brought forth public ridicule. These include nude encounter groups, sensory awakening sessions, screaming and crying sessions, and a broad array of activities which have been labeled "touch-and-feel" marathons—usually conducted blindfolded, but with no other restrictions! The sponsorship of these kinds of encounter groups varies from apparently respectable organizations such as the WTL and Esalen Institute to ad hoc groups of untrained practitioners.

Well-known and respected scholars and practitioners continue to experiment with these newer forms of awareness and learning. Thus one cannot conclude that they are all without merit. The evidence on the effects of these groups is not in yet. What the untrained encounter-group buffs (no pun) do along these lines is less than what is usually accepted as scientific experimentation. Nonetheless, many who do not know much about these activities other than the sensations they read about in newspapers and magazines and who do not care to try to understand the newer, experimental forms of learning, lump the amateurs and professionals together and ridicule them as if they were one group of "nuts."

Wide variation in qualifications of trainers

Another source of concern involves the qualifications of those who conduct sensitivity sessions. At one extreme are those formally educated in the behavioral sciences who have received special training and are certified by NTL Institute or other recognized professional organizations. At the other extreme we find apparently well-meaning but untrained and unprofessional zealots and experimenters. These are usually people fresh from some type of T-group experience themselves who are extremely eager to convert others or at least have others experience the same things they found particularly exhilarating and satisfying. Much of this type of nonprofessional activity took place during the late sixties and early seventies, and seems to have abated considerably since then. Nonetheless, it did give T-groups a poor image among the very cautious.

Insufficient attention to carryover back on the job

This criticism is not unique to sensitivity training. Nearly everybody in the field of training is concerned with whether that which is taught will be applied by participants on the job. In the case of sensitivity training, this concern takes on a new dimension: namely, what results if attendees really do return to their job imbued with the values learned and an increased level of awareness. Now, can the organization live with the new level of openness? Can it tolerate people telling each other how they feel? Is it desirable for employees to analyze and question every bit of their own and their fellow workers' behavior?

Selecting a T-Group

A great amount of care should be exercised in selecting a T-group. Both programs and candidates should be carefully screened to determine whether they are appropriate for each other. Moreover, the organization should consider whether it will benefit from having its members attend a sensitivity session. House (1967, pp. 23–26, 29–30) cites these questions to help guide managers in determining when T-group training is appropriate to achieve their specific objectives.

1. Are the changes that T-group training induces the kind required for more effective (leader) behavior? Will the organization reward the new behavior and as a result will the individual be more or less effective, satisfied, and accepted?

2. Can the organization tolerate the changes in the individual if the T-group is successful?

3. Can the candidate tolerate the anxiety involved in the T-group process?

4. What are the credentials of the T-group leaders? Is the leader capable of conducting an emotional learning process (as opposed to cognitive learning)? An advanced academic degree even in psychology is not by itself an indication of a trainee's qualification.

House also recommends the following guidance to ensure a maximum protection of the individual attending sensitivity training and at the same time to provide for a maximum freedom for needed changes within the organization.

1. Careful study of performance requirements before deciding to use T-groups, to ensure that changes induced by the effective T-group are actually required for effective performance and are changes which the organization will support when the individual returns to the job.

2. Careful preselection of participating individuals by means of adequate psychometric instruments to screen out as effectively as is possible any persons for whom this method might prove potentially overwhelming.

3. Careful explanation, to those selected for participation, of the goals and the process of T-group training in order to allow withdrawal of any individual who prefers not to invest psychically in the program, and to provide a mental framework which will facilitate the learning process of those who attend.

4. Careful selection of the T-group leader, to ensure that he has adequate training to conduct group emotional learning sessions that deliberately induce anxiety, interpersonal feedback, intrapersonal introspection, and experimentation with new methods of behavior.

5. Continued research to further elaborate the relationships between individual characteristics and conditions of use of T-groups which will result in greater refinement of the methodology and isolate those situations where the method can most effectively be employed.

6. Provision of reserve precautionary procedures to be instituted in the event that a program, once begun, fails to fulfill the expectations of either the organization or members of the group itself. Such precautions would include alternative methods for accomplishing the desired changes as well as provisions for the safety and well-being of individuals enrolled in an organization-sponsored program of behavioral re-training.

EFFECTIVENESS OF THE VARIOUS TRAINING METHODS

The relative effectiveness of the various methods for achieving particular training objectives is a major concern of training professionals as they face the questions as to which method to use to teach this or that concept, or skill, or personal characteristic. The training literature contains only a little helpful information along these lines. The research studies which have been carried out to determine the relative effectiveness of training methods are quite limited in scope. Most compare only two methods for producing one or more types of learning. This is largely due to the fact that this type of research is quite complex and to study more than just a few variables at a time requires a very cumbersome research design.

Carroll, Paine, and Ivancevich (1972) have provided the literature with a comprehensive summary of what is popularly believed by training directors and what is known regarding the effectiveness of various training methods. By means of mailed questionnaires, they obtained judgments of the relative effectiveness of nine different training methods for achieving six kinds of training objectives. These judgments were obtained from 117 training directors of the 200 corporations in the United States with the largest numbers of employees. The questionnaire asked the training directors to rate the effectiveness of the nine methods studied for achieving six different objectives, using the following five-point scale:

    5 = highly effective
    4 = quite effective
    3 = moderately effective
    2 = limited effective
    1 = not effective

Figure 5-1 presents the results of their study.

Carroll, Paine, and Ivancevich went further in their study and compared these collective judgments with the research findings contained in the literature. While there was some agreement between the judgments of the training directors and the research findings, there were glaring differences too. Most notable was the judgment that the lecture method has been found to be much more effective in causing the acquisition of knowledge and being acceptable to trainees than the training directors gave it credit for.

According to the survey of the literature by Carroll, Paine, and Ivancevich, plus some additional research completed since, a number of generalizations can be made. It should be kept in mind, however, that these generalizations are based upon research studies involving all kinds of groups learning various kinds of subject matter. They are not limited to groups of managers learning management.

1. For the acquisition of knowledge (learning a given amount of information in a set time):

  a) Programed instruction is superior to the conventional lecture method (Nash 1971; Schramm 1964).

  b) There is no difference between the effectiveness of the lecture and the conference (discussion) method (Buxton 1956; Hill 1960; Stovall 1958; Watson 1975); the conventional lecture and the television lecture (*Business Week* 1959; Schramm 1962); the lecture and the case-study method (Watson 1975).

  c) Conventional lecture is superior to film (Andrew 1954).

Training method	Knowledge acquisition		Changing attitudes		Problem-solving skills		Interpersonal skills		Participant acceptance		Knowledge retention	
	Mean	Mean rank	Mean	Mean rank	Mean	Mean rank	Mean	Mean rank	Mean	Mean rank	Mean	Mean rank
Case study	3.56	2	3.43	4	3.69	1	3.02	4	3.80	2	3.48	2
Conference (discussion) method	3.33	3	3.54	3	3.26	4	3.21	3	4.16	1	3.32	5
Lecture (with questions)	2.53	9	2.20	8	2.00	9	1.90	8	2.74	8	2.49	8
Business games	3.00	6	2.73	5	3.58	2	2.50	5	3.78	3	3.26	6
Movie films	3.16	4	2.50	6	2.24	7	2.19	6	3.44	5	2.67	7
Programed instruction	4.03	1	2.22	7	2.56	6	2.11	7	3.28	7	3.74	1
Role playing	2.93	7	3.56	2	3.27	3	3.68	2	3.56	4	3.37	4
Sensitivity training (T-group)	2.77	8	3.96	1	2.98	5	3.95	1	3.33	6	3.44	3
Television lecture	3.10	5	1.99	9	2.01	8	1.81	9	2.74	9	2.47	9

Fig. 5-1. Ratings of training directors on effectiveness of alternative training methods for various training objectives. (Source: Stephen J. Carroll, Jr., Frank T. Paine, and John J. Ivancevich, "The relative effectiveness of training methods—expert opinion and research." *Personnel Psychology* **25**, No. 3, August 1972, p. 498. Reprinted by permission.)

2. For changing attitudes:

a) The conference (discussion) method is superior to the lecture method (Butler 1966; Silber 1962).

b) The discussion method is superior to the lecture method (Bond 1956; Levine and Butler 1952; Lewin 1968).

c) Role playing can be effective for changing attitudes (Festinger and Carlsmith 1959; Harvey and Beverly 1961).

d) The case-study method is superior to the lecture method (Butler 1967; Watson 1975).

e) Sensitivity training can produce attitude changes (Schultz and Allen 1966; Smith 1964) and behavior change (Boyd and Ellis 1962; Bunker 1965; Miles 1965; Underwood 1965; Valiquet 1964).

3. For teaching problem-solving skills:

a) The case-study method is effective (Fox 1963; Solem 1960).

b) Role playing is effective (Maier 1953; Maier and Hoffman 1960; Maier and Maier 1957; Maier and Solem 1952; Solem 1960).

c) Role playing is more effective than case study for getting trainees to accept solutions to problems (Solem 1960).

4. For teaching interpersonal skills:

a) Sensitivity training is effective (Campbell and Dunnette 1970).

b) Role playing is effective for those directly involved (Bolda and Lawshe 1962; Maier et al. 1960, 1957; Van Schaack 1957).

5. For participant acceptance:
Few generalizations can be made about participant acceptance. Some studies indicate that participants prefer the lecture to discussion; other studies indicate that the lecture and discussion are equally acceptable. Perhaps much depends upon the participants themselves and their needs and expectations. In general, supervisors and managers enjoy the participative methods, but this is not to say that they dislike the lecture.

a) Students taught by the case-study method perceive the learning climate to be better and have a more favorable overall reaction to the instructor than do students who are taught by the lecture method (Watson 1975).

b) Role-playing receives good acceptance (Bolda 1962).

6. For knowledge retention:

a) Material retained is proportional to amount learned (Crow 1953; Verner et al. 1967).

b) Lecture and discussion are equally good (Dietrick 1960; Verner et al. 1967).

Table 5-1. Usefulness of training methods for achieving training objectives.

Training method	Acquisition of knowledge	Changing attitudes	Problem-solving skills	Interpersonal skills	Participant acceptance	Knowledge retention
Business games	NA	A[2]	A[3]	NA[6]	A	A
Case study	A[1]	A	A	NA[7]	A	A
Conference (discussion) method	A	A	NA	NA	A	A
Lecture (with questions)	A	NA	NA	NA	A	A
Movie films	A	NA	NA	NA	A	A
Programed instruction	A	NA	NA[4]	NA	A	A
Role playing	NA	A	A	A	A	A
Sensitivity training (T-group)	NA	A	A[5]	A	A	A
Television lecture	A	NA	NA	NA	A	A

A = Acceptable

NA = Not acceptable

[1] The case discussions are typically supplemented with short lectures. As a consequence, a fair number of points can be made.

[2] Games can be acceptable for altering attitudes provided there is ample post-game analysis of actions and the thinking that led to the actions. If people reflect on their beliefs and experience, their attitudes may change.

[3] Games may also be effective in teaching problem-solving skills provided there is post-game analysis of decisions made.

[4] In general, most programed instruction does not aim to help people develop this problem-solving skill, rather it is typically designed to teach facts and information. This need not always be the case. Programed instructional exercises can be designed to teach problem-solving skills.

[5] Sensitivity training does not usually aim to teach problem-solving skills. However, depending upon the nature of the T-group and the discussion that occurs, T-groups can be useful in teaching problem-solving skills in individual or personal problems or human-relations problems.

[6] Games may be used as an experience for trainees to reflect upon thus enabling them to gain greater insights into their own and their group's behavior and the effectiveness of each.

[7] Case studies usually do not allow participants to practice interpersonal skills or receive feedback on their actions and behavior. Thus they are typically not effective here.

c) Movie films and lecture and discussion methods are equally good (Sodnovitch et al. 1961; Vander Meer 1948; Verner et al. 1967).

d) Television lecture, conventional lecture, and discussion approach are equally good (Klausmeier 1961; Kumata 1960).

e) Programed instruction, conventional lecture, and discussion method are equally good (Nash 1971).

There appears to be little use in trying to rank-order the various training methods in terms of their effectiveness. Whether one is more or less effective than another is of minimal value. What is important, however, is which methods are effective or not effective in reaching various training objectives. Table 5-1 shows acceptable methods for achieving various objectives. Seven important exceptions and limitations are footnoted in Table 5-1.

In practice, there are several good alternative training methods that might be used to achieve some particular objective. Therefore, it seems to make sense for program planners to consider the advantages and limitations associated with each individual case in question and to make the decision as to which method to use with regard to the unique circumstances of the situation, rather than to follow some dogmatic guide that purports to tell which one is best. It is likely that no method is best. A certain amount of variety of methods is an important factor to consider too.

REFERENCES

Allen, Louis A. "The T-group: Short Cut or Short Circuit?" *Business Horizons* 16, No. 4, 1973, pp. 53–64.

Andlinger, G. R. "Business Games—Play One!" *Harvard Business Review* 36, No. 2, 1958, pp. 115–125.

_____. "Looking Around: What Can Business Games Do?" *Harvard Business Review* 36, No. 4, 1958, pp. 147–160.

Andrew, Gwen A. "A Study of the Effectiveness of a Workshop for Mental Health Education." *Mental Hygiene* 38, No. 1, April 1954, pp. 267–278.

Andrews, Kenneth R. *The Case Method of Teaching Human Relations and Administration.* Cambridge, Mass.: Harvard University Press, 1953.

Argyris, Chris. "Conditions for Competence Acquisition and Therapy." *Journal of Applied Behavioral Science* 3, No. 2, 1967, pp. 147–177.

_____. "In Defense of Laboratory Education." *Training Directors Journal* 17, No. 10, 1963, pp. 25–30.

_____. *Interpersonal Competence and Organizational Effectiveness.* Homewood, Ill.: Irwin-Dorsey, 1962.

_____. "T-Groups for Organizational Effectiveness." *Harvard Business Review* 42, No. 2, 1964, pp. 60–74.

Bass, Bernard M. "Reactions to Twelve Angry Men as a Measure of Sensitivity Training." *Journal of Applied Psychology* 46, No. 2, 1962, pp. 120–124.

Bennett, Willard E. "The Lecture as a Management Training Technique." *Personnel* 32, No. 6, 1956, pp. 497–506.

Bennis, Warren G. "Goals and Meta Goals of Laboratory Training." *NTL Human Relations Training News* 6, No. 3, 1962, pp. 1–4.

Bolda, R. A., and Lawshe, C. H. "Evaluation of Role Playing." *Personnel Administration* 25, No. 2, 1962, pp. 40–42.

Bond, Betty W. "The Group Discussion-Decision Approach—An Appraisal of Its Use in Health Education." *Dissertation Abstracts* 16, 1956, p. 903.

Boyd, J. B., and Ellis, J. D. *Findings of Research into Senior Management Seminars.* Toronto: The Hydro-Electric Power Commission of Toronto, 1962. Cited by J. P. Campbell and M. D. Dunnette, "Effectiveness of T-Group Experiences in Managerial Training and Development," *Psychological Bulletin* 70, 1968, pp. 73–104.

Bradford, Leland P.; Gibb, Jack R.; and Benne, Kenneth D. (eds.). *T-group Theory and Laboratory Method: Innovation in Re-education.* New York: Wiley, 1964.

Bradford, Leland P., and Lippitt, Ronald. "Role Playing in Supervisory Training." *Personnel* 22, No. 6, 1946, pp. 358–369.

Brown, D. S. "The Lecture." *Journal of the American Society of Training and Development* 14, No. 1, 1960, pp. 17–22.

Bunker, Douglas R. "Individual Applications of Laboratory Training." *Journal of Applied Behavioral Science* 1, No. 2, 1965, pp. 131–148.

Business Week. "In Business Education, The Game is the Thing." July 25, 1959, pp. 56–58, 63, 64.

Butler, Elmer D. "An Experimental Study of the Case Method in Teaching the Social Foundations of Education." *Dissertation Abstracts* 27, 1967, p. 2912.

Butler, John L. "A Study of the Effectiveness of Lecture Versus Conference Teaching Techniques in Adult Education." *Dissertation Abstracts* 26, 1966, p. 3712.

Buxton, Claud E. *College Teaching: A Psychologist's View.* New York: Harcourt-Brace, 1956.

Campbell, John P., and Dunnette, Marvin D. "Effectiveness of T-group Experiences in Managerial Training and Development." *Psychological Bulletin* 70, No. 2, 1968, pp. 73–104.

Campbell, John P.; Dunnette, Marvin D.; Lawler, Edward E., III; and Weick, Karl E., Jr. *Managerial Behavior, Performance and Effectiveness.* New York: McGraw-Hill, 1970.

Carlson, John G. H., and Misshauk, Michael J. *Introduction to Gaming: Management Decision Simulations.* New York: Wiley, 1972.

Carpenter, Clarence R., and Greenhill, L. "An Investigation of Closed Circuit Television for Teaching University Courses." Instructional Television Project Report No. 2, University Park, Pennsylvania, Pennsylvania State University, 1958.

Carroll, Stephen J., Jr.; Paine, Frank T.; and Ivancevich, John J. "The Relative Effectiveness of Training Methods—Expert Opinion and Research." *Personnel Psychology* 25, No. 3, 1972, pp. 495–509.

Copeland, Melvin T. "The Genesis of the Case Method in Business Instruction," pp. 25–33 in *The Case Study Method at the Harvard Business School*, Malcolm P. McNair (ed.). New York: McGraw-Hill, 1954.

Corsini, Raymond J. "Role Playing: Its Use in Industry." *Advanced Management Journal* 25, No. 2, 1960, pp. 20–23.

Corsini, Raymond; Shaw, Malcom; and Blake, Robert. *Role Playing in Business and Industry*. Glencoe, N.Y.: The Free Press of Glencoe, 1961.

Craft, Clifford J. "Management Games" (Chapter 14, pp. 267–284) in *Training and Development Handbook*, Robert L. Craig and Lester R. Bittel (eds.). New York: McGraw-Hill, 1967.

Craig, Robert L., and Bittel, Lester R. (eds.). *Training and Development Handbook*. New York: McGraw-Hill, 1967.

Crow, Richard R. "Group Training in Higher Management Development." *Personnel* 29, No. 6, May 1953, pp. 457–460.

Dietrick, D. C. "Review of Research" in Richard J. Hill, *A Comparative Study of Lecture and Discussion Methods*. White Plains, NY: The Fund for Adult Education, 1960, pp. 90–118.

Dill, William R. "What Business Games Do Best." *Business Horizons* 4, No. 3, 1961, pp. 55–64.

Dill, William R., and Doppelt, Neil. "The Acquisition of Experience in a Complex Management Game." *Management Science* 10, No. 1, 1963, pp. 30–46.

Dunnette, Marvin D. "Should Your People Take Sensitivity Training?" *Innovation* 14, 1970, pp. 6, 44–46, 52–55.

Elms, Alan. *Role Playing, Rewards and Attitude Change*. New York: Van Nostrand, 1969.

Festinger, Leon, and Carlsmith, James M. "Cognitive Consequences of Forced Compliance." *Journal of Abnormal and Social Psychology* 58, 1959, pp. 203–210.

Fox, William M. "A Measure of the Effectiveness of the Case Method in Teaching Human Relations." *Personnel Administration* 26, No. 4, 1963, pp. 53–57.

French, John R. P., Jr. "Role-Playing as a Method of Training Foremen," in J. L. Moreno (ed.), *Group Psychotherapy*. Beacon, NY: Beacon House, 1945, pp. 172–187.

Fulmer, R. M. "Lectures Can Produce Lethal Lethargy." *Administrative Management* XXXI, No. 4, 1970, pp. 76–78.

Gambatese, Joseph N. "Training Methods Test Executive Judgment." *Nation's Business* 43, No. 6, 1955, pp. 72–73.

Golembiewski, Robert T. "The Laboratory Approach to Organization Change; Schema of a Method." *Public Administration Review* XXVII, No. 3, 1967, pp. 211–223.

Golembiewski, Robert T., and Blumberg, Arthur (eds.). *Sensitivity Training and the Laboratory Approach*. Itasca, Ill.: Peacock, 1970.

Graham, Robert G., and Gray, Clifford E. *Business Games Handbook.* New York: American Management Association, 1969.

Gragg, Charles. "Because Wisdom Can't Be Told." *Harvard Alumni Bulletin,* October 19, 1940.

Greene, J. R., and Sisson, R. L. *Dynamic Management Decision Games.* New York: Wiley, 1959.

Greenlaw, Paul S.; Harron, Lowell W.; and Rawdon, Richard H. *Business Simulations.* Englewood Cliffs, NJ: Prentice-Hall, 1962.

Greenlaw, Paul S., and Knight, Stanford S. "The Human Factor in Business Games." *Business Horizons* 3, No. 3, 1960, pp. 55–61.

Haas, Kenneth B., and Ewing, Claude H. *Tested Training Techniques.* New York: Prentice-Hall, 1950.

Harvey, O. V. and Beverly, George "Some Personality Correlates of Concept Change Through Role Play." *Journal of Abnormal and Social Psychology* 63, 1961, pp. 125–130.

Hill, Richard J. *A Comparative Study of Lecture and Discussion Methods.* White Plains, NY: Fund for Adult Education, 1960.

House, Robert J. *Management Development: Design, Evaluation and Implementation.* Ann Arbor: University of Michigan, 1967.

_____. "T-Group Education and Leadership Effectiveness." *Personnel Psychology* 20, No 1, 1967, pp. 1–32.

_____. "T-Group Training: Good or Bad?" *Business Horizons* XII, No. 6, 1969, pp. 69–77.

Huse, Edgar F. *Organization Development and Change.* New York: West-Publishing, 1975.

Jaffee, Cabot L. *Problems in Supervision: An In-Basket Training Exercise.* Reading, Mass.: Addison-Wesley, 1968.

Joyce, Robert. "In-Basket Programs." *Training in Business and Industry* 8, No. 2, 1971, pp. 40–44.

Kalman, J. Cohen, and Rhenman, Eric. "The Role of Management Games in Education and Research." *Management Science* 7, No. 2, 1961, pp. 131–166.

Kibbee, Joel M.; Craft, Clifford J.; and Nanus, Burt. *Management Games.* New York: Reinhold, 1961.

Klausmeier, Herbert J. *Learning and Human Abilities.* New York: Harper and Row, 1961.

Klaw, Spencer. "Two Weeks in a T-Group." *Fortune* 64, No. 2, 1961, pp. 114–117.

Kumata, H. "A Decade of Teaching by Television," in W. Schramm (ed.), *The Impact of Educational Television.* Urbana: University of Illinois Press, 1960, pp. 176–192.

Lerda, Louis W. "Conference Methods," (Chapter 9 pp. 154–173) in *Training and Development Handbook,* Robert L. Craig and Lester R. Bittel (eds.). New York: McGraw-Hill, 1967.

Levine, Jacob, and Butler, John. "Lecture vs. Group Decision in Changing Behavior." *Journal of Applied Psychology* **36**, No. 1, 1952, pp. 29–33.

Lewin, Kurt. "Group Decision and Social Change," in *Readings in Social Psychology,* E. E. Maccoley, T. M. Newcombe, and E. L. Hartley (eds.). New York: Holt, 1968, pp. 197–211.

Lowell, Mildred. *The Management of Libraries and Information Centers,* 4. Metuchen, NJ: Scarecrow Press, 1968.

Lopez, Felix M., Jr. *Evaluating Executive Decision Making, The In-Basket Technique.* American Management Association Research Study 75. New York: AMA, 1975.

Lynton, Rolf P., and Pareek, Udai. *Training for Development.* Homewood, Ill.: Irwin-Dorsey, 1967.

McDonald, John, and Ricciardi, Frank. "The Business Decision Game." *Fortune* **58**, No. 3, 1958, pp. 140–142.

McGehee, William, and Thayer, Paul. *Training in Business and Industry.* New York: Wiley, 1961.

McKenney, James L. *Simulation Games for Management Development.* Boston: Graduate School of Business Administration, Division of Research, Harvard University, 1967.

McNair, Malcom P. (ed.). *The Case Method at the Harvard Business School.* New York: McGraw-Hill, 1954.

Maliver, Bruce L. *The Encounter Game.* New York: Stein and Day, 1973.

Marshall, Donald L. "The Incident Process of Supervisory Training: Case Study of Experience in a Small Plant." *Personnel* **31**, No. 2, 1954, pp. 134–139.

Maier, Norman R. F. "An Experimental Test of the Effect of Training on Discussion Leadership." *Human Relations* **VI**, No. 2, 1953, pp. 161–173.

_____. *Principles of Human Relations.* New York: Wiley, 1952.

_____. *Psychology in Industry.* New York: Houghton Mifflin, 1946.

Maier, Norman R. F., and Hoffman, L. R. "Quality of First and Second Solutions in Group Problem Solving." *Journal of Applied Psychology* **44**, No. 4, 1960, pp. 278–283.

_____. "Using Trained Developmental Discussion Leaders to Improve Further the Quality of Group Decisions." *Journal of Applied Psychology* **44**, No. 4, 1960, pp. 247–251.

Maier, Norman R. F., and Maier, Richard A. "An Experimental Test of the Effects of 'Developmental' vs. 'Free' Discussions on the Quality of Group Decisions." *Journal of Applied Psychology* **41**, No. 5, 1957, pp. 320–323.

Maier, Norman R. F., and Solem, Allen R. "The Contribution of the Discussion Leader to the Quality of Group Thinking." *Human Relations* **V**, No. 3, 1952, pp. 277–288.

Maier, Norman R. F.; Solem, Allen R.; and Maier, Ayesha A. *Supervisory and Executive Development.* New York: Wiley, 1957.

Meyer, Herbert H. "The Validity of the In-Basket Test as a Measure of Managerial Performance." *Personnel Psychology* **23**, No. 3, 1970, pp. 297–307.

Miles, Matthew B. "Change During and Following Laboratory Training: A Clinical Experimental Study." *Journal of Applied Behavioral Science* 1, No. 3, 1965, pp. 215–242.

Nanus, Burt. "Management Games: An Answer to Critics." *Journal of Industrial Engineering* 13, No. 6, 1962, pp. 467–469.

Nash, Allan; Muczyk, Jan P.; and Vettori, Frank L. "The Relative Practical Effectiveness of Programmed Instruction." *Personnel Psychology* 24, No. 3, Autumn 1971, pp. 397–418.

Newport, M. Gene. "A Review of Training Fundamentals." *Training and Development Journal* 22, No. 10, 1968, pp. 17–21.

Nicholson, Scott. "Training by the Case-study Method." *Management Record*, The National Industrial Conference Board, Inc., New York, XVIII, No. 4, 1956, pp. 118–120, 147–150.

Odiorne, George S. "The Trouble with Sensitivity Training." *Training Director's Journal* 17, No. 10, 1963, pp. 9–20.

O'Donnell, Walter G. "Role Playing as a Practical Training Technique." *Personnel* 29, No. 3, 1952, pp. 275–288.

Ogg, Elizabeth. *Sensitivity Training and Encounter Groups*. Public Affairs Pamphlet No. 474, Public Affairs Committee, New York, 1972.

Pigors, Paul. "Case Method" (Chapter 10, pp. 174–205) in *Training and Development Handbook*, Robert L. Craig and Lester R. Bittel (eds.). New York: McGraw-Hill, 1967.

Pigors, Paul. "Case Method" (Chapter 10, pp. 174–205) in *Training and Development cess*. New York: McGraw-Hill, 1967.

_____. *Director's Manual: The Incident Process*. Washington, D.C.: Bureau of National Affairs, 1955.

Planty, Earl G. "Some Suggestions for Senior Seminar Teachers Using the Case Study Buzz Group Method of Teaching." Senior Seminar in General Management, unpublished paper, 1968.

_____. "Teaching Methods for Business Education." Senior Seminar in General Management, unpublished paper, 1967.

Planty, Earl G; McCord, William S.; and Efferson, Carlos. *Training Employees and Managers*. New York: Ronald Press, 1948.

"Problem Solving Conferences." Conference Board Reports, Studies in Personnel Policy No. 176, N.I.C.B., New York, 1960.

Rogers, Rolf E. *Organization Theory*. Boston: Allyn and Bacon, 1975.

Schein, Edgar H., and Bennis, Warren G. (eds.). *Personal and Organizational Change Through Group Methods*. New York: Wiley, 1965.

Schramm, Wilbur L. *The Research on Programmed Instruction: An Annotated Bibliography*. Washington, D.C.: U.S. Department of Health, Education and Welfare, Office of Education, 1964.

_____. "What We Know About Learning from Instructional Television." *Educational Television—The Next Ten Years*. Stanford: Stanford University Press, 1962, pp. 52–74.

Schrieskeim, Janet F., and Schrieskeim, Chester A. "The Effectiveness of Business Games in Management Training." *Training and Development Journal* **28**, No. 5, 1974, pp. 14–17.

Schultz, William C., and Allen, Vernon L. "The Effects of a T-Group on Interpersonal Behavior." *Journal of Applied Behavioral Science* **2**, No. 3, 1966, pp. 265–286.

Seashore, Charles. "What is Sensitivity Training?" *NTL Institute News and Reports,* April 1968, also in *Public Administration News: Management Forum* **XVIII**, No. 2, 1968, Section 11, also in Robert T. Golembiewski and Arthur Blumberg, *Sensitivity Training and the Laboratory Approach,* pp. 14–17. Itasca, Ill.: Peacock, 1970.

Shepherd, Herbert A., and Bennis, Warren G. "A Theory of Training by Group Methods." *Human Relations* **IX**, No. 4, 1956, pp. 403–414.

Shostrom, Everett L. "Group Therapy: Let the Buyer Beware." *Psychology Today* **2**, No. 12, 1969, pp. 36–40.

Silber, Mark B. "A Comparative Study of Three Methods of Effective Attitude Change." *Dissertation Abstracts* **22**, 1962, p. 2488.

Sodnovitch, J. M., and Pophorn, W. J. *Retention Value of Filmed Science Courses.* Kansas State College of Pittsburgh, 1961.

Solem, A. R. "Human Relations Training: Comparisons of Case Study and Role Playing." *Personnel Administration* **23**, No. 5, 1960, pp. 29–37.

Smith, P. N. "Attitude Changes Associated with Training in Human Relations." *British Journal of Social and Clinical Psychology* **3**, 1964, pp. 104–113.

Stone, S. I. "The Incident Process." *Journal of Society of Training and Development,* March 1959, pp. 17–26.

Stovall, Thomas F. "Lecture vs. Discussion." *Phi Delta Kappan* **XXXIX**, No. 6, 1958, pp. 255–258.

Tiffen, Joseph. *Industrial Psychology.* New York: Prentice-Hall, 1952.

Underwood, W. J. "Evaluation of Laboratory Method Training." *Training Director's Journal* **19**, 1965, pp. 34–40.

Valiquet, I. M. "Contribution to the Evaluation of a Management Development Program." Unpublished Masters Thesis. Massachusetts Institute of Technology, 1964.

Van Schaack, H., Jr. "Naturalistic Role Playing: A Method of Interview Training for Student Personnel Administrators." *Dissertation Abstracts* **17**, 1957, p. 801.

Vander Meer, A. W. Relative Effectiveness of Exclusive Film Instruction, films plus study guide, and typical instructional methods. Progress Report #10. *Instructional Film Program.* State College, PA: Pennsylvania State College, 1948.

Verner, Coolie and Gary Dickinson. "The Lecture, An Analysis and Review of Research." *Adult Education* **XVII**, No. 2, 1967, pp. 85–100.

Watson, Charles E. "The Effectiveness of the Case Study Method." *College Student Journal* **9**, No. 2, 1975, pp. 109–116.

Yoder, Dale. *Personnel Management and Industrial Relations.* Englewood Cliffs, NJ: Prentice-Hall, 1970.

Zelko, Harold P. "Conference Leadership Training." *Personnel* **29**, No. 1, 1952, pp. 37–42.

_____. "The Lecture" (Chapter 8, pp. 141–153) in *Training and Development Handbook*, Robert L. Craig and Lester R. Bittel (eds.). New York: McGraw-Hill, 1967.

Zoll, Allen A. III. *Dynamic Management Education*. Reading, Mass.: Addison-Wesley, 1969.

Zif, Jay Jehiel, and Otlewski, Robert E. *Contract Negotiations*. Toronto, Ontario: Collier-MacMillan Ltd., 1970.

6

The Role of the Program
Coordinator

So important and critical to the success and impact of a training program is the role of the program coodinator that it deserves a chapter of its own. Briefly stated, the coordinator's role is to implement the training plan. Very often the coordinator is heavily involved in the planning process, if not the master mind behind it. However, the coordinator's major contribution is to implement the plan by carefully scheduling and controlling all aspects of the training program, minute by minute, to assure that everything happens as it should and the program runs smoothly. This includes everything from assuring the quality and timely serving of mid-morning coffee to briefing instructors and discussion leaders about the program so that they will be able to emphasize the right points in their lectures and discussions.

Sometimes these functions are carried out by a program director; in other cases it is the training director or training manager who performs these functions; and sometimes they are carried out by the program moderator. Regardless of the title used, the role and responsibilities remain the same—that is, to implement the training program plan smoothly and effectively. This chapter addresses the person or persons who perform in this capacity, what the job involves, and how to do it.

STYLES OF COORDINATION

The coordinator's role may be carried out at one of, or somewhere between, two extremes. At one extreme the coordinator performs basically a scheduling function and serves as host. He or she schedules various speakers and instructors to cover specific subjects, but does not go into any degree of detail with regard to specific aspects of the subjects that should be stressed. He or she does not take the responsibility of making the course content relevant to the needs and wants of the participants. These and other similar questions and details, such as selection of cases, exercises, and reading assignments, are left entirely to the various discussion leaders. In short, the coordinator, in this instance, does not get involved in planning and orchestrating the learning content and process. Moreover, he or she stays as far away as possible from the day-to-day details such as scheduling breaks, checking on meals and equipment, and keeping the program on schedule. The coordinator abdicates a leadership role and allows the group members to fend for themselves. Also, he or she stays away from the group as much as possible.

The coordinator will introduce speakers and may be at a few of the meals, but his or her main concern and attention does not lie with overseeing the interactions of the participants and building a cohesive group, mainly for two reasons. One, he or she does not understand how cohesive groups can be used to facilitate learning by "unfreezing" their members and encouraging them to try out new approaches; and two, he or she does not have the knowledge and skill to do this.

At the other extreme, the coordinator performs planning and orchestrating functions that assure the entire experience produces the optimal changes and improvements for those participating. Functioning in this fashion, the coordinator is heavily involved in designing and planning the entire program. She or he is thorough in researching the program's participants and their needs and expectations. She or he works closely with the carefully selected faculty (with whom she or he is acquainted) to advise them of the training needs of the group and is not hesitant about suggesting cases or reading material for the faculty to use. Moreover, the coordinator combines the various subject areas so that the program's content is consistent and does not contain gaps, overlaps, or contradictions. As the training program progresses, the coordinator oversees all matters to ensure that everything runs as planned. She or he maintains a close watch over the participants to observe their learning progress and their emotional adjustments to it and works to arrange the various conditions and interpersonal relationships so that the training's impact is maximized. In short, the coordinator stays on top of every phase of the training program by her or his own efforts or through the assistance of attentive and well-trained associates.

Experience shows that the best management development programs are those which are run by coordinators who perform their jobs as described by the second extreme. What follows here is a detailed description of what this kind of program coordinator does as he or she plans and coordinates the implementation of a typical live-in program.

MONTHS BEFORE THE PROGRAM STARTS

Three to six months before the program is held, the coordinator and his or her staff (provided there is a staff) engage in a study of needs. If the program they plan is open to the general public through subscription, and if the participants are obviously not known because they have not yet registered, then the study of needs will have to be based on the typical registrants who have attended in the past. In these cases the study of needs may involve a survey of the training directors from companies that in the past have sent one or more participants. Many university-sponsored executive programs are thoroughly known by corporate line executives and training directors since these executives frequently serve on advisory boards to these programs and periodically offer suggestions and guidance to their directors. Many training directors have attended or visited these programs regularly and so can recommend appropriate programs for managers and executives in their organization who are slated for training.

If the program is for a specifically defined population, as would be the case in an organization's in-house program, then the needs survey will involve interviews with the members of this population and their superiors. This the program coordinator does. He or she might even have one or more of the teachers to be used in the program assist in this process so that they can gain first-hand knowledge of the needs and so that some of the doubt, suspicion, and mistrust trainees may have about training and those who conduct it can be removed. If the program coordinator is an "insider," such as the local training manager, he or she works closely with top management and other key people to assure their acceptance and support of the program. If the program coordinator is an "outsider," such as consultant or someone from the corporate headquarters, he or she works closely with the local personnel manager or training director as well as with higher ups and involves them in all phases of the program as appropriate.

Once the study of needs has been completed and the training purposes and objectives have been reviewed and approved by the appropriate people, the coordinator moves on to the next step—i.e., identifying and selecting the proper case studies, articles, exercises, films, etc. for the program. The program coordinator often does this; however, it is preferred that the various instructors and discussion leaders do this themselves, under the coordinator's guidance. In this phase of the program planning, new cases are written or old ones are revised to depict the industry (or industries), work settings, and management levels represented by the program's attendees. Steps are taken to shape the program to the needs of the group.

Depending upon the type of program and the availability of conference meeting space and room accommodations, the coordinator selects the training site and makes the necessary reservations for meeting rooms, hotel, and dining accommodations. In some cases, 6 to 9 months lead time is required to obtain the space and facilities needed. In other cases, reservations must be made 12 to 18 months in advance. It is important that the necessary space and facilities be secured far enough in advance to assure that they are adequate for the needs and comfort of the group.

Two to four months before the program is to be held (assuming that it is an in-house program), the course schedule and materials should be presented to top management for approval, which should not be difficult to obtain because the planners have been working closely with top management all along. This material should include brief statements of purposes for each section, a daily schedule showing topics and instructors, a course outline showing case studies and reading assignments, and a copy of each of the materials to be used.

Two months before the program is to be held, the training staff should begin reproducing ample quantities of this material. Three ring binders and dividers should be ordered and the notebook material should be collated. The notebooks should be completely assembled and inspected at least two weeks prior to the start of the program to assure that all materials are present. The conscientious coordinator realizes that this is an important deadline to meet, since there are many other important details that will require his or her attention (as well as that of the staff) during the week before the course is to begin.

A month in advance of the program all participants are identified. If the program is open to the public by subscription, the applications for enrollment will most likely contain requests for biographical data such as name, address, position title, company, previous experience, family, hobbies, and outside interests and activities. The biographical data is typed and reproduced along with a photograph of each participant for inclusion in the notebooks. The biographies will help the staff and participants to become acquainted and will also help the class to become a closely knit group quickly.

A letter which explains the program and how it will be conducted is sent to each participant a month before the course is to be held. If the program is open to the public, this will be the second letter that the participants receive (the first letter was a formal acceptance to the program). If the program is an in-house course, this letter is probably the first formal communication each participant receives regarding the course. This letter is extremely important because it helps to shape the participants' expectations about the program and establishes the climate or tone of the program and the work standards that will be required. Not only does it contain factual data and information, but it also carries emotional, unwritten messages, including such things as the coordinator's interest in the participants and their comfort, the seriousness of the course, the extent to which the participants can be themselves at the program, and some assurance that participants will not be subject to the threat of embarrassment or intimidation. This letter is carefully composed by the coordinator, who reads it over several times before sending it and is sensitive to the emotional impact it will have on those who will receive it.

To some readers, this may sound like nonsense and may involve too much "humanizing." To others, it is just "gobbledygook." Those who feel this way should pause a moment and consider the following illustration. The Hypocase Company has planned a supervisory training program for its supervisors. Typical supervisors are between 45 and 50 years old and have been with the company 20 to 25 years, and in the supervisor's position for 10 to 15 years. They have many years of experience, but little contact with training or formal education. They do not read very much or well. They did graduate from high school, but never cared for it much. They have biases against education and learning, believing that "experience is what really counts." They are suspicious about what the training department may try to do to them. They fear being embarrassed or looking bad in front of others, especially peers. Understandably, they try to cover up their feelings arising out of perceived inadequacies in themselves regarding learning and from their less than satisfactory experiences in school 20 or 30 years earlier. They may exhibit defensive and hostile attitudes toward learning. Moreover, these hypothetical supervisors have heard via the grapevine and from their bosses that they will soon be attending a management course for the company's supervisors. They may feel that the company is having the course because they have been performing their jobs inadequately. Thus they will most likely be defensive of the way in which they do their jobs.

The letter announcing the course can go a long way in either alleviating all anxieties and defensiveness or accentuating them, depending upon how it is written. One can hope to do a reasonable job of predicting the impact of the course anouncement letter only by placing himself or herself in the shoes of the reader, by understanding and empathizing with the reader, and by reading the letter and reacting to it emotionally as the reader might. Particular care should be taken to assure that the letter does not convey a condescending tone or carry with it the implied message, "We in the training department have all the answers you dummies need, and we will be around to straighten you fellows out in a few weeks." It should express the fact that none of the participants will be put on the spot or embarrassed or examined by lengthy tests. It should imply that the people who attend will be treated as adults.

In addition to dispelling any fears and anxieties the participants may have, the letter should create support and enthusiasm for the program. It should be an early demonstration that the training staff is organized, has done its homework, and has prepared a serious and meaningful learning experience. These, then, are the emotional messages the announcing letter should convey. It should contain factual information as well. Namely, it should explain the following to the participants:

1. The purpose or purposes of the course

2. Top management's support (frequently the letter goes out over the top manager's signature to convey this)

3. The daily schedule including topics to be covered and the faculty who will teach them

4. Assignments

5. Travel information or a request for participants to inform the training staff of their travel plans (e.g., airline arrival times and flight number) so that they can be met at the local airport, train depot, or bus terminal

6. A map of the training site and directions on how to get there

7. The starting times of events and the locations where participants should gather

8. What to wear and what to bring

9. A description of the dining and living accommodations and nearby recreational facilities

10. Whom to contact if they have any further questions or requests

Some programs request participants to read articles and cases before they arrive. These preprogram assignments are sometimes included in the announcing letter. From experience, training directors have found that not everybody will complete preprogram study assignments, especially if they are too time consuming. However, it is usually a good idea to send participants some reading materials and cases before the program begins, along with a description of the case-study method and how it works. In total, these materials should be limited to not more than 25-30 typewritten pages. By receiving preprogram assignments participants will quickly get the message that the program will be demanding and should not be considered a vacation away from work. Most participants will make an honest attempt to complete the assignments and hence will reduce some of the work load they would otherwise have to face while at the program. Even if every person does not complete each assignment beforehand, an important step has been taken—that is, setting the standard of hard work.

Two examples of preprogram letters to participants, which illustrate the ideas just discussed, are shown in Figs. 6-1 and 6-2.

Three to four weeks prior to the program the coordinator contacts the faculty again, sending them the biographies of the participants and additional insights he or she has gathered pertaining to the participants' expectations and needs. The coordinator sends the faculty the final program schedule and a brief synopsis of what each instructor plans to cover during her or his session, including reading assignments and case studies or other exercises. The coordinator also determines from the faculty what their audio-visual equipment needs are and promptly begins to secure these items. The coordinator also determines the faculty's travel plans and lodging and dining needs.

Mr. John Smith
Production Supervisor
Indianapolis Plant

Dear John:

There's no question about it--your job as a supervisor is a
tough one. It's demanding and filled with problems. You know
this and we know it too. And, we also know that our company is
dedicated to quality products, quality performance, and constant
improvement. This includes on-going improvement in the ways in
which everyone in the company does his or her job--from the
president on down. This is why it is company policy to give
everyone plenty of opportunities to improve and update his or
her job knowledge and skills. To carry out this policy, every
one of our company's managers has already or will soon attend
a management-development program.

Sometime next month you and your fellow supervisors will attend
one of the four, one-week training sessions in supervisory
management. From (date) to (date) you will be relieved of your
normal duties to attend our supervisory-management program.

This same program has been run for other Amco supervisors at
Dallas, Pittsburgh, Louisville, and Waterbury. It covers many
important topics including:
> The roles and responsibilities of the supervisor
> Leadership
> Goal setting
> Work planning
> Organizing
> Delegating
> Motivation
> Communication
> Discipline
> Work standards
> Methods improvement
> Employee orientation and training

This program is not run like a school. We are all adults.
Therefore, much of the learning will involve a sharing of our
many ideas and methods that have been tested over our many
years of experience. Everyone will be expected to contribute
his or her best thinking to the discussions. There will be
reading and work assignments. Some you will do on your own in
the evenings. Most will be done during the formal sessions.
There will be no examinations or lengthy written assignments.
No one will be quizzed or put on the spot.

Fig. 6–1. Preprogram letter.

The reactions of the people who have already participated in
this program are very favorable. They found it interesting,
practical, and quite helpful. Here are some comments they
have written about the program:

"Top management is finally realizing the difficult
position held by their first-line supervisors."

"Very interesting. I gained good knowledge about
managing and our own jobs . . . also about getting things done."

"I gained some very good ideas from this program.
It taught me to have a better understanding of my men."

"I think it is a very helpful and enlightening
program."

"Every member of management should attend this
program. It is very helpful."

"Everything was of the highest order. This was my
first taste of any type of formal education."

"We got to the heart of the problems of management."

Soon you will receive more information about this program
including reading materials and assignments.

Cordially,

James Jones
Training Director

Mr. John Doe
1776 Parke Lane
Cleveland, Ohio

Dear Mr. Doe:

The start of the Miami University Executive Development Program
for Library Administrators is just three weeks away. We look
forward to your visit to Oxford and participation in the program.
Enclosed is a daily program schedule and a map of the campus.
The following information, we trust, will be useful.

Travel - Miami University in Oxford, Ohio is located in south-
west Ohio, roughly between Cincinnati and Dayton. It may be
reached by U.S. 27 or state highways 732 or 73. Dayton and
Cincinnati Airports are the nearest public airports. Car
rentals are available at both. There will be parking space
available on campus. Please advise our office of your travel
plans so that we can meet your flight and drive you to campus.
We have several vans available.

Time and Dates - The program officially commences with a welcome
dinner at 6:00 p.m. in the Heritage Room (3rd floor) of the
University Center on Sunday evening, August 10. Should your
travel arrangements preclude your arrival in time for the
dinner, please let us know when we can expect you. Travel
schedules may be such that it would be more convenient for you
to arrive Saturday, August 9. If so, please alert me so that
I can arrange to have your room ready then.

The program will end with a luncheon and graduation exercise at
noon on Saturday, August 16. I urge you to stay through the
entire program. To leave early would be like buying a product
with important parts missing. To miss the last building block
in the program would be like buying a house without a roof. We
can make arrangements for you to stay the evening of August 16
if necessary.

We are very punctual and will begin and end our sessions on time.

Room - Morris Hall is air conditioned. When you arrive in
Oxford your first stop should be Morris Hall. Each participant
will have a private room at Morris Hall (see map enclosed).
We will be there all Sunday afternoon (or on Saturday if you
indicate you plans to be such) to register you and help you
get settled.

Meals - Meals will be served in the Zebra Room at the University
Center (see map). Breakfast will be served cafeteria style.
Lunch and dinner will be served.

Fig. 6–2. Preprogram letter.

<u>Classroom</u> - Classes will be held in the School of Business Administration Building, Laws Hall. Laws Hall is also air conditioned.

<u>Dress</u> - While it is advisable to bring one nice outfit, most of the time dress will be casual. Shorts are O.K., too. Thunderstorms are common during this time of the year, so bring rain gear.

<u>Evening Case Studies</u> - For the most part, we will be using the Harvard Case Study Method of Instruction. You will be assigned to a small study group (buzz group) each evening from Sunday to Thursday. Groups will study, analyze, discuss, and prepare group case reports, which they will present orally to the assembled class the following day. Usually case-study preparation requires 2 to 3 hours. Participants generally elect to do this after dinner.

We are working hard to make your stay at Miami University both profitable and enjoyable. We look forward to seeing you at dinner on August 10. If you have any questions or concerns, please write or call (513) 529-4129.

Cordially,

Joe Smith
Director

During the next few weeks the coordinator gathers and assembles the necessary resources and materials. He or she maintains a file on the travel plans of participants and faculty and makes arrangements for them to be met at airports, bus terminals, and railroad depots. He or she also firms up commitments for meeting-room space, lodging, and meal service and goes over menus and arranges for coffee breaks with those who perform these services.

DAYS BEFORE THE PROGRAM STARTS

A day or two before the program begins the coordinator and staff double check arrangements, facilities, and equipment. Projectors are checked over to assure that they will work properly and that each has a spare bulb. An inventory is made of supplies. The conference-room checklist (presented in Chapter 4) is reviewed to assure that everything is ready and in its place. A final meeting is held with the staff so each person knows what she or he is to do. Bulletin boards near the meeting room and sleeping rooms are organized to display schedules of meals, classes, and events. Announcements and schedules are posted on bulletin boards, even though they are also included in each participant's notebook. This helps to assure that the various communications are received. The day before the program starts the coordinator has the meeting room and buzz-group rooms set up with tables and chairs. Notebooks, name place cards, ash trays, announcements, etc. are neatly placed on the conference room tables. Everything is now in its place. Equipment and materials have been checked. Everything and everyone is ready.

THE FIRST DAY OF THE PROGRAM

The beginning day of the program has arrived. The coordinator has enjoyed a long, restful night's sleep for she or he will need it. Today will be long and hectic. If the program is scheduled to begin in the morning, the coordinator and staff are present an hour before the scheduled starting time to give everything a last minute check and to welcome the early arriving participants. Many of the non-live-in programs are scheduled to run for five to six consecutive days. Participants commute daily to the program, which may run from 8:30 A.M. to 4:30 P.M. As participants arrive on the first morning, the coordinator welcomes them and encourages them to find their place as designated by the name place cards. The coordinator has each person wear a lapel name tag. (The coordinator too wears a lapel name tag at all times to set a good example.)

If the program is a live-in type course, then the schedule is different. These programs usually begin with a social hour, followed by a dinner, a short welcome speech, and orientation. At this type of program the training staff is busy running a shuttle service to meet arriving participants and instructors and bring them to the conference center from the local airport. If possible the program coordinator meets the arriving instructors at the airport. This provides a chance to visit and to discuss the program.

Upon arriving at the training site, participants are made welcome and are assured that things have been well planned and are in good order. Each participant finds a short, personal note at the check-in desk welcoming him or her to the program and inviting him or her to the social hour and dinner at a specified time and location. Directions are also provided so that the participants do not feel lost or confused. A couple of the early arriving participants meet and decide to take a ride around the area and to visit a few of the local attractions before the formal activities begin. They are provided with courteous directions by a knowledgeable person at the check-in desk. One man from Dubuque arrives without his luggage and is quite upset. The airline he traveled on failed to transfer his baggage during a plane change in Chicago. This is one of the kinds of problems the staff is not surprised to encounter. A call is made to the baggage handling section at the local airport, where a claim report is filed on the missing luggage. They estimate that it will be 8:00 or 9:00 A.M. the next morning before this man's bags can be delivered to the conference center. This isn't much consolation to the participant, but he tries to make the best of it. In the meanwhile one of the training staff offers to drive him to a local drugstore where he may purchase toilet articles. An extra set of pajamas and robe along with other articles of clothing are secured for him to use until his things arrive.

During the remainder of the afternoon things run smoothly. A record is kept of those who have arrived.

By 4:30 P.M. all of the participants and the two instructors who are scheduled to teach for the first few days have arrived. The coordinator breathes a sign of relief and goes to the reception area; the reception is scheduled to begin at 5:00 P.M. There the coordinator finds things are in good hands. One staff member has a well-stocked bar neatly organized; there are plenty of clean glasses and lots of ice.

Five o'clock arrives and a couple of participants stick their heads into the room as if to ask, "Is this the right place?" The coordinator and staff assure them it is and welcome them. By 5:15 most of the guests have arrived. The staff mixes with the crowd to say hello to each. The instructors also mingle with the participants. At 5:45, the coordinator sends an assistant to check on the dining room to make sure that everything is ready for the 6:00 P.M. dinner. He or she notices that the man from Dubuque is pretty well into his third old fashioned and has ceased worrying about his missing luggage.

Six P.M. arrives. Time for dinner. The bar is promptly closed and guests quickly file out of the room and toward the dining room where they are seated. Service begins immediately. The staff and the instructors do not sit together. Instead, they spread out among the participants. By 6:50 the group is just finishing dessert and after-dinner coffee. A few minutes thereafter the coordinator, who is known to all by now, rises and suggests a break. He or she asks the group to assemble in the meeting room, located nearby, at 7:00 P.M., sharp. The group is polite and respectful of the schedule. The participants disperse quickly.

The welcome and orientation is scheduled to be brief and not run longer than 45 minutes. If it is an in-house program, the local top-level manager is present to say a few words of welcome. Her or his presence is very important because it conveys top management's interest and support of the training. The top-manager may speak for 12 to 15 minutes to welcome participants, to explain current problems, plans, policies, and opportunities, and to underscore the importance of the training.

During the orientation, the program coordinator reviews the nature and purposes of the program, the daily schedule, the course subject areas, the work-load demands and expectations, the methods of instruction, and the first assignment and case-study preparation, which is scheduled for that evening. The coordinator also explains the case-study method, what it involves, how it works and the demands it places on learners. She or he also orients participants so they know where the various meeting rooms and other facilities are located and explains the dining schedule and where participants can obtain laundry service and sundries. The coordinator makes a special point of encouraging participants to feel free to consult the staff, or the coordinator, if they have questions or problems. The orientation session concludes at 7:49 P.M., a few minutes later than planned, but no one seems to be restless. One interesting question, posed to the top manager, required a long answer and additional discussion that was not planned, but everyone seemed interested. The participants leave the meeting room with bulging notebooks in hand and head for their respective buzz-group rooms, where they will meet for the next two hours or so to prepare tomorrow's cases.

Later that evening the coordinator and the instructors visit each of the buzz groups individually. They may answer questions and clarify what the groups are supposed to do in their case analyses. They demonstrate, by their presence, the importance of the buzz-group discussions and thorough case analysis and preparation. Their presence also gives participants the feeling that the faculty is working hard and with them to make the learning experience as thorough and fulfilling as possible. A few of the participants ask the instructors to give their views and answers to the questions during their visit. The experienced instructors politely decline, since they know wisdom cannot be told and that the skills of insight, judgment, and analysis must be learned by doing. They jokingly respond to requests for answers with a statement such as, "You wouldn't want your buddies back at the office to find out you get your answers to tough questions from 'eggheads' like me would you?" The participant who asked the question smiles, shaking his head "no" and thinks, "this instructor is O.K."

Frequently, visits to the buzz groups clue instructors in on what to expect from the group the next day. Sometimes what instructors learn here will require them to bone up on one or two additional points for their presentation the next day. Sometimes the visits will forewarn them as to what to expect the next day in class so that they will not be surprised and appear ill-prepared.

THE FIRST DAY OF INSTRUCTION

The following morning finds the coordinator having an early breakfast with three or four early-rising participants. The coordinator and staff will eat all their meals with the group for several reasons: to keep in touch with the participants so as to know their moods and feelings and how they are reacting to the learning and the various discussion leaders; to give participants the feeling that there is someone in charge and running things in an organized way; to provide participants with an outlet to express their needs and feelings and handle their individual problems and requests as they may arise; and to continually keep watch over the food's quality and service.

Midway through the breakfast hour, the discussion leader who will handle the morning session arrives for breakfast. The coordinator joins her or him for another cup of coffee. They chat about the group and eventually agree on several additional modifications to the first session which appear to be appropriate. The coordinator reminds the discussion leader of the coffee break and luncheon schedules. They both know that it is important to keep things running on schedule. These details will be reviewed by the coordinator for each discussion leader who teaches on the program.

It is now thirty minutes before the first morning session is scheduled to begin. The coordinator excuses himself or herself from the breakfast table and heads toward the meeting room. Arriving there he or she discovers that everything is in order except for water pitchers and ash trays and asks an assistant to take care of this right away. The coordinator then double checks on the ventilation and air conditioning. Everything seems to be in order.

A minute or two before the scheduled starting time, the entire group has arrived and all have found their places. The discussion leader has arranged his or her materials and has just finished writing the purposes and objectives of this session on the chalkboard. The coordinator stands before the group joking with several of the participants and answering the questions of others.

Then, as the clock strikes the chimes signifying the starting time, the coordinator formally greets the group. He or she welcomes the participants and the morning's discussion leader and makes several announcements, including the election of class officers that will take place at the end of the formal session the following afternoon. Finally, as she or he introduces the discussion leader, the coordinator stresses the discussion leader's academic contributions and practical experiences. She or he brings out those things about the discussion leader that the participants will value most and will give them the feeling that the discussion leader is competent and credible and will provide them with useful ideas and insights.

The time taken for making announcements and introducing the discussion leader is brief, lasting only 5 to 10 minutes. These things completed, the coordinator takes a seat at the back of the room. She or he will sit here throughout most of the program to keep an eye on how the learning progresses and to be alert to any problems the participants may have in understanding or accepting the ideas and concepts taught. The coordinator observes each session so that she or he knows what has been covered and how it has been treated as the program unfolds. Some may argue, and for very good reasons, that the coordinator should not appear to be checking up too closely on the various discussion leaders, who should be treated as the professionals they are. There are, however, several benefits to be derived from sitting in throughout the entire program:

1. It gives the coordinator a better idea as to exactly what has been covered in each session than he or she would get if hearing about it second-hand.

2. By knowing what has been covered, and how it has been received, the coordinator can do a good job of briefing subsequent discussion leaders to tie the program's subject matter together.

3. It gives the coordinator a basis to judge the teaching effectiveness of each speaker.

4. It allows the coordinator an opportunity to keep a close watch on the group's learning as it progresses and a first-hand knowledge of what the participants might be talking about as they discuss what occurred in class.

5. It demonstrates to the group that the coordinator is one of them and is available and approachable.

The beginning session of the program is entitled the *Work of the Manager*. The aims of this session are: to give participants an overall picture of the roles and responsibilities of the manager; to let them see how their views of management compare with others; and to suggest areas where each participant might profit through improving. In this first session, participants learn about some of their values and beliefs regarding management. This is accomplished by means of a case study and a couple of short, written exercises.

The discussion leader spends 15–20 minutes at the beginning of his or her session explaining what will be covered and how it will be done. The discussion leader "warms" the group so that they will be receptive to what he or she will teach. Next the discussion leader gives a short lecture and an overview of the content and then turns to the participants' case analyses and presentations. He or she listens to each report, makes appropriate comments, and raises thought provoking questions. The last case-study report is concluded on schedule. Coffee and rolls have arrived and everything is ready for the morning break. The coordinator has checked that all is in order and signals the discussion leader it is time to stop for coffee.

The remainder of the day runs as planned. A few of the participants spend the recreational period just before dinner on the tennis courts, while most of the others find refreshment in the nearby, inviting pool.

The evening social hour runs from 5:00–6:00 P.M. A few of the participants arrive at the social hour somewhat disturbed over what was covered in the day's sessions. They speak about how impractical the ideas they heard discussed seem to them and how they probably wouldn't apply where they work. The coordinator, staff, and discussion leaders are prepared for this. They know that it can be very disturbing and upsetting for someone, particularly a dogmatic person, to have ideas challenged and to learn about how some of her or his values and attitudes cause her or him to perceive things and perform the job as a manager in ways unlike most of the other successful managers who are there. To this person, these revelations are challenging to the self-image which she or he, in turn, strives to maintain. Thus it is not unusual for these people who are challenged and upset to be critical of the program and its instructors, or to argue with the staff or the instructors, or to withdraw and avoid contact, or to complain about the work load and reading assignments, or to drink more than they normally do, or to exhibit any number of what many would consider to be irrational behaviors.

One of the main reasons for having a social hour before dinner each night is to provide an outlet for the expression of these feelings. One giant in the field of executive development said, in support of the value of the nightly social hour, "All day long the participants are getting clobbered and challenged by the instructors. Their ideas are challenged and held up to scrutiny. Their most dearly held beliefs are shaken. The social hour, then, is a time for the tables to be turned, where the participants can 'clobber' the faculty and unleash their disgruntled feelings on those who evoked them. It is a good time to clear the air." This thinking is known and accepted by the coordinator, staff, and all instructors. And each is prepared to handle these expressions of irrational, emotional behavior in the best possible way—that is, by listening and understanding and neither agreeing nor disagreeing. This is what Rogers and Roethlisberger (1952) say is the most powerful way to change deep-seated, fixed, emotional opinions. It is nondirective counseling and the coordinator and staff are skilled at it. If they were to argue with the participants as they express their emotional reactions, learning and change would be minimal. Rogers and Roethlisberger (1952, p. 47) write, "If I can listen to what he can tell me, if I can understand how it seems to him, if I can see its personal meaning for him, if I can see the emotional flavor which it has for him, then I will be releasing potent forces of change in him." By listening with understanding and by reflecting the feelings participants express, the coordinator and staff release potent forces of change. When participants can get those things that bother and upset them off their chests, then and only then will they be willing to accept new ideas and concepts and abandon old ones with which the new ideas conflicted. And thus individual growth and development occurs.

Dinner that first evening runs as scheduled. At a few minutes after 7:00, the participants are in their buzz groups and hard at work discussing and preparing their analyses of the cases for the following day. And again, as was done the previous evening, as it will be the pattern every evening, the coordinator, staff, and the instructors spend a few minutes individually visiting each buzz group.

During the evening the coordinator also makes a point of telephoning each of the next day's speakers who are not staying overnight with the group to remind them of their next day's assignment and to brief them on the group and what has gone on up until then.

Later that evening the coordinator and staff, and very likely the instructors who taught that day, gather to review how things are progressing. They go over the schedule, the service, the rooms, the meals, the supplies, what went on during the day's sessions, and most importantly the participants. They review their observations of each participant and ask the following kinds of questions: How is she or he reacting to the program? How is she or he adjusting to the schedule? Is he or she participating actively in the buzz-group discussions and in the formal class sessions during the day? Is he or she fitting in with the group or is he or she a loner? These meetings will be held every three or four days. During them, decisions might be made to adjust the schedule, change the menu somewhat, make alterations in the program's content as the needs and interests of the group dictate, change things that will increase group cohesiveness or effectiveness, counsel particular individuals who need help adjusting or accepting the course, or bring the loners or isolates into the group so they are part of it, etc.

This attention to how well participants are fitting into the group and responding to the learning is given because the coordinator and staff see effective management training as both an intellectual and emotional experience with the latter aspect being their prime concern. Unlike most other disciplines which involve merely acquiring knowledge, management education also involves the teaching of certain skills and personal characteristics as explained in Chapter 2. The knowledge, skills and personal characteristics (behaviors) taught are frequently novel and contrary, even sharply contradictory, to those held and practiced by participants. The willingness to understand, accept, and put into practice these new approaches does not come easily. Traditional teaching methods and educational philosophies are ineffective at this task. Instead, self-discovery with encouragement and support from a closely knit group are the keys. As long as the group is cohesive and all participants feel a part of it, the group will be influential in helping its members to learn and accept what is taught.

THE DAYS THAT FOLLOW

The second full day of the program runs according to the previous day's schedule. The coordinator and staff have developed a routine with which they now feel comfortable, one they will maintain throughout the program.

As planned, the group elects class officers at the end of the second day of classes—a president, a vice-president, and an activities coordinator. There will be a special announcement and congratulations party for these people during the evening social hour. The election of officers is an important step in developing a strong, effective, cohesive group. It places those who have emerged as informal leaders into conspicuous positions of influence which the others have acknowledged through their votes. It helps the group feel more like a group. It legitimatizes the leadership actions that these emergent leaders might not be so inclined to take were they not elected. It gives the group members a few "inside people" to whom they can voice their feelings and complaints, and who in turn can approach the program coordinator as the group's representatives with regards to anything from food and schedule to work load and teaching quality. These roles and responsibilities are outlined and discussed by the coordinator with the newly elected group of officers later that evening. Moreover, the coordinator solicits their assistance in observing the other participants and in helping each one to become and feel a part of the group.

One of the discussion leaders finishes the last session he or she is scheduled to teach on the program at the conclusion of the second day's classroom activities. The coordinator has arranged with an assistant to drive the discussion leader to the airport. But before the two depart, the coordinator gives the discussion leader a check for his or her services, along with a form that details travel expenses. It is important to pay people for their services as soon as possible.

The third full day of the program begins with a few announcements made by the group's newly elected leaders during the first few minutes of the morning class session. A golf tournament, they announce, is being planned for next Saturday afternoon and a few other members of the group want to get tickets for an upcoming concert. Arrangements for these and other activities start to shape up.

The remainder of the third day goes as planned, following the established daily schedule, but the emotional tone of the group shows evidence of negative feelings. A few of the participants have voiced strong differences of opinion regarding some of the things the discussion leaders said and with a few of the ideas contained in the reading materials. Most of these remarks, however, have been made among the group members outside of class. But at one point in the third day's afternoon session, a particularly disgruntled and vocal participant openly challenged the discussion leader. Many of the participants are complaining that the schedule is too demanding, that there is just too much work, and the case studies are too long. Some complain that they feel that they are not getting straight answers and that the faculty discussion leaders should simply tell them how to manage and handle the cases instead of bothering them with long and tiring case-study assignments where they have to figure out the answers themselves. Some participants are even bothered because they feel that the case method is too vague and never concludes anything definite and concrete.

By the time the social hour arrives that evening the participants feel they are unanimous in their dissatisfaction. They are beginning to joke among themselves more than they did the evening before. Some even go beyond their normal limit of drinks. Silently, the word is passed among the group that there will be a late meeting for all participants after the buzz-group work to voice complaints to the class officers who will, in turn, bring these to the attention of the coordinator.

The coordinator and staff are neither surprised nor unaware that this occurs. They do not try to put a stop to it. They do not pretend it doesn't exist. Instead, they have planned on it happening and are fully prepared to handle it. They know that the case-study method causes discomfort because it forces participants to analyze complex situations and to decide on courses of action which will be subjected to scrutiny by the teacher and members from the other buzz groups in class the next day. Instead of teaching entirely content, the program is designed to teach processes as well. In fact the course is about one-third content and about two-thirds process. The latter involves such things as awareness of self and others, how to analyze management situations, how to be creative in generating alternative courses of action, and how to present ideas clearly and convincingly. The skills of insight, judgment, and decision making are sharpened. And all these things are learned the only way they can be learned, by experience followed by evaluative critique that is frequently aggravating and painful.

These negative reactions and expressions of dissatisfaction are signals which tell the coordinator that two important things have occurred: (1) the participants are beginning to understand the content taught, and (2) they are working hard in their buzz groups and profiting from this experience. It is critical for the coordinator to assure that this learning continues and the development process is furthered. If the coordinator fights the expressed feelings of dissatisfaction, she or he will stop the learning process and quite likely cause a revolt which might take the form of the group refusing to do the assignments and individuals attending only those classes they feel like going to. If the coordinator gives in completely to the group's demands to make things easier and lighten the work load by eliminating cases and reading material, the participants will be short changed by receiving a flimsy learning experience. This would be like designing a bridge and trying to build it leaving out half the required parts. The coordinator must avoid these two extremes. Instead, she or he has to let the participants know that she or he understands how they feel and will stand beside them and work with them and provide support and encouragement as they continue with the processes of learning and individual growth and development. And the coordinator has to continue to build a strong group that will maintain a climate for continued learning and experimentation with new ideas and behaviors and that will also provide encouragement and support to its members as they do this. Thus the participants should take a share of the responsibility for their own development.

At breakfast the next morning, the class officers make a point of sitting with the coordinator at a private table which has been arranged. Here they can talk without interruption. They exchange a few polite pleasantries at first as if to say, "We are really nice people." Then they get on with what they want to say to the coordinator. They explain that the group has expressed dissatisfaction with some of the things that have gone on. They try to make it plain that they all like the coordinator and appreciate all his or her effort. They say they like the program, generally speaking, and see that it has tremendous value. But they are unhappy about some of the concepts and those who taught them. And they feel the work load is too stiff. Throughout all this the coordinator listens attentively. He or she feeds back what is heard and sensed and promises to go to work on their grievances. Breakfast ends on a pleasant note. The officers feel good because the coordinator listened to what they had to say. Deep down they feel that she or he is genuinely and sincerely dedicated to making the program the best it can possibly be. As a consequence they are inclined to work with the coordinator and be supportive of his or her decisions and actions.

The morning session has purposely been scheduled to allow time for the coordinator to discuss with the group how they feel about the program and their learning to date. This time slot is specifically reserved, although not announced to the group, as a time when the coordinator can remove the obstacles to self-analysis and experimentation with new concepts and behaviors. It is a time when new group norms of openness, trust, and the willingness to experiment with the course content emerge and, hopefully, will become accepted. To do this, the coordinator begins the morning session with an announcement that the scheduled topic will be reorganized and condensed to make time for more important matters.

The coordinator levels with the entire group about the breakfast meeting with the class officers and compliments them on their directness and frankness. This not only builds greater respect for these leaders and further legitimizes their role, but it also serves to establish the norm of openness and honesty. The coordinator goes on and reflects to the entire group what the leaders told him or her and how he or she senses they and others in the group feel. By so doing, the coordinator demonstrates to the entire group that he or she is interested in and values what they have to say, is concerned and cares about their feelings, is willing to listen and work out the problem, and accepts and respects their views and feelings. Next the coordinator talks briefly about the nature of the subject matter and how complex and subtle it is and how it is a discipline where there are no perfect answers. She or he again makes a plea for the group to consider all different methods and philosophies and to be open to the benefits they might bring, as well as to their problems and drawbacks. She or he reviews the nature of the case method and reemphasizes its value in the teaching process as opposed to the acquisition of content. The latter is what most people, because of their previous experiences with education, equate with learning.

Then the coordinator gets to the heart of the message—i.e., resistance to the learning. She or he talks about the tendency people have to reject or resist new ideas and practices and tells about different forms of resistance by giving examples of it from his or her personal life and from family and friends. This is done in a personal, down-to-earth manner and not in a pedantic, theoretical, condescending way. The coordinator goes on to ask the participants to think about how they are resisting the program's content. By this time, the group is beginning to relax. They feel, "This person is honest and direct. We can be direct and level with him or her now, too."

Sensing that the group is with her or him, the coordinator suggests that it would be a good time for the group to level and make known how they feel about the program and their learning to date. To do this, the coordinator asks everyone to take out a piece of paper and respond anonymously to the following questions, which are written on the chalkboard.

1.   What do you like most about the program?

2.   What do you like least or dislike about the program?

3.   How do you feel about your learning progress to date?

4.   How or in what ways have I (a participant) resisted the content? That is, what have I done to show my resistance?

5.   Write anything else you wish to make known to the program coordinator.

The coordinator asks the group to work on this exercise, giving them 20–30 minutes. Nearly everyone eagerly gets to work on the assignment. One or two others who do not quite feel the same as the majority and who appear to scoff at "all this nonsense," sit with somewhat bored expressions and idly scratch out a few lines. The others feverishly fill their papers with pent-up feelings, so eager are they to release and make them known.

As the last person finishes writing, the coordinator collects the papers and places them in a pile on the table in the front of the room. One person pipes up, "Are you really going to read them?" The coordinator smiles and says, "Yes. Right now. Aloud." One by one, the coordinator reads aloud the participants' comments. He or she does so with empathy and genuineness. Never does he or she rebut or disagree with or play down what someone has written. The coordinator neither agrees nor disagrees with what is read and shows neither shock nor embarrassment. He or she does not become annoyed or angry. The coordinator simply reads aloud what the participants have written.

Nearly everyone writes something positive about the program. There is overwhelming support for it. A majority of the papers report one or more criticism. Some are stated bluntly. Most everyone expresses the feeling that he or she is learning something important at the program. However, many go on to say that they want something "more practical," something they can use back on the job. What they are really asking for here are answers to the problems they have struggled with for years and with which they will probably have to live for a long time simply because these problems are too large and too complex to handle or possibly because they are simply unsolvable.

The responses participants give to the question "How have I resisted the course content?" bring on a new dimension of honesty and openness to the program. They also are the source of humorous relief to an otherwise emotionally charged ordeal. A few of the comments made are comical, even laughable, and the group seizes upon this opportunity for laughter as an outlet. One woman writes that she has resisted some of the concepts taught by refusing to read the assigned reading material. Another participant says that he showed his resistance by overdrinking at the social hour. Two others admit to the noisy, early-morning prank of rolling empty soft-drink bottles down the stairs of the lodge. A few others say that they showed their resistance by refusing to sit and eat with the discussion leader, who was "tough" on their case study analysis and conclusions the day before. Although seemingly childish, these kinds of behaviors are not unusual for mature, responsible, successful, highly respected executives, so intense are their reactions to the learning experience.

The expression of feelings brings a sense of relief to the group. It gets participants to see that they have been resisting some of the program content and that they are not alone or unique in how they feel. It allows participants to take a look at themselves in a nonthreatening way and maybe even laugh a bit at what they see. In short, this experience "clears the air." Unbelievable as it may seem to many, it works almost like magic in transforming a hostile, upset, irrational emotional climate to one that is positive, calm, and rational. Yet, most importantly, this "air-clearing" experience removes the forces that can prevent participants from understanding and accepting new ideas and from changing to become even more effective managers.

Last, the coordinator turns to some of the requests she or he has received to reduce the work load. These have suggested eliminating case-study and reading assignments and reducing the number of formal sessions. The coordinator asks how hard the group members work at their jobs back home. All admit that they put in 9 to 12 hours each day. He asks them if the work load of the seminar is really "that" tough. Most, now that the air is clear, answer they don't think so. The coordinator goes on to make an appeal for the need to have a learning experience that is meaningful and complete; one that has enough substance to cause meaningful and lasting change and improvement. He or she uses the analogy of trying to build a bridge with only some of the specified parts and then expecting it to work as it should. They all agree with the coordinator on this point. Finally, she or he appeals to the group to go along with the plan as other groups in previous sessions of the program have. This last appeal causes an emergent leader of the group to say, "If other groups in the past could handle this work load, we sure the hell can too." Others quickly agree. The group quickly rallies to meet the challenge to work at least as hard, if not harder, than previous groups. Thus a new norm—namely, hard work—emerges and becomes an important determinant of each person's good standing within the group.

At lunch following the morning gripe session there are no obvious signs of dissatisfaction. The members of the group appear to have positive attitudes toward the program and its content and instructors. A few even compliment the coordinator on what she or he did that morning. Many others remark on how well the remainder of the morning session went. A few have asked about the evening's buzz-group assignment, as if to say, "We are really going to work hard from now on."

During the next several days the program runs pretty much as planned. The coordinator maintains the pace of the program and continues to oversee all the important details. He or she clips from the daily newspapers and other periodicals current events which are pertinent to the various topics and sessions. By bringing current news and illustrations of concepts relevant to the program, he or she gives participants the feeling that the program is up to date and not just a canned course that everyone else in the past has had. Instead, it is fresh, new, alive; it is as up-to-date and abreast of the times and the field as possible. And to many executives, this is a valued attribute for a program to have.

Each instructor who teaches receives a thorough briefing from the coordinator on what has occurred at the program to date, the characteristics and mood of the group, the content that has been covered and how it has been received, the interests and needs the group members have voiced that they have, and what content will be coming up later in the program. The coordinator may suggest one or two changes in the discussion leader's assignment or presentation depending upon the group's needs.

The coordinator and staff are present throughout the entire program. They are available to the participants to provide them with information, to solve minor problems, and to give them the feeling that everything is running under control. The coordinator and staff work to make sure participants are not burdened with other matters and thus unable to devote their full attention and energies to the program.

Two or three days before the conclusion of the program the coordinator begins plans for the participants' return home. She or he learns, for instance, that most of the participants who came by air will need boxes in which they can pack the course books and notebooks and other items they purchased for their families since they have no more room in their suitcases. He or she has planned for this request and already has a supply of sturdy cardboard boxes and packaging tape and twine.

Each participant provides the coordinator's staff with his or her travel plans home. Transportation arrangements are then made to provide transportation to the airport for all who need a ride. These and any other similar kinds of courtesies, remove concern from the minds of the participants, which allows them to concentrate more completely on the program.

THE LAST DAY

The final day of the program is scheduled to begin at the usual, morning starting time. The final session, entitled, *Future Managerial Challenges and Self-Development Plans to Meet These* will run until the morning coffee break. After the break, the coordinator will talk for 30–45 minutes to summarize the major themes and messages covered during the program. When this is concluded, participants will have approximately an hour to complete a course evaluation form. A graduation luncheon and presentation-of-certificates ceremony will follow.

The experienced, guiding hand of the coordinator is evident as each of the scheduled last-day events runs according to plan. The graduation ceremony is a warmly received highlight of the program. It provides the participants with recognition for their accomplishment of completing a rigorous course and an exhilarating learning experience. Each person is justifiably proud.

The ceremony ends on time and the group members begin to shake hands and say goodby. Cars are ready and loaded to whisk away to the airport two or three who are scheduled to depart on early afternoon flights. The coordinator finishes saying goodby to a few others who want to chat for a short while after lunch.

Now the participants have all departed. The coordinator begins the process of getting equipment and supplies back to where they came from. Tables and chairs, audio-visual equipment, extra books and notebooks and papers must be stored or filed in their proper places. This takes the better part of the afternoon.

That evening the coordinator feels a little lonesome for those with whom she or he had come accustomed to seeing and talking with every day for the past few weeks and seems at quite a loss for what to do. He or she reviews the comments the participants made on their program evaluation forms. These reassure him or her that the course was successful and well received. The coordinator also notices several suggestions which will help improve the program the next time it is presented. These evaluation forms will be tabulated and summarized by staff members and will be included in a brief report on the program, which she or he will write during the next several days.

AFTER THE PROGRAM

On the first business day following the conclusion of the program the coordinator sends a personalized letter to each participant. In the letter, he or she thanks the participants for their contributions to the program and wishes them well as they apply the concepts gained from the course on their jobs. These letters are a gesture made by the coordinator not only to say "thank-you" and "good-bye," but also to build a strong tie of friendship and support for the program and to encourage participants to continue their personal growth and development.

A few days after handling these chores and clearing up several other pressing matters, the coordinator escapes for a few days of much-needed and deserved vacation and rest. The coordinator and the staff are tired. They have been on the go from early to late day after day solving minor problems, checking and double checking on details, and doing whatever needed doing, with scarcely any time for themselves. But the payoff has been worthwhile—a successful program.

REFERENCE

Rogers, Carl R., and Roethlisberger, Fritz J. "Barriers and Gateways to Communication." *Harvard Business Review* 30, No. 4, 1952, pp. 46–52.

7

Getting Management Training to Pay Off

Over the past thirty years, there has been an enormous increase in the amount of management training. As a result, many people have improved their knowledge and understanding of management. Unfortunately, many of the potential benefits these educational experiences can bring are never fully realized because attendees of management training courses and seminars all too frequently apply only a small part of their increased knowledge when they return to their jobs. One approach that promises to help overcome this problem is a method of continuing, on the job, the learning begun in the formal training program. In short, this approach consists of assisting managers learn how to increase their skill in diagnosing situations and to apply the management theories and contingent principles learned at the training program in their work situations.

Whereas the understanding and acceptance of concepts and contingent principles can generally be advanced to satisfactory levels during a formal training program, the ability to be consistently successful in applying them typically cannot. It is extremely difficult for practicing managers to acquire adequate skill and competence in the application of management theories and generalizations anywhere else but on the job.

THE PAYOFF: CASE HISTORIES OF HOW
MANAGERS APPLIED WHAT THEY LEARNED

Part of a two-week supervisory management course conducted for first- and second-level supervisors of an internationally known United States corporation was an assignment for each participant to identify a problem, apply the appropriate principles and concepts learned at the course to solve it, and report on the results. Based on actual reports, here are some examples of how several of these supervisors were successful in applying what they had learned.

Clarence H. found that goal setting and motivation go hand in hand. People are motivated when they are working to reach clear cut goals and their progress is reported back to them regularly so they can see what they have accomplished (Likert 1961).

When Clarence returned to work after participating in the first week of the Supervisory Management Program, he began communicating the importance of goals to his people. He discussed how well his group had been reaching goals in the past and announced the goals for each day of the upcoming month. These goals he posted daily.

At the end of the first day, his group produced 14 percent below the established goal of 17,000 board feet per shift, but the next few days showed improvement. On the last day of the first week, his men produced only 2.9 per cent below the goal for that day. And then, half way through the second week, his group surpassed the daily goal by ½ per cent.

Clarence reported that goal setting did a lot to lift the morale and motivation of his people and increased their interest in production. Frequently they ask, "How are we doing? Are we going to make our target today?" Clarence believes that within a few more months his people will be ready and able to set their own production goals and suggest improvements in how to reach these more easily and economically.

Ben P. applied the concepts of work planning, communications, motivation and group participation in the overhaul of a Harnischfeger, Model 2100, 15-yard shovel. In his report Ben stated, "The whole principle of this project was to encourage everyone involved . . . salaried bosses, five-day bosses, and the men to work together to reach one goal . . . to overhaul the shovel in 38 days."

Ben worked out an initial plan to overhaul the shovel using the Gantt Chart technique. He then gathered his people together to enlist their ideas and suggestions. Here is what Ben writes, "I held a meeting with all of my bosses and explained the complete plan to them. They were not only very interested, but volunteered all of their help and cooperation required in order to make the project succeed. Next, I called in the men who would be working on this project and explained the details of this plan to them. They were told that if they needed further information, not to be afraid to come in and talk it over. It was quite surprising how the men took to this. When a question was raised, they came in and talked it over. As the project continued, the chart was plotted from day to day. Progress was reported back to the men periodically and meetings were held to discuss problems.

The results of Ben's approach were fantastic. In the past, the average down-time for overhauling this type of shovel had been sixty days. Ben's initial plan cut the time to 38 days. Amazingly, his people beat this plan by 8 days. Thus Ben got the shovel back into operation in 30 days instead of the normal sixty. When operating at full capacity this machine will dig an average of 12,000 to 16,000 tons of material per eight hour shift. Ben's efforts amounted to a savings of well over $90,000.

Jim F. was successful in helping two of his men who had excessive absences. One man had been absent for 51 out of the last 305 shifts, or about one day in six.

Talking with each man privately, Jim started out by having *them tell him* about any of their personal problems that would cause them to be absent from work. He *didn't* judge what they said by telling them their excuses were "no good." Rather, he let them tell him how they felt. By using communications skills (Rogers et al. 1952), he allowed these men to express their feelings and, by so doing, he conveyed his sincere interest in them.

After having the opportunity to express their feelings, the men were ready to hear what Jim had to say. Very calmly, Jim explained to each man the importance of their jobs. He showed them how they fit into the operation and the important roles they played. Next, he turned to another very important matter—money. Using simple arithmetic, Jim showed each man how much money they lost as a result of their absences. They were surprised.

Seventeen weeks after starting to solve this problem, Jim reported that their absences have fallen to only 2–3 days each over the past four months. He reinforced this good behavior by feeding back to these men what the change has meant to them in terms of dollars and to the company in terms of produc-tion.

Jim B. found success in orienting a new employee. Knowing that a new man was to be assigned to him, he prepared himself by reading over the recom-mended procedures for orientation. The next day this is what he did.

In the changehouse before work, he introduced the new man to those with whom he would be working. Then, on the way to the job, he found out about the new man's background including his past jobs and interests. Upon getting to the job, Jim explained to the new man what he would be doing and how this work fit into the overall mission. He also emphasized the importance of the new man's work. Jim knew that there were just too many new things for the new man to learn all in one day and that the first day for any new person is confusing. So, Jim focused his efforts on reducing the new man's anxiety, giving him encouragement, and creating a climate where he would feel free to ask questions (Gommersall et al. 1966). It took several days, plus some follow up on Jim's part by asking the new man's co-workers how he was coming along.

The results were as could be expected. The man fit in well and has been doing a good job from the start.

Claude H. found that a good way to build motivation is to give recognition for good work. Claude was using a well-established principle from psychology—"The law of effect" (Thorndike 1912). This is a principle formulated by Thorndike. It says, in part, that people will tend to continue to behave in those ways in which they are rewarded.

One of the underground miners working for Claude had done an especially fine job of timbering and Claude took the time to look over the work and compliment him on it, saying, "That's a good job." Claude reported that this individual really brightened up. He told Claude, "That's the first time anyone ever said that. Nobody ever cared before." Claude reported that the man's motivation and morale showed definite signs of improvement from that time on.

PROBLEMS MANAGERS FACE WHEN APPLYING RECENTLY LEARNED THEORIES AND CONTINGENT PRINCIPLES ON THE JOB

Unlike the performance of manual skills, the practice of management does not require precision in following rather specific, well-defined procedures. Instead it involves the application of many subtle, complex concepts and theories in real-life situations where psychological barriers and human factors are often present. If this were not the case, the teaching of management would be considerably easier and involve nothing more than having people learn to perform prescribed mechanical routines.

The problems described below are the ones found to be the most common reasons why the application of recently learned management theories and principles is so difficult.

Making Theories and Contingent Principles
Operational for Individual Situations

Upon hearing of or learning about management theories and principles, managers frequently ask, "Where can they be applied?" Although they can grasp a concept or theory, they often have difficulty in identifying the particular situations in their own work when they should apply the management knowledge which they already possess and understand. There are no simple solutions to this problem. Every situation is to some extent unique, and the particular circumstances surrounding each will determine when and how a theory or principle can be applied successfully. Beyond the problem of determining when a principle should be applied in a particular situation lies a larger stumbling block. This is, how do you make a theory operational? What are the things you must do in the process of applying it? Attendees of management training programs generally feel that time spent answering these questions is very worthwhile.

Identifying Principles That can be Applied

Another difficulty many managers have after completing a management course is to identify the specific principles, theories, or concepts that were covered. At best, they can vaguely identify only a few; beyond that, their responses to the question, "What concepts and contingent principles did you learn at the seminar that you can apply?" are usually broad statements, such as:

1. A manager should always be working toward goals.

2. I should listen more.

3. Being tough isn't the best way to motivate people.

4. Planning is important.

If training is to cause changed behavior, it is essential that learners know the specific theories and principles which they can and should apply. For this reason, it seems advisable to devote some portion of the formal training program to identifying the specific concepts and contingent principles covered.

Anyone planning and coordinating a management seminar should spend some time during and especially at its conclusion, to obtain participant feedback to discover how well participants can identify the specific principles or generalizations covered. In most cases, the results from this exercise will be valuable aids for seminar leaders to better understand the learning that has taken place and perhaps suggest areas for improvement for future teaching.

Inadequate Drive and Follow-Through

The lack of drive and persistence to follow through and complete tasks is one of the most common human failings. The manager returning from a training program will have to overcome this tendency to procrastinate if she or he is to do a conscientious job of applying newly acquired knowledge (Mee 1969). But in addition to this common human failing, he or she is faced with the distraction of everyday problems and concerns, which usually further divert attention and energies from systematically applying recently learned management knowledge. In the presence of pressure, people generally revert to doing their work and coping with problems in the ways in which they have in the past. It is generally when people are free from pressure or are completely convinced that their old ways of solving problems are not effective that they will experiment, trying out new approaches.

Level of Understanding

An adequate level of understanding of theories and principles is necessary for their correct and successful application. Ideally, this is accomplished at the formal training program. However, this end might not be completely achieved for every principle that an individual might wish or need to apply. In these cases, or in situations where a person's understanding recedes over time through forgetting, additional learning must be continued after the formal program.

Unwillingness to Try Out New Knowledge

Managers may be unwilling to believe that the theories and principles they learned at a training program will actually work. This is especially true in cases where there are sharp contradictions between these theories and the manager's values and attitudes. It is also true if these managers have been relatively successful in their jobs using methods considerably different from the ones they have just learned. Unwillingness to try out recently learned management theories and principles can also be caused by a lack of self-confidence on the part of the manager that he or she can successfully apply the newly learned concepts.

Negative Attitudes

The challenge posed by negative attitudes held by superiors, peers, subordinates, and even the trainees themselves toward newly acquired knowledge and attempts at its application can be a most formidable one. Negative attitudes often give rise to social pressure which can be an extremely strong force in controlling and modifying behavior. This type of social pressure can completely shut off a person's attempts to apply new ideas, or at least quickly stop her or him from trying to apply these ideas over an extended period. Here are some of the more common ways in which negative attitudes toward a manager's acquisition and application of newly acquired management knowledge can arise.

1.   Superiors and peers may develop negative attitudes toward a person's training if they feel that they have been ignored by higher management and will not have the same or similar opportunity to attend a training program.

2.   Superiors might be caused to feel insecure and become negative if their subordinates attend management development programs and they do not. In these situations, supervisors often feel that subordinates have learned about recently developed management theories and practices which they do not yet know. This can be uncomfortable for these superiors.

3.   Negative attitudes can also develop if those receiving the training return to work and openly discuss ideas and concepts learned at the program, which superiors and peers neither understand nor agree with.

4.   Subordinates of individuals who have attended a management training program might sometimes suspect that their bosses have learned devious ways

to manipulate them. This can cause negative attitudes which might lead to their uncooperative behavior.

5.   Subordinates can develop negative attitudes toward their superiors if they attempt to apply newly acquired knowledge too quickly or abruptly, before they are ready to accept and adjust to the new methods.

Near the conclusion of the formal training program, time should be spent on increasing participants' understanding of these sources of negative attitudes and how to prevent and deal with them.

Obvious actual negative attitudes sometimes occur, but they are not nearly as common as imagined negative attitudes. In one company, where all first- and second-level supervisors (about 120) completed a two-week supervisory management course, the author conducted a post-program survey to study the impact the training had. In the course of this survey, the remark, "I'd like to apply what we discussed, but my boss keeps me from it," was encountered on numerous occasions. Each time this or a similar comment was made the person was asked, "Tell me, how does your boss prevent you from applying what you learned at the program?" Not a single one of those interviewed had an answer. Most simply replied, "I don't know." Inquiring further each was asked, "Have you ever tried applying what you learned and found either direct or indirect disapproval from your boss?" None had.

One conclusion that might be drawn from this experience is that imagined disapproval from one's superior can be just as effective in modifying behavior as actual, outright disapproval. Subordinates, interested in building and preserving a favorable image of themselves in the bosses' eyes, will often be very sensitive to their superiors' methods and opinions. Thus subordinates often try to emulate these as they manage.

It is hard to believe that this conclusion fully explains the existence of the imagined negative attitudes. Perhaps the statements claiming disapproval from superiors was more of an excuse for the subordinates' lack of motivation to practice what they learned than an identification of an influence over which they had no control. Or it might be their own resistance to recently learned theories and principles. Some people, unable or unwilling to publicly reject the content of a training session, do so by cutting off the application step. They show their resistance or rejection to the idea by stopping when the time arrives to apply the learning. They say, "It's all theory. It won't work here."

Discouragement

The skillful application of management theories and principles is not easily acquired. Many repeated attempts at applying any particular theory or principle are often needed before an adequate mastery is reached. This can be discouraging in the early stages of learning and may even lead people to the incorrect conclusion that the principle failed because it is not valid. People returning fresh from management training programs should be prepared to encounter only partial success at applying their new knowledge as they begin using it. Moreover, they should be prepared to overcome possible discouragement and be willing to learn from their own mistakes.

A SYSTEM FOR TEACHING APPLICATION

One system which has been found successful for teaching application of management theory consists of three phases: (1) formal seminar training, (2) a procedure to follow for applying principles on the job, and (3) assistance and support while making the effort to apply. This system contains a variety of methods specifically aimed at overcoming the problems described earlier. It is also designed to provide a framework and climate to stimulate and promote on-going learning and application of good management practices when one returns to the job from classroom training.

Formal Seminar Training

The training seminar is the first step in this learning process. In the classroom, participants cannot only learn about and come to understand concepts and contingent principles, but they can learn to accept and believe in them too. For this deep-seated learning to occur, the practical value of the theories and generalizations taught must be convincingly illustrated so that trainees can accept them as having utility and in particular situations even being superior to their old methods of managing. In addition to this, the following should occur at the training seminar so that participants may become more able to diagnose situations and apply the concepts taught.

1.   Heavy emphasis should be given to teaching diagnostic and problem-solving skills and to the personal characteristics which enable and encourage managers to perform thorough diagnoses of situations and apply concepts and contingent principles successfully. To neglect these two areas is to invite failure for the management development process.

2.   The teaching of each topic must contain illustrations, similar to the ones in this chapter, of how other managers have applied the concepts being taught.

3.   Part of the formal seminar should include opportunities for participants to think about and discuss how they might apply the principles and theories which they are learning. Participants should be permitted to practice applying their new knowledge in simulated exercises during the formal seminar, too.

4.   Principles being taught should be specifically identified. This can be done by the program coordinator, by the discussion leaders, or better still, by the participants themselves. Suggestions and aids for on-the-job application of each principle should be provided also. The list of principles and suggestions for their application should be reproduced and distributed at the end of the

formal program. Table 7-1 gives several examples of contingent principles and suggestions for their application.

Table 7-1. Suggestions for applying contingent principles. (From Charles E. Watson, "Getting Management Training to Pay Off," *Business Horizons,* January–February 1974. Reprinted by permission.)

Contingent principle or generalization	Suggestions for application
Setting management objectives	*How to establish objectives*
Management should be goal-oriented. Without objectives there is no logical basis for action. Objectives should, therefore, be established.	1. Identify the major missions of your organizational unit by identifying why it exists, the purpose it serves, and role it should play within the total organization.
	2. Identify each specific end result that your organizational unit is responsible for accomplishing.
	3. An end result is a future condition that you would like to see prevail. Carefully think through what it should be like.
	4. Describe each of the following desired future conditions in writing. Make sure these descriptions are:
	a) Organizationally appropriate— a future condition that should logically be caused to exist by your organizational unit
	b) Attainable—within reach but challenging
	c) Specific—clear not confusing or ambiguous
	d) Measurable—written in quantifiable terms or established professional standards
	e) Coordinated—consistent with other objectives set in the organization
Employee induction and training	*How to induct a new employee*
It is important that new employees be properly inducted so that they have a good attitude toward you, their work, and the company.	1. Learn all you can about the person— skills, interests, experience, past work, etc.

Table 7-1. *cont'd.*

Contingent principle or generalization	Suggestions for application

2. Let her or him know what is expected—rules, policies, work expectations, standards, etc.

3. Explain how this job fits into the whole operation and acquaint him or her with the overall operation. Stress the importance of his or her job.

4. Assign a sponsor for the new employee.

5. Keep in close contact with the new employee. Discuss the employee's progress with her or him in a helpful way.

6. Encourage the new employee to talk out any problems and do your best to see that they are solved.

7. Deal with discipline problems before they become bad habits.

8. Reduce the new employee's anxiety by explaining that chances for success are quite good. Help the new employee to feel that his questions are welcome.

Decision making

It is not easy to make the "best" decision, the one that best serves to advance or achieve the goals of the organization. It should be the choice that will bring the greatest profit, the highest productivity, the surest gain, the least cost, etc.

How to make a decision

1. Always keep the goals of your organization in mind when confronted with a decision, no matter how small.

2. Try to develop all the possible alternative solutions, courses of action, choices, etc. If appropriate, seek assistance from your subordinates and peers to do this.

3. Think through to identify the probable consequences for each alternative.

4. Rank the probable consequences in the order of their desirability.

Table 7-1. *cont'd.*

Contingent principle or generalization	Suggestions for application
	5. Select the course of action that best serves to advance or achieve the goals of your organization as determined in step 4, above.
Counseling employees	*How to counsel an employee*
Nondirective counseling can release potent forces of change within the individual who receives it.	1. Treat the other person with genuine kindness and respect.
	2. Be prepared to hear unpleasant or confused statements. Don't act startled at what you may hear. Conversely, the employee may be reluctant to talk.
	3. Be aware of the employee's feelings and attitudes in addition to logic. Don't criticize or argue. Be neutral. Don't agree or disagree.
	4. Try to experience what he or she feels. Reflect the employee's feelings, not his or her logic. Don't try to reason with her or him or ask suspicious questions. Just reflect the employee's feelings.

It should be emphasized here that there are definite limits to which these guides suggesting ways for applying management concepts and contingent principles can and should be relied upon. They should be presented and used only as suggestions and not as required prescriptions.

Management is a complex process and should be understood as such by those who practice it. It cannot be boiled down to a set of tidy principles and corresponding easy-to-follow recipes; quite the contrary. The application of management concepts and contingent principles must be adjusted to fit the unique circumstances of every situation.

Surely one of the objectives of any management training program should be for trainees to become more able to bridge the gap between understanding theory and the application of theory in a wide variety of unique situations. Guides suggesting how to apply theories such as the ones presented here should not be set forth as *the* way in which theories should be applied. It is unrealistic, in the first place, to suggest there is only one best way to apply a concept or theory. And, in the second place, if guides are overly relied upon, it might restrict trainees from developing their ability to identify and understand unique parameters of given situations and creatively develop appropriate approaches for the application of management theory in light of them. Instead, suggestions for the application of management principle should only be used as supplemental aids for assisting learning managers in their beginning attempts at applying recently learned knowledge.

A Procedure to Follow for Applying Principles on the Job

Beginning attempts at applying newly learned theories and generalizations can be made easier if trainees have a well-structured procedure to follow. This can provide helpful guidance and motivation by making the process of applying principles easier and less confusing. One approach which has successfully helped managers learn how to apply recently learned management principles and theories consists of the following eight-step assignment. Part of a management training program should include this exercise. A three-hour session during the program should be devoted to explaining and having participants begin working on this assignment.

The assignment

Step 1   Identify a work problem to solve through the application of the appropriate principles and concepts covered in the formal management seminar.

Step 2   Report to the other participants at the seminar the work problem you intend to solve and the principles you intend to apply to solve it.

Step 3   Study the problem you intend to solve. Identify exactly what the problem is. Analyze and identify its causes. Identify more carefully the appropriate principles you think will solve it. Study these principles by reviewing your notes and readings. If your boss, or peers, or both are familiar with the new knowledge which you intend to apply, discuss the problem you have identified and solution you have worked out to solve it with them.

Step 4   Plan the steps you will take in solving the problem through applying the appropriate principle(s).

Step 5   Execute your plan.

Step 6   Carefully observe the results and make notes of these.

Step 7   Analyze the results. Ask yourself what did I learn from this? What did I do well? What should I have done differently, and why? How should I handle problems like this or apply this principle again, in the future?

Step 8   Prepare a report to be delivered to seminar participants at some future date on how you carried out Steps 1–7.

Assistance and Support

The third phase, assistance and support, consists of motivational incentives and methods for overcoming negative attitudes, forgetting, fear, and discouragement. Assistance and support from training and development specialists and higher levels of management helps trainees complete the assignment described above and encourages continued efforts toward situation diagnosis and application of concepts. Lower-level managers are, in general, not as independent and self-starting as top-level managers. As a result, a much smaller proportion do a good job in handling an assignment to apply a principle and report on it. Ths suggests that lower-level managers need a great deal of assistance and support while learning to apply whereas top level managers do not. The assistance and support phase entails the following:

1.   Management training opportunities should be periodically available to all who want them. No one should be left out. It is generally best to start at or near the top levels of the organization with formal training programs. These levels receive training first, the next lower levels next, and so forth down through the organization. By making training available to everyone an attitude is created in the organization that each person can and should improve. This also carries with it the implied message that training and development are company policy. This "message" is supported further by having the top levels of management participate in training before lower levels of management do. The attendance of higher level managers is a signal to those at lower levels that training is important and that it should cause certain changes in their behavior on the job. Moreover, when top-level managers know and understand what "good" management is, they are better able to provide needed guidance to their subordinates as they apply what they too have learned from the same training which their superiors have received. Also, higher levels of managers are likely to be supportive of their subordinate's attempts to practice good management if they (the higher levels) have received management training first.

2.   There should be recognition of and sympathy for the problems typically encountered by returning participants who will attempt to apply what they have learned. Near the conclusion of the formal program, these problems should be described and discussed so that the attendees will be prepared to face them. These include: the challenge to continue to know and understand and believe in concepts and theories learned; the challenge of their own possible negative attitudes (real or imagined) and those of superiors, peers, and subordinates; and the challenge to live with and learn from failures.

3.   Attendees of programs should be encouraged to gather informally (at lunch, for example) when they return to their jobs after the formal seminar, to discuss problems, share experiences, and learn from each other how and where principles can be applied.

4.   Help should be provided to people to continually update their knowledge through having periodic opportunities to attend training programs and seminars of their choice.

5.   Through coaching and counseling, training managers, personnel managers, and willing bosses should assist trainees in carrying out the application assignment and the continued systematic application of principles.

6.   Top management should be kept advised of the assignment to apply principles. They may even be provided with a list of problems each person intends to solve. Top management should communicate its support of this exercise.

7.   Success stories such as the ones at the beginning of this article should be written, based on reports generated. These can be reproduced and distributed, or printed in house organs, or included in management newsletters.

8.   Top mangement should recognize outstanding success stories. This can be done by sending the best ones to key corporate officials to read. Top management may choose to write letters of congratulation in recognition of these success stories. A recognition dinner may even be held once a year to honor the most outstanding success stories as judged by a committee.

TRAINING: NOT AN ISOLATED PROCESS

Training promises to provide immediate and tangible benefits when it includes the teaching of application of management principles and theories on the job and when the application of such receives strong support from top management. Training must be part of a deliberately designed process of organizational development. It cannot, by itself, bring about desired improvements. The organization's norms must be supportive of sound managerial analyses and the application of appropriate concepts and theories. The suggestions outlined here are illustrative of the things the organizational climate should contain and what some of the organizational development activities should include.

REFERENCES

Gommersall, Earl R., and Myers, M. Scott. "Breakthrough in On-The-Job Training." *Harvard Business Review* 44, No. 4, 1966, pp. 62–72.

Likert, Rensis. *New Patterns of Management.* New York: McGraw-Hill, 1961.

Mee, John F. "The Zeigarnik Effect." *Business Horizons* 12, No. 3, 1969, pp. 53–55.

Rogers, Carl L., and Roethlisberger, F. J. "Barriers and Gateways to Communication." *Harvard Business Review* 30, No. 4, 1952, pp. 46–52.

Thorndike, Edward L. *Education.* New York: MacMillan Co., 1912.

8

Evaluating
the Training Effort

From time to time, every training director faces the nagging questions: What has been the impact and value of the training effort? Does training really do any good? Does it modify behavior? Does it help an organization meet its goals? Is it worth the money spent for it? Why is it even done? The answers to these and other questions relating to the impact and values of training are not easily found. And, even when they are found, they are often subject to problems of measurement and subjective interpretations that vary markedly.

The evaluation of training is relatively straightforward when it is in manual production operations, where results and output can be measured in terms of quantity and quality. But management training is different because it involves the development of conceptual and judgment and problem-solving skills and the ability to work with others. While the acquisition or improvement of these kinds of knowledge and skills may lead to increased efficiency and better morale, the causal relationships between learning and improved performance is not easily ascertained. Sometimes a manager's success or failure can be determined by external factors beyond her or his control and thus not be a function of management knowledge and skills at all.

Some people, therefore, prefer not to involve themselves with evaluating the impacts of training at all. Instead, they accept on faith that training is worthwhile. Others believe that when it comes to training, not a penny should be spent unless and until its value can be proven to exceed its cost substantially in terms of concrete measures—preferably dollars and cents.

Both of the extreme positions regarding the evaluation of training just mentioned are lacking. Accepting the value of training simply on the basis of some faith that it is good and worthwhile is downright irresponsible. By neglecting to evaluate his or her endeavors the doer demonstrates that he or she is unconcerned with the quality and significance of his or her work. To accept training as having only so much value as can be scientifically measured in quantitative terms is naive because it says that dollars and cents are all that matter and that one should only act when she or he enjoys complete certainty. This level of certainty simply does not exist in our complex world. Somewhere between these two extremes lies a reasonable approach to the matter of obtaining a sound judgment of the worth of management training. For to evaluate management training is simply this: to assess its value or worth in terms of its overall costs and benefits.

Whether the training effort is evaluated as thoroughly and scientifically as is possible or not deliberately evaluated at all, the evaluation of its overall worth still occurs through those who have decision-making and budget-allocation responsibilities. Hence, because evaluation occurs formally or otherwise, the question need not be raised as to whether to evaluate training. Instead, the question that needs to be answered is, what should be the level of quality and thoroughness of the evaluation? This chapter will not attempt to make a case for evaluation. Most all training directors already appreciate the need for good evaluation. They do, however, frequently encounter difficulties in operationalizing the idea. Therefore, this chapter will suggest how to go about the matter of evaluation intelligently, so as to obtain a correct judgment of the quality of training and its worth in both monetary and non-monetary terms.

EVALUATION: A PHASE OF THE CONTROL PROCESS

At a minimum, it seems reasonable to expect those who teach management to practice sound management themselves. A well-planned and executed control system is an important aspect of good management. Essentially, the control process involves measuring actual performance, comparing it to planned performance or goals, and then taking whatever corrective action is deemed necessary and worthwhile to cause actual performance to conform to that which is planned. Sometimes the control process is future oriented in that it attempts to predict what actual performance will be, before the fact, based upon early warnings, which serve as "leading indicators" or harbingers. This type of control may be more costly and complex, but it does offer the advantage of the chance for early corrections before performance has been completed and irrevocable mistakes have been made.

Control need not always involve identifying and correcting substandard performance. It may also spot performance which exceeds excessively that which is needed and planned. In these instances, modifications may be made so as to reduce the extent and quality of actual performance and thus yield a savings of the resources being devoted to the work or project involved.

The costs of taking corrective actions should always be evaluated in light of the expected benefits. When actual performance falls below planned performance and various corrective actions are contemplated, the question of which one to choose should always be made in light of its costs and the expected benefits. It may be that the benefits derived from bringing substandard performance up to the level planned do not appreciably offset the additional cost required. In these cases, it is wise to revise the performance expectations.

Rarely is one able to forsee all of the eventual consequences, good and bad, at the outset of most any endeavor. Control systems should be concerned with all consequences to some degree and not just those that are identified as initial objectives. Managers should avoid constricting their attention to measuring only the progress made toward initially defined objectives and evaluating the worth of a project in these terms. It may be that more significant consequences result from their work, other than those anticipated and planned for. A well-conceived control system should include an evaluation of these outcomes too.

Figure 8–1 depicts a control system that embodies these ideas. The evaluation of training is only a portion of the entire control system. It involves Steps 2, 3, and 4, while planning essentially involves Steps 5, 6, 7, and 1.

Some may choose to differentiate between validation (i.e., an attempt to ascertain whether training achieved specified behavioral and learning objectives) and evaluation (i.e., the assessment of the total value of training). The usefulness of making such a distinction, however, seems questionable. The concept of evaluation, as it is used here, embodies both of these considerations and seeks to answer essentially three questions.

1. Did the training achieve what it was supposed to achieve?

2. Could the training be done more effectively and efficiently?

3. What has been the overall significance and value of the training?

One of the important messages that this chapter attempts to convey is that evaluation should encompass various outcomes and consequences of training. It should be thorough and systematic. Another important message is that evaluation should not be "tagged-on" to the training effort as an "afterthought." Instead, it should be thought through carefully during the planning phase. It used to be popular in the field of management to refer to planning and controlling as the *Siamese twins of management.* This was meant to convey the idea that a good plan does not exist unless there are good controls and conversely that controls cannot exist in the absence of a plan. The two are inseparable.

By designing the evaluation system during the planning phase of a training course, several benefits result. First, it tends to cause the plan and its implementation to be taken more seriously than it might be otherwise because people tend to respect those things that are inspected. Second, it causes greater

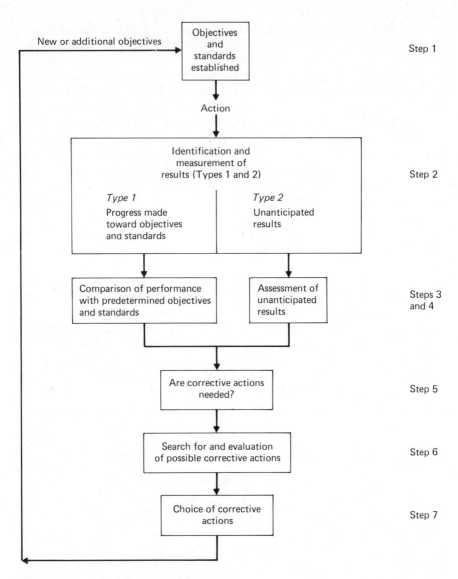

Fig. 8–1. A control-system model.

thought to be taken in establishing program goals and standards. And, when objectives and standards become more specifically defined, better plans can be formulated. This, in turn, increases the likelihood of success. Third, it raises the level of professionalism of the training staff and brings it greater respect and recognition from others. And, last, it increases the likelihood of improvements being made in future training programs because it causes a commitment to inspecting and evaluating results and overcoming the areas of deficiency discovered. Doing this requires that those responsible for the training face up to performance deficiencies, which they might choose to cover up or ignore by not bothering to evaluate them if the evaluation plan were not drawn up until after the training was completed.

WHO WANTS EVALUATION INFORMATION?

When training occurs in an organization, several people or groups of people want information about its evaluation for various reasons. Trainees want information on what and how much they learned and benefited from the training and how they might improve in their work as a result. They also want to know how their perceptions and reactions to the training compare with those of other trainees. They may be eager to pick up on the group's norms, which will influence whether they accept or reject what was taught.

Teachers want evaluation information so they can improve their classroom performance and teaching effectiveness. They want to know what they did or failed to do that trainees liked and enjoyed or disliked and did not enjoy. They want to know to what extent they stimulated the students' enthusiasm and their learning of the material presented. They want to know, specifically, what it was they did or failed to do that led to this level of interest and learning. They want to know which points and messages got across and which ones did not and why. They want to know what it was their students found difficult to grasp and what was easy. And they want to know which teaching methods, examples, and exercises were most stimulating and most productive in causing learning to take place.

Training directors (or program coordinators) need a wealth of evaluation information too. They want much of the same information the instructors want, so that they can advise them and other future program instructors what will or will not be effective. They want to know which instructors contributed to the program's success and acceptance and which detracted from it. They want to know which topics or sessions trainees got a great deal of value from and which they benefited little from. They want to know how the instructors and trainees regarded the physical facilities, including the conference room, case-study rooms, sleeping rooms, and dining areas. They want to know whether the physical facilities and the services were an asset or a liability? They also want to know how the participants enjoyed the food if any meals were served in connection with the program. They want to know which processes, methods, and sequences of topics were most effective in causing learning, so that they can do a better job of designing future programs. They want to know how much was learned and how much of it is being applied by the trainees on their jobs. And they want information on the learning and benefits of training so that they can demonstrate the contribution training makes to the organization to other department heads and higher-ups in management.

Some of this evaluation information can be gathered only after the training has been completed. Other parts of it can and should be collected during the training program, so that immediate adjustments can be made on the spot while they can still do some good. This is why it is so important for the program coordinator to be present with eyes and ears open during the program discussed in Chapter 6.

The trainees' supervisors will want to know the values derived from the training in return for the time their people have been away from work and the money spent from their unit's budgets to support the training. They want to know the extent to which their subordinates have developed and the ways their units have become better off because of it.

The chief executive officer wants to know how the training has helped the organization to better meet its goals, the extent to which employees have become enriched from their learning, and how much more they are committed to the organization and their own development and career success. And if the chief executive officer is an enlightened manager and values her or his employees as much as she or he values profits, she or he will want to know the extent to which the training has enriched their lives so they gain greater self satisfaction and enjoyment from their work.

WHAT DOES A SUITABLE EVALUATION INVOLVE?

When the question, "What constitutes a suitable evaluation of management training?" is raised, a variety of conflicting answers and viewpoints can be found. Some argue that evaluation is an impossible task because it is too complex; therefore, it should not even be contemplated. Instead, the benefits of training should be assumed to exist, and therefore training is accepted to be worth its cost just as a college education is accepted as having value. This group holds that experimental conditions, free from contaminations and distortions, are impossible and, hence, should not be bothered with.

Others feel that the trainees and others with whom they associate frequently on the job are the best source of information about the value of training. This group feels that the opinions of trainees are an adequate measure of a program's worth especially when they are supplemented with opinions of trainers, superiors, subordinates, and peers.

Still others accept the opinions of trainees and those who observe them frequently as a minimum source of information to evaluate the worth of training. This group believes that evaluation ought to be a systematic search aimed at determining whether progress is being made toward stated objectives at reasonable speed and expense (Korb 1956). Accordingly, evaluation should consist of several criteria including: measures of changes in attitudes and knowledge; self-reports made by trainees on how they have benefited from the training and how they have used the concepts and techniques they learned; analyses of employee records such as performance appraisals and supervisors' comments; and performance measures of production, bottlenecks, problems, and employee morale and satisfaction with their supervisors and managers. This group realizes the futility of trying to find certainty and complete objectivity in evaluations. Yet these people are undaunted in their quest for a realistic and useful estimate of the worth of training. This group wants undeniable evidence that behavioral changes in all participants have occurred as a result of the training and that these changes are the sole source of improved organizational performance—particularly profits.

And still others insist on absolute, concrete measures as the only suitable sort of evaluation evidence. These people argue that training must prove its worth in strict economic terms, and if management development cannot be demonstrated to contribute to the economic goals of the organization, it should not be carried out.

It may sound ironic (since these opinions do vary so widely), but there are elements of merit contained in each of these positions. One conclusion that may be drawn from the fact that there are wide differences of opinion as to what constitutes a suitable evaluation is that different people see the need for evaluation differently because they have different reasons for it. For example, an instructor may be satisfied with evaluation information that includes participant reactions to his or her presentation and some measures of the learning that occurred. This is because he or she views the need for evaluation to be something that will enable him or her to do a more effective job of teaching and do so in a more acceptable manner to participants. A chief executive officer will likely not be interested in this type of evaluation information. Instead, she or he will be more interested in broader issues and will want to know the extent to which training has assisted the organization in meeting its overall objectives. In general, she or he wants to know the overall value of training and whether it has been worth the cost.

It seems pointless, therefore, to argue whether evaluation should be done at all or whether evaluation should consist of measures of trainee reactions, or measures of increases in knowledge and skills, or measures of changes in behavior, or economic measures of training benefits, etcetera, since each of these measures are important for different reasons and useful to different people who have an interest in knowing about some part of or the whole value of training. Rather, evaluation ought to include as much information about each of these areas as practicable.

The training literature contains several statements of what can be considered thorough approaches to evaluation. Perhaps the three best evaluation plans are those of Korb (1956), Kirkpatrick (1967), and Hamblin (1974). They are fundamentally alike and serve as the basis of the approach presented in this chapter.

According to Korb, management training can be measured with respect to three sets of criteria:

1. In-course evalution of participants' progress. This is an appraisal of the effects of management training at the "training-room" level. More specifically it involves an assessment of:

    a) increased knowledge;

    b) acquired skills;

    c) changes in expressed attitudes;

    d) indications of interest;

    e) degree of participation;

    f) acceptance of training given.

    In short, this set of criteria is used to measure the effectiveness of the training as a process.

2. Impact on the participants after training. This is an appraisal of the effects of training as revealed by subsequent, modified behavior on the job. It involves measures of:

    a) the transfer of instruction into changed behaviors and attitudes on the job;

    b) the extent and duration of such change;

    c) whether the changes are positive, contributing to improved efficiency, production, and employee satisfaction;

    d) whether progress has been made in meeting the specific objectives of the training.

    This set of criteria is used to determine the effect of the training on people in the organization.

3. Impact on the organization. This involves a determination of the extent to which training has played a part in organizational success. The kinds of things that indicate significant contributions to organizational success include:

    a) an improved supervisory and management force;

    b) improved interdepartmental functioning;

    c) improved productivity and morale;

    d) improved communication, vertically and horizontally;

    e) greater customer or public satisfaction with goods produced or services rendered;

f)   an adequate reservoir of talent to meet present promotion and future expansion needs.

This level of assessment is usually done by higher levels of management. It puts into perspective the ultimate goals of training.

Kirkpatrick's (1976) approach to training evaluation involves measuring the effectiveness of a training program in terms of four criteria:

1.   Reaction—How well did the participants like the program?

2.   Learning—What principles, facts, and techniques were learned?

3.   Behavior—What changes in job behavior resulted from the training?

4.   Results—What were the tangible results of the training program in terms of reduced cost, improved quality, improved quantity, etc.?

Hamblin's (1974) work on training evaluation, published some fifteen years after Kirkpatrick's, extends Kirkpatrick's ideas one step further. Picking up where Kirkpatrick left off, Hamblin added a fifth criteria—ultimate value. Hamblin's evaluation scheme thus involves five levels of training evaluation which he labels: reactions; learning; job behavior; organization; and ultimate value.

It seems doubtful that substantial improvements can be made upon the excellent work of Korb, Kirkpatrick, and Hamblin in recommending sets of evaluation criteria to assess more thoroughly the value of a training program. So a composite of their thinking is set forth here as a set of criteria for evaluating management-training programs. It consists of five areas for evaluation.

1.   Reactions—Reactions of participants to the learning experience and to those who presented it (i.e., coordinators and teachers). Reactions of program coordinator and the various teachers in the program regarding the learning environment and experience. Reactions consist of opinions and conclusions based on first-hand observations. They may be collected during, immediately after, or several months after the training occurs.

2.   Learning—Measures of changes in attitudes, knowledge, and skills of the trainees. These changes may be measured immediately after the training experience to determine a program's immediate impact and several weeks or months later to measure retention.

3.   Job behavior—An assessment of how trainees behave differently because of their training. The biggest question this aspect of the evaluation process aims to answer is, how and to what extent have trainees applied the various concepts and processes taught? It also seeks to determine who among the trainees have been changed as a result of the training.

4.   Organizational impact—This involves assessing the effects of attitude and behavioral changes caused by the training on both the functioning and the

ability to function of the organization to which the trainees belong. The aim of this phase of evaluation is to ascertain both quantitative and qualitative changes in organizational performance which can be attributed to the training directly or indirectly.

5.   Additional outcomes—Other results or by-products of the training not identified or assessed by the other four areas. This includes such things as the social value of training. To what extent do trainees feel better about themselves? Has the training helped people satisfy some of their personal goals? Has it assisted them in their career development? Whereas organizational impact refers to an assessment of contributions of training to the organization's performance or capacity to perform along the lines or in the direction it has chosen to head or would like to head, the assessment of additional outcomes involves an examination of the impacts training has had on the organization's performance or capacity to perform with respect to measures it presently does not use.

Three things should be said about this set of training evaluation criteria. First, the definitions of these five criteria are somewhat imprecise. It would take forever to define in complete detail exactly what should be included or excluded in each area. Therefore, it is up to those who are responsible for evaluating programs to start with this or some other set of criteria and define as completely and precisely as they think necessary what will be examined in each area.

Second, the outcomes identified and measured with respect to all five of these criteria areas include both desirable and undesirable consequences.

And third, both the anticipated and the unanticipated outcomes within each of the five criteria areas should be identified and measured.

A LOGICAL APPROACH TO COLLECTING, ORGANIZING, AND INTERPRETING EVALUATION DATA

A logical approach to collecting, organizing, and interpreting evaluation data is necessary in order to provide useful information to those who need it. A couple of important questions should be raised. The first question that should be answered when planning how a training intervention will be evaluated is, "Who needs what kinds of evaluation information?" There must be some reason or reasons why these various people want particular kinds of evaluation information. These people should know what they will do with this information once they get it. The one exception to this is when training produces unanticipated results that have significance and, therefore, should be assessed and included in the evaluation report.

A second question that needs to be answered is, "What are the various ways one can go about collecting the needed information?" There are sometimes various ways of collecting essentially the same kinds of information.

Each approach should be evaluated in light of the possible distortions associated with it, the specificity of the information obtained and the form it takes, how usable it may be, and the time required and the difficulty involved in obtaining it. These factors should be considered in deciding on the best ways to collect the information needed.

Once data are collected, they must be tabulated and organized into a useful form. Again, it is essential that those who prepare evaluation reports know how their readers will use the evaluation information. For example, if those who prepare the evaluation reports know the questions their readers have, they can generally do a better job of organizing and presenting evaluation information so that it is readily understood and provides the users with needed answers.

Frequently evaluation data do not provide a complete picture and full understanding of what occurred. Other factors and extenuating circumstances often need to be considered along with raw, evaluation data. Sometimes, too, those who are close to the training see and understand things about it that others who are not so involved do not. For these reasons, it is useful to provide interpretations of the evaluation data reported. Sometimes there may even be two or more possible interpretations that might be made from the same data. Those who prepare evaluation reports should state that these various interpretations might be given and then go on to state which interpretations they choose and why.

The key to a logical evaluation approach is to always keep in mind who needs what information and for what reasons and then to collect it by the best possible way and report it in an easily understood and usable fashion.

TECHNIQUES OF INFORMATION GATHERING AND INTERPRETATION

This section will suggest the various techniques that can be used to gather the information needed to answer questions typically asked within each of the five areas of evaluation discussed earlier. It will also describe some of the problems and shortcomings frequently encountered when using many of these techniques and in interpreting the information obtained.

Some purists might scoff at many of the techniques suggested here, calling them unscientific and crude. To some extent, these criticisms are justified, especially when the information obtained by them is accepted as being free from error and proof positive that training has or has not been effective. The point is simply this: measurements are only as good, or precise, as the instruments used to obtain them. Crude measures may be good enough to provide only rough approximations. But this does not mean the aims of evaluation cannot be met. Maybe rough approximations are good enough to provide the usable information needed for making the decisions which could not be made any better or would not be made any differently if more precise and scientific information were obtained.

One thing will become apparent through reading the remainder of this chapter, which takes up the issue of evaluating training programs with respect to the five areas identified earlier. Namely, it becomes increasingly difficult to identify and measure objectively the results of training within each of the five areas or levels. That is, it is more difficult to measure job behavior than it is to measure learning, and it is more difficult to measure learning than it is to measure reactions. This is so because as one attempts to evaluate training with respect to the five areas in the order they are presented here, she or he finds that for each of these levels it becomes increasingly difficult to specify what to look for in each, the techniques and methods available become less objective and less precise, and the possibilities and magnitudes of outside distorting influences which prevent one from concluding that particular changes were caused from the training become greater.

Gathering and Interpreting Reactions to Training

The most commonly used method of evaluating management training is to collect participant reactions to it. This approach to evaluation is simple, fast, and straightforward. It does suffer, however, from a major fallacy because of the ways in which the information generated is frequently interpreted. Specifically, some people labor under the misconception that management training has value and is instrumental in improving managerial effectiveness if those who received the training say they liked it and thought it was worthwhile. The obvious deficiency with this sort of reasoning is that there are no objective measures of changes in attitudes and learning and the degree to which these changes have, in turn, led to improvements in managerial performance. This is not to say, though, that reactions cannot be useful sources of information for evaluating training. They can be, but only for specific facets of training.

The reactions of participants, the program's coordinator, and the program's instructor are a useful source of information to help assess the acceptance of and support for training, to evaluate training as a process, and to identify perceptions of what was learned or accomplished. Typical questions which reactions to training can go a long way in answering include the following:

1.   Will training get, or continue to get, support from those for whom it is intended and their superiors? Is it perceived as being useful? If those who experience training react favorably, it seems likely that they will support it and will encourage others to support it. To get this kind of information, participants could be asked what their overall reaction to the training was; whether they felt it was worthwhile in terms of its cost and their time away from work; how well it measured up to their expectations; and whether they think others would profit from it.

2. Was the training relevant? Did it meet the needs of the participants? These questions may be answered by obtaining the reactions of participants and perhaps the reactions of some of their superiors who have first-hand knowledge of the training. The kinds of things that need to be determined in answering these questions are: Was the training practical? Was it thorough? Did it contain new and useful ideas? Which of the topics were most helpful? Which were least helpful? Which topics should be expanded? Which ones reduced or eliminated? Should other topics be included which are not now included?

3. Was the quality of teaching acceptable? Were there any problems with the ways in which the various instructors performed? What can instructors do to improve? These and similar questions may be answered by collecting reactions from participants and the program coordinator.

4. Were the teaching methods and materials stimulating and effective? Was the quality and quantity of the materials appropriate? Here, the perceptions of participants should comprise the primary source of data. This can be supplemented with the perceptions of instructors and the program coordinator. The kinds of questions that should be asked here are: Which of the teaching methods most helped learning? Which ones least helped learning? Which cases and readings were most useful? Which ones were least useful? Which ones should be eliminated?

5. Were the physical facilities and the services employed satisfactory? This question is asked to determine whether the facilities and services used were of a quality so as to add to and not detract from the learning that the program was designed to produce. Opinions from participants, the program coordinator and the various teachers should be polled to determine both positive and negative aspects of the conference room, sleeping accommodations, meals, meal service, transportation, and recreational facilities.

6. Was the program well-planned and organized? Were its many parts and phases well-coordinated? The purpose of asking these kinds of questions is to spot problems that can detract from a good learning situation. Here, participants should be polled to see if they felt the program ran smoothly and without irritating annoyances, delays, and foul-ups which can quickly and decisively sour a group's attitude and enthusiasm toward the learning experience. Included here might also be questions aimed at finding out how thorough and timely were the many communications which were used to tell participants of the daily activities and where and when they were to occur.

7. What did the participants perceive they learned? Perceptions of what someone thinks he or she learned are important because they indicate what that person felt he or she gained from the learning experience and, hence, what he or she will be likely to tell others when explaining what the training was

about. This, in turn, helps shape their perception of the training and its worth. These perceptions also give a fair indication as to what was learned.

Reactions to training can be collected best by using two methods, questionnaire and interview. The advantages of questionnaires are: they can be completed quickly and easily; they provide a source of direct information from participants; they can be completed anonymously, thereby helping to ensure nonfiltered data; and the results can be tabulated and summarized easily. For the most part, questionnaires contain either objective questions or at least very specific questions. Thus the people surveyed respond to essentially the same stimuli.

Interviews have other advantages. They permit greater depth and insight as to how people feel and why. Since they are oral, much more data may be collected since most people rather express themselves verbally than in writing.

Although questionnaires do not permit getting in-depth information, that which they do obtain is usually sufficient. If those who review the data collected by questionnaires find a need to learn more about specific points, then they can always follow up with interviews.

Typically, questionnaires are administered at the conclusion of a program. Some feel that this is a good time to gather reactions because they are fresh in the minds of participants and because those who are to be sampled are a captive audience. Sometimes participants, weary from sitting and anxious to go home, suggest that they be permitted to take the program evaluation questionnaires home so they can think over what they want to say more thoroughly. Research evidence does not exist to show whether responses to questionnaires differ depending upon when they were completed. It is a great deal more difficult to assure a 100 percent response when participants are allowed to take the questionnaires home, however. Moreover, it is doubtful whether they will actually take more time and care than they would if they were to complete them at the training site. If questionnaires are completed at the end of the program, it is necessary to give participants ample time so that they can do a thorough and conscientious job and not feel rushed. Their minds may be occupied to some extent with the thought of traveling home, which distracts the participants from giving their full attention to the questionnaire. But even if they complete the questionnaires at some later time, who is to say that their minds will not be diverted by some other matters.

Questionnaire design considerations

The construction of a good questionnaire is not a simple matter. It must be of a reasonable length so as to collect adequate data and, at the same time, not be a burden. It also must contain specific questions so that each one is interpreted in the same way by those who complete it.

Most questionnaires that seek to gather reactions contain scales to assess the degree to which people liked or disliked or found value or did not find value in something. A sizeable portion of the scales appearing on the questionnaires used today to obtain reactions are poorly constructed. In general, they suffer from two kinds of shortcomings. The first kind of problem is that they contain too many points or intervals. Depending upon what it is that people are asked to respond to, very few are able to discriminate between more than five points or intervals. And, in some cases, three points or intervals is the limit. As a good rule of thumb, a five-point scale is most practical. Ten- and twenty-point scales are ridiculous.

A second kind of problem is that scales are sometimes biased upwards or downwards and do not contain categories that reflect the range of responses possible. Here are a couple of examples:

Tell what you thought about X. Check the appropriate point on the scale.

Fantastic	Great	Good	O.K.	Bad

This scale is poor because it is nearly impossible to distinguish between "fantastic" and "great." It is also biased to obtain favorable responses since there are more positive responses possible than negative responses.

Tell what you thought about Z.

Extremely bad	Moderately bad	Slightly bad	Neutral	Fantastic

This scale is deficient because it does not contain two items between the neutral reaction and the most favorable reaction. There should be an equal number of positive and negative reactions. The labels used for the categories are not consistent. "Fantastic" should be replaced with "good" and there should be three categories, slightly good, moderately good, and extremely good. The wording on the scale points is also very important. It needs to make sense and be shown to be interpreted uniformly by all who read it.

Those who wish to learn more about questionnaire construction and scaling techniques than is covered by the few tips presented here should consult a good book in research methods in the social sciences. University and major public libraries usually contain several excellent ones.

Examples of questionnaires

The major portion of the reaction data will come from the participants themselves. Given at the conclusion of a program and scheduled to permit respondents adequate time to complete it, this questionnaire can provide a wealth of important information. Portions of it may be completed by the program coordinator and by the instructors to supplement the participants' reactions. (See Table 8-1.)

Table 8-1. Management development program participant evaluation form.

1. I found the quality of this program to be (select one):

   |———————————|———————————|———————————|———————————|———————————|
   Poor   Below   Average   Above   Outstanding
                average   average

2. Briefly state your overall feelings about this program.

   _____

   _____

   _____

3. To what extent did this program measure up to your expectations?

   |———————————|———————————|———————————|———————————|———————————|
   Far less   Somewhat   Met expec-   Somewhat   Far exceeded
   than expected less than   tations   more than   expectations
                 expected   expected

4. Do you feel that this program was worthwhile in terms of its cost and your time away from normal job duties?

   Yes _____   No _____   Undecided _____

5. Would you recommend this program to your peers?

   Yes _____   No _____   Undecided

6. Rate the program using the following code: 5 = outstanding; 4 = above average; 3 = average or neutral; 2 = below average; 1 = poor.

	Rating
a) Practical value	_____
b) Thoroughness	_____
c) New ideas gained	_____
d) Helpful to self-development	_____
e) Relevance to job	_____

7. Which topics did you find *most* helpful?

   _____

   _____

   Why?_____

8. Which topics did you find *least* helpful?

   _____

   _____

   Why?_____

Table 8-1. *cont'd.*

9. Which topics would you recommend eliminating? _____

_____

Why?_____

10. Which topics would you recommend enlarging and devoting more time and emphasis to? _____

_____

Why?_____

11. What other topics should the seminar cover that it does not now include?

_____

_____

12. Rate the *content* of each session, in terms of value to you, using the following code: 5 = very valuable; 4 = valuable; 3 = undecided; 2 = little value; 1 = no value.

Session	*Rating*
a) Leadership	_____
b) Planning	_____
c) Motivation	_____
d) Communication	_____
e) Controls	_____

13. Rate each of the program's instructors, in terms of their *teaching effectiveness* (getting ideas across), using the following code: 5 = extremely effective; 4 = effective; 3 = neutral; 2 = somewhat ineffective; 1 = extremely ineffective.

Instructor	*Rating*
a) A	_____
b) B	_____
c) C	_____
d) D	_____
e) E	_____

14. Would you recommend eliminating any of the instructors from future programs?

Instructor's Name	*Reason*
_____	_____
_____	_____

15. Would you recommend that any of the instructors have a greater portion of the teaching responsibility than they now do? Which instructors? _____

_____

Table 8-1. *cont'd.*

16.   What do you feel are the *greatest strengths* and the *greatest weaknesses* of each program instructor?

    a) Instructor A: greatest strength: _____

                                    _____

                                    greatest weakness: _____

                                    _____

    b) Instructor B: greatest strength: _____

                                    greatest weakness: _____

                                    _____

    c) Instructor C: greatest strength: _____

                                    greatest weakness: _____

                                    _____

    d) Instructor D: greatest strength: _____

                                    greatest weakness: _____

                                    _____

    e) Instructor E: greatest strength: _____

                                    greatest weakness: _____

                                    _____

17.   Which of the teaching methods did you find particularly *effective?* _____

_____

Why? _____

18.   Which (if any) of the teaching methods did you find particularly *ineffective?*

_____

_____

Why? _____

Table 8-1. *cont'd.*

19. Which of the case studies were *most* useful? _____

    _____

20. Which of the case studies were *least* useful? _____

    _____

    Would you recommend eliminating any of these? _____

    Which ones? _____

21. Which of the readings were most useful? _____

    _____

22. Which of the readings were least useful? _____

    _____

    Would you recommend eliminating any of these? _____

    Which ones? _____

23. How satisfied were you with the *quality* of the materials and assignments?

Very dissatisfied	Dissatisfied	Neutral	Satisfied	Very satisfied

24. What are your feelings about the *quantity* of materials and assignments?

Far less than there should be	Less than there should be	Just right	More than there should be	Far more than there should be

25. How satisfied were you with the following facilities and services? (Code: 5 = very satisfied; 4 = satisfied; 3 = neutral; 2 = dissatisfied; 1 = very dissatisfied)

Facilities and services	Rating
a) Conference room	_____
b) Buzz-group/case-study rooms	_____
c) Sleeping rooms	_____
d) Quality of food	_____
e) Quality of food service	_____
f) Recreation facilities and activities	_____
g) Transportation arrangements	_____
h) Other _____	_____

Table 8–1. *cont'd.*

26. Do you have any suggestions for improving the facilities and services? What are they?_____

_____

27. How do you rate the organization and coordination of the program?

```
|——————|——————|——————|——————|——————|
```

| Terrible (too many foul-ups, much confusion) | Less than adequate | Adequate | More than adequate | Excellent (everything ran perfectly) |

28. Answer the following questions regarding the program's coordination:

	Yes	No	Undecided
a) Was there a friendly atmosphere?	____	____	_____
b) Did things run smoothly?	____	____	_____
c) Were questions and concerns answered?	____	____	_____
d) Was the daily schedule well-thought-out?	____	____	_____
e) Were communications clear and adequate?	____	____	_____

29. How do you think this program could be improved?

_____

_____

_____

30. Think over the subject-content covered. Give one or two key ideas you gained from each.

Session	*Key ideas or concepts*
a) Leadership	_____
	_____
b) Planning	_____
	_____
c) Motivation	_____
	_____
d) Communication	_____
	_____

Table 8-1. *cont'd.*

   e) Controls

It was mentioned earlier that one of the benefits of obtaining reactions is to improve teaching effectiveness. Some organizations use a separate, instructor-evaluation form to help pinpoint their areas of strength and weakness, which can be used to assist the instructors in improving themselves. These should be completed by participants and the program coordinator right after the instructor finishes her or his session. (See Table 8-2).

Table 8-2. Instructor-evaluation form.

Name _____   *Subject*_____

*Date*_____   *Course*_____

Check the appropriate rating for each item listed.

	Excellent	Very good	Adequate	Needs to improve	Poor
1. How well did the individual "break the ice"—get the group warmed up to him or her?					
2. How well did the individual introduce her or his topic and generate interest and enthusiasm?					
3. How well did the individual outline goals and purposes?					
4. How well did he or she keep the session alive and interesting?					
5. How well did the individual encourage group participation?					
6. How well did she or he clarify key points?					

Table 8–2. *cont'd.*

		Excellent	Very good	Adequate	Needs to improve	Poor
7.	How well did he or she welcome and answer questions?					
8.	How well did he or she come across personally?					
9.	How well did the individual summarize and wrap up at the end of his or her session?					
10.	To what extent was her or his presentation clear and logical?					

11.   What is your overall rating of this teacher?

```
|-------+-------|-------+-------|-------+-------|-------+-------|
  Excellent    Very        Average      Below         Poor
               good                    average
```

12.   Was there a good balance between instructor inputs (lecture) and participant inputs (involvement via discussion and case-study reports)?
Yes _____   No _____   Undecided _____

13.   Explain the ways in which this instructor could have been more effective in

a) public speaking: _____

_____

b) organization: _____

_____

c) responses to questions: _____

_____

d) attitude toward participants: _____

_____

14.   What other suggestions do you have to help this instructor improve? _____

_____

_____

A problem frequently encountered in evaluating the worth of the topics covered in a management program and the teaching effectiveness of those who teach them is that these evaluations are often largely a function of the perceived importance of the topics. Thus an instructor who covers less popular subject matter usually does not receive as high a rating as another instructor who covers a very popular topic. Fast (1974) has developed a technique to eliminate this source of bias, which involves having participants complete a questionnaire in which they identify the relative degree of importance of the various training objectives and then rate the extent to which each was fulfilled. The degree of importance rating and degree of fulfillment evaluation scores are then multiplied to give an Index of Objective Fulfillment Score.

At the beginning of a program, participants are given the questionnaire (see Fig. 8-2) and asked to select the objectives that they feel are important and to rate these by completing columns 1 and 2. At the end of the program they complete column 3. Column 4 is completed next by computing the degree of fulfillment for each objective.

Summarizing and interpreting the data

The tabulation of reaction data collected by questionnaires is not a complicated process. A good procedure to follow is to prepare tabulation sheets for each of the objective questions. Clerical assistants can type all the responses to each of the fill-in type questions on separate sheets of paper so that one can read all the responses to the same question and thus can quickly obtain a feel as to how everyone felt regarding that particular item. For formal reports, it may be useful to prepare bar charts or other data displays which show the number and percentage of people who responded to the objective questions in the various ways possible. For example:

Overall, I found the quality of the program to be:

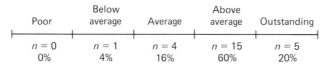

	Poor	Below average	Average	Above average	Outstanding
	$n = 0$	$n = 1$	$n = 4$	$n = 15$	$n = 5$
	0%	4%	16%	60%	20%

$n = 25$ participants

Some people go beyond this by taking an additional step of computing a weighted score or average value for this kind of data. This is done by assigning weights for each of the categories (poor = 1; below average = 2; average = 3; above average = 4; outstanding = 5) and multiplying the number of responses obtained in each category times the respective weight and then dividing the sum of these values by the total number of responses. These weighted index scores (or average scores) give a rough measure of participant reactions, but

Systems Design Workshop

Your Name _____

Objectives
Check those that are important to you. (Ignore those that are not)

Be able to:

	✔ *Degree of importance* × *Weight each checked objective for its importance to you, allocating exactly 100 points *among* all of those checked. A total of 100 points *must* be assigned.	*Degree of fulfillment* = **Rate *each* objective you checked (from 0–10) to indicate how well it was fulfilled.	*Index of objective fulfillment*
1. Identify and describe the various elements in the systems development process and understand their significance.			
2. Understand the use and value of systems feasibility studies.			
3. Identify essential considerations (critical factors) in a systems design problem.			
4. Design a management report.			
5. Design an input form.			

6. Develop an overall systems flow.

7. Understand the objectives and techniques of designing input/output controls.

8. Select among and be able to use basic data base structures.

9. Prepare an oral presentation of design recommendations for management.

10. Exchange ideas with other participants.

100   TOTAL =

*If you checked only one objective, assign all 100 points to it; if you checked two objectives, spread the 100 points between them, etc.

**0 is unsatisfactory; 1–2 poor; 3–4 below average; 5 average; 6 above average; 7 good; 8 very good; 9–10 excellent.

Fig. 8-2. Objective-fulfillment measure. (From Dorothy Fast, "A New Approach to Quantifying Training Program Effectiveness." Reproduced by special permission from the September 1974 *Training and Development Journal.* Copyright 1974 by the American Society for Training and Development, Inc.)

are not statistically appropriate. The display of information shown in the previous example provides a much more complete picture of respondent reactions than does some weighted index score or mean score.

Three statistical terms which are frequently used when discussing distribution data are the mean, the median, and the mode. Strictly speaking, all of these are averages, although most people use the words *average* and *mean* interchangeably. The *mean*, or arithmetic mean, is the average score, and it is computed by summing the values of all scores and then dividing this total by the number of scores. The *median* is that point on a distribution range that one half of the population is above and the other half of the population is below. The *mode* is the value on a distribution range that corresponds to the highest point on the distribution curve. In practice, the arithmetic mean and the median are the most frequently used of the three terms.

Once data are tabulated and summarized, the big problem of interpretation arises. One of the reasons why the point was made regarding the importance of having the program coordinator present throughout as much of the program as possible is to assure accurate interpretation of the data collected. There are no formulas available to follow in interpreting participant response data. However, the most important thing that should be kept in mind by those who have this responsibility is that there are always reasons for responses being what they are and that they should not be accepted at face value or without some thought as to why they are as they are. In other words, time should be taken to discover and understand these reasons.

Measures of Learning

Favorable reactions to a program and to those who presented it are indications that participants liked the experience, but positive reactions are negligible assurance that any learning actually occurred. Many people have attended meetings or lectures where the speaker generated considerable enthusiasm and was cheered and applauded for her or his "terrific performance." Yet, a careful analysis of what the audience actually gained in terms of learning revealed that nothing of value was acquired. Training should be more than a source of entertainment. Hence, it is important to get adequate measures of what was actually learned and retained from the training experience. *Learning* is defined here to include increased knowledge of facts, concepts, and techniques; acquired skills in diagnosing situations and applying appropriately the knowledge learned; and changes in expressed attitudes including acceptance of the training content. It does not include on-the-job use of the newly acquired knowledge, skills, and attitudes. This is determined in the third area of evaluation—job behavior. Evaluation of learning provides information about the effectiveness of training as a process. It shows the immediate results of training; however, it does not reveal whether the training brought about better management in practice.

Design of the measurement process

The more systematic and objective the process for measuring learning becomes, the greater the credibility of the conclusions as to the extent to which training resulted in any learning. There appear to be essentially three general approaches:

1. A common-sense approach, which essentially involves a nonsystematically collected sample of feelings, opinions, and conclusions based upon observations.

2. A systematic approach, which consists of collecting indicators and evidences. The evidences to be collected is decided upon in advance, before the training occurs. It includes judgments which can be shown to be logically derived from observations and inferences. These may be collected by means of interviews, questionnaires, and group discussions.

3. An experimental approach, which attempts to study changes of knowledge, skills, and attitudes under controlled conditions.

It is this last method which has the greatest degree of acceptance among training professionals because of its thoroughness and objectivity and is therefore recommended here.

The most basic approach to measuring learning would be to test for it after the training. However, this method does not permit one to attribute the levels of knowledge and skills and the attitudes measured to being caused by the training per se. The levels of knowledge revealed by such measures may or may not have been caused by the training. What needs to be done is to measure changes in knowledge, skills, and attitudes. This requires both before and after measures. Differences detected between before-training measurements and after-training measurements may be attributed to the training. But this approach is not without weaknesses and limitations. Perhaps the changes detected were caused by the training, or perhaps they were caused by other things going on in the organization at the same time as the training. What is needed in order to rule out the latter as a possible explanation is to have a control group which is measured at the same times the experimental group is measured.

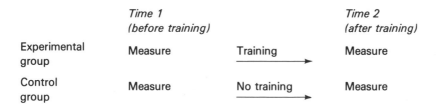

	Time 1 (before training)		Time 2 (after training)
Experimental group	Measure	Training ⟶	Measure
Control group	Measure	No training ⟶	Measure

A question that should receive attention in assessing changes is, "Are these changes significant?" In other words, are the changes large enough so that one can conclude with a reasonable degree of confidence that they were, in fact, caused by the training itself and are not just small random variations in measurement scores because of slight changes in the people being measured and how they happened to respond to tests on one particular day or because of the limitations of the measurement instruments and procedures. In other words, a 1 percent or 2 percent increase in learning may be due to training, or it may be simply a random variation in those being measured. A 50 percent or 90 percent increase in learning, however, is likely due to the training intervention and most probably not influenced dramatically by random variations in the people being measured. Most good texts in tests and measurements explain this concept in depth and suggest ways of avoiding erroneous conclusions about the impacts of training.

Validity and reliability of tests

In selecting or constructing measuring instruments (i.e., tests), two factors should be considered—*validity* and *reliability.* A test is valid when it measures what it claims to measure and not something else. As an illustration, suppose a test were constructed to measure how much people know about planning and are able to plan. If the test were valid, it would measure just these things and nothing else. People who receive higher scores than others on this test would do so simply because they have greater knowledge and skills in planning—not because they can read the test faster or have more knowledge of things not related to planning.

Nearly every personnel director is familiar with the concept and the importance of the predictive validity of tests. This is a measure of how well tests are able to predict performance as measured by some specific criteria. The ability of a test to predict is expressed as the correlation between test scores and the specific criteria used to measure performance. This is called the *correlation coefficient of validity.*

The purpose of testing for learning is not to predict but to measure it directly. The test itself stands as a measure of what it is supposed to measure. This presents the need for what is known as *content validity.* A test that has content validity is one that actually measures what it claims to measure. In other words, those people who receive higher test scores than others do in fact have a greater knowledge of whatever the test claims to measure than those who receive lower test scores. Content validity is not determined or measured statistically. The literature on tests and measurements suggests two things be done to assure that a test has content validity.

1.   Care should be taken in collecting and selecting test items. They should be a representative sample of information being tested for.

2. The test should be constructed in a "sensible" fashion. Most good texts in tests and measurements contain additional information on techniques to assure test validity.

The reliability of a test is its stability or consistency of measurement. A highly reliable test will yield the same score on an individual when two or more measurements are made. In other words the scores a person receives on the test will not change appreciably from one testing to another. The degree to which a test is reliable can be expressed in terms of the correlation between two measurements of the same thing. This is known as the *correlation coefficient of reliability*. As a general rule of thumb a test ought to have a reliability coefficient of 0.9 or above.

There are two other problems associated with testing. One is the ever-present danger that the act of measurement will change the thing being measured. The other is that people may learn something from taking the before-training tests, or they may become "test wise" and able to do a better job on the same test when they take it for a second time after the training. In other words, the application of a test makes it unsuitable for further use with the same subjects.

Comparable forms (call them A and B) of the same test may be used to overcome this second problem. In this procedure, the group takes form A of the test before training and form B after the training. Since the forms are comparable, differences in scores between A and B may be attributed to the training.

This technique, however, does not solve the first problem of people being changed because of the act of measurement. The suggested procedure for controlling this problem is to set up a second control group, which receives no before-course measure and does not receive training.

Another complicating factor that can distort evaluation findings is the so-called *Hawthorne effect* or the fact that people may change because they feel important and special by being singled out to receive training. To guard against this phenomenon, yet another control group might be used which receives a placebo training experience instead of the real training. Thus the experimental desing necessary to guard against the contaminating influences just mentioned involves an experimental group and three control groups.

	Time 1 (before training)		Time 2 (after training)
Experimental group	Measure	Training →	Measure
Control group 1	Measure	No training →	Measure
Control group 2	(No measure)	No training →	Measure
Control group 3	Measure	Placebo training →	Measure

Quite obviously this design becomes quite complex and cumbersome to work with, yet it is required in order to do a sound job of accurately measuring the effects of training. However, it is not without problems, which will be discussed later in the chapter in the section entitled "Evaluation: The Practical Dimension."

Types of tests

Oral, written, and performance tests are the three ways of measuring learning. Oral tests consist of direct questions, which are asked to determine what people feel, think, and know. Written tests may be subjective or objective. Performance tests place people in mock situations and require them to demonstrate their knowledge, skills, and attitudes through doing something. Since each of these approaches has its own unique advantages and drawbacks, they all should be considered in planning the measurement system.

In practice, most measurements of learning are made using written tests, because they can be administered in less time, are capable of obtaining greater amounts of data, and can be scored and tabulated faster and with greater objectivity than can oral and performance tests. There are several types of written tests. The ones most commonly used are essay, objective, true-false, multiple-choice, matching, and completion. Each has unique characteristics and is more or less appropriate for obtaining different kinds of information.

In designing a measurement plan, one should consider the various types of tests and use the ones that will provide the necessary data at the least cost and time (Berry 1969). One also needs to consider the ability and confidence trainees have in taking tests. Obviously, groups of people who have college educations will be much more skilled in test taking and self-expression than others who have never attended college. Another thing that should be considered in selecting tests is the question of whether widely known and used standard tests such as How Supervise? and the "Leadership Opinion Questionnaire" should be used, whether other tests should be constructed by those who conduct the training, or whether some combination of the two should be used. The answer to this question depends upon the specific purposes of the training and the extent to which standard measures will provide a fair reflection of what the training involved. It will also depend, to a lesser extent, on the need for evaluation and the time and other resources which can be devoted to it. Those who have expertise in test construction know all too well the enormous difficulties and time required to construct a good test. Yet this may be the best, if not the only, way to do an adequate job of evaluating training at the learning level, because of the unique objectives of the program in question and because suitable standardized tests simply may not exist.

Knowledge

Knowledge can be measured by oral, written, or performance tests. Usually, it is measured by written tests because far more can be measured and in less time than by oral or performance tests. And, as a practical matter, it is rarely convenient to spend more than a couple of hours of participants' time to administer before- and after-training measurements. Oral tests and, to a lesser extent, performance tests, particularly when they are used as pretraining measurements, have a potential for embarrassing participants who may not know the correct answers to the examiner's questions. This embarrassment can turn quickly to sour attitudes toward training and those who present it.

Too much testing turns people off and is unnecessary. Typically, it is practical to get across only about three to five fundamental ideas in a half-day session of training. Thus in a five-full-days program the number of concepts covered may range somewhere between 30 and 50. This makes it possible to test, in some fashion, for all of the principle ideas covered without resorting to more than a couple of hours of testing. And, if one perceives a suitable test as involving a reasonably representative sample of knowledge, as opposed to a measure of all of it, then the number of key concepts tested for might be reduced to 15–25.

Learning objectives for each session should serve as the guide to constructing a suitable mechanism for measuring changes in knowledge. Objectives help to eliminate nonpertinent and unimportant test questions and thus help prevent the construction of overly long tests. Tests constructed with regard to only the key learning objectives of each session are also useful for pinpointing how successful each teacher was in achieving the learning objectives of his or her particular unit of instruction.

Short answer essay tests are best for testing for knowledge. They should be kept simple and specific so that they can be answered satisfactorily in 3 to 5 lines. They should resemble straightforward questions which can be answered directly. This permits the test to cover a fair number of different points and areas. Long essay exams call for greater skills in self-expression, organization of thought, and imagination, and therefore tend not to be as valid as short-answer essay exams. People in management-training programs will be outraged at the thought of being required to write one- to two-page answers to each essay exam question. Most would refuse.

It is useful when establishing a scoring system to mark the short answer essay on a scale of 0-3:

0 = missed the question entirely

1 = said something correct, but little of it

2 = was essentially correct, but lacked an important point or was slightly in error with regard to some aspect

3 = completely correct; adequately answered the question

Grading scales of more than 5 points, such as those which assign 0-10 points per question, pose serious grading difficulties. In practice, it is too difficult for a grader to discriminate between more than five intervals. Essay tests have the advantage of determining what people know without giving them clues as to what the correct answers are. They avoid the possibility of guessing and, if graded by a competent person, are difficult to bluff through successfully.

True-false and mutiple choice are the best kinds of objective tests to use for adult groups. Matching and completion tests are perceived as being too picky because they require people to know the "correct word" or phrase. True-false and multiple-choice tests can be used to some extent to determine how well people understand concepts or particular facets of concepts, but they are also somewhat limited since they can give away the correct answers and invite guessing.

One last word might be said on behalf of testing and that is its motivational effects on learning. If people know they are going to be tested, they are more likely to pay closer attention to what is going on and try to learn more than they would otherwise. There is a great deal of controversy about the value of grading and grades. Testing is slightly a different matter and learning is not too different from other kinds of human performance which usually increase when there are standards and expectations.

Skills

In evaluating knowledge alone, one is unable to tell whether those who possess the knowledge have the skills needed to apply it. Skills must be evaluated in their own right as an important dimension of learning. To a very large extent, the measurement of skills is also a measure of the knowledge and perhaps even a measure of the participant's attitudes toward or acceptance of this knowledge. Moreover, to some extent the measurement of skills is also a measure of a person's characteristics—for example, her or his tendency to choose to use the skill in a given situation.

In general, performance tests are the only adequate instruments for measuring skills. Oral and written tests are not appropriate. As a result and since performance tests require considerable time and are potentially embarrassing, it is very difficult to conduct much, if any, pretraining testing of skills of all of the participants. As a practical matter, therefore, a couple of good alternatives should be considered—either to measure the skills of a representative sample of participants before training or to measure the skills of participants during the training as they begin to learn them.

The actual measurement of skills is often a problem to instructors since there are no easy steps or rules to follow to do it, nor is there much in the way of standardized instruments. Thus it will be necessary for most instructors to tailor-make their own measurement instruments. It does make sense, however, to attempt to measure skills as objectively as possible. To do this, the following steps are advised. (See Fig. 8–3)

Person being evaluated _____

Date _____ Course _____

Observer_____

Critical dimensions of skill	Rating scale	Relative importance (expressed as a percentage)
Critical dimension 1	├──┼──┼──┼──┤	_____
Critical dimension 2	├─────┼─────┤	_____
Critical dimension 3	├───────┤	_____
.		
.		
.		
Critical dimension *n*	├──┼──┼──┼──┤	_____
	Total	100%
Overall rating of skill	_____	

Fig. 8–3. Skill-rating form (hypothetical skill).

1.   Identify the skill to be measured.

2.   Define as completely and clearly as possible what the skill is. This will consist largely of descriptions of how people will and will not behave as they perform the skill correctly.

3.   Identify the critical dimensions of the skill. These are the various, specific behaviors that compose it.

4.   If possible, assign some kind of values of relative importance to each of the critical dimensions. This may be too difficult because of the obvious controversies that might arise over which aspects are more or less important than others. Actually the only utility in doing this is to cause instructors to think about their priorities in teaching the various critical dimensions of a skill and to give corresponding attention and emphasis to helping participants learn these.

5.   Prepare rating forms to record observations of participants when their skills are being measured. The rating forms will need to be developed in ways that are appropriate and make sense in terms of the skills being measured. They should include separate rating scales for each of the critical dimensions of the skills. Each of these scales may consist of two or more points. Each should be labeled with behavioral descriptions and not evaluations as to how well it was performed.

For example, one critical dimension of interviewing skill might be eye contact made by interviewer. A scale with behavioral descriptions for this dimension might be:

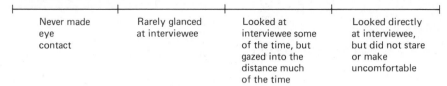

A scale with evaluations would be:

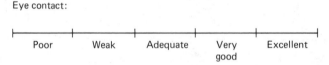

6.   Involve groups of two to five trained observers to record behaviors and to measure skills.

It might be helpful to make a distinction between purely mental skills and performance skills. The latter involve some combination of thinking and doing. Purely mental skills involve such things as problem solving, situational analysis, critical thinking, and decision making. Performance skills include things such as interviewing, listening with empathy and understanding, communicating, motivating, and planning.

The mental skills can be measured by rating people's performance on case-study analyses, problem solving, in-basket exercises, and the like, which require thinking, analyzing, insight judgment, and problem solving. Performance skills can be measured by rating people's performance on role-playing situations, exercises, games, and in-basket exercises, which require actions as well as decisions.

Perhaps the best source of help available to instructors who wish to measure skills are assessment centers. These include many already well-tested instruments for measuring particular skills, which may be directly applicable to their existing training needs, or at least they may serve as good examples that can be adapted to other specific situations and needs. Assessment-center measures will also provide instructors with helpful ideas on how to develop scoring measures as well.

Attitudes

To a large extent, people's actions are governed by their attitudes. Therefore, nearly every management-training program has attitude objectives in addition to knowledge and skill objectives.

The literature defines an attitude as an enduring system of three components which center about a single object (including people) or situations. These include: (1) the cognitive component or the beliefs about the object or situation; (2) the feeling component, or the affect connected with the object or situation; and (3) the action tendency component, or the disposition to take action with respect to the object or situation. Each of the three components may differ in terms of valence and multiplicity. *Valence* in the degree of favorability or unfavorability with respect to the object or situation. *Multiplicity* is the variation in the number and kind of the elements making up the components.

Measuring attitudes is a difficult process. Attitudes exist only in peoples' minds and are usually not highly visible or obvious. The measurement of attitudes is necessarily indirect. They can be measured only on the basis of inferences drawn from the responses of an individual toward the object or situation (Kretch 1962). It is unrealistic to think that it is possible to measure attitudes accurately by simply asking people to tell what their attitudes are. This does not mean to imply that a direct approach to attitude measurement is impossible. To a limited extent it may be possible, but there are enormous difficulties associated with it. For one thing, people do not fully know what their attitudes are. While they may be conscious of large portions of their attitudes, some remaining portions remain hidden from their view in the subconscious part of their minds. For another thing, people are frequently not willing to reveal their true attitudes. Instead, they will reveal only a portion of their attitudes. For many different reasons they may deliberately or nondeliberately disguise or distort those attitudes that they choose to reveal. This frequently occurs when those who are being studied reveal their attitudes in such a fashion (or so distort those which they do reveal) that their attitudes will appear in accordance with what they perceive either to be "appropriate" or what they perceive those who are studying the attitudes want to observe. Distortions caused by these forces are particularly likely when attitudes are measured after a training program which more or less suggests to participants what the "correct attitudes and correct ways" to handle situations are.

To summarize what has been said, attitudes are very difficult to measure because:

1. they are hidden in peoples' minds, and they are not overt;

2. they must be inferred, and inferences are frequently subject to distortions and errors;

3. people cannot simply tell others what their true attitudes really are because some portions of their attitudes are not known, even to themselves; and

4. when people do reveal their attitudes they often distort what they reveal.

These difficulties should not be completely discouraging to those charged with the task of attitude measurement. A thorough understanding of these problems can serve as the basis for developing methods and approaches so that attitudes can be measured as accurately as possible.

The two ways in which attitudes can be measured are: by the direct approach, where people are simply asked to reveal their attitudes; and by the indirect approach, where attitudes are inferred from observed behavior.

The direct approach usually involves paper-and-pencil measurement instruments which are completed by the individuals being studied. While it is possible to obtain these kinds of data orally, in practice this procedure is too cumbersome and time consuming. Much more can be collected by written measurements such as questionnaires and objective diagnostic tests.

There are two good questionnaire design approaches to attitude measurement. Both involve having respondents indicate their choices on objective scale items which most nearly or most closely reflect their attitudes. The first involves a series of statements about the object with regard to which attitudes are being measured. These various statements are different so that respondents can distinguish between them, and they cover the range of possible reactions toward the object. Respondents are asked to indicate the response that most closely reflects their attitude.

Example: Select the statement which most nearly reflects your belief about the way in which a manager should behave.

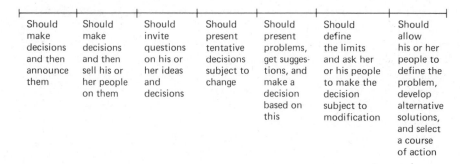

Should make decisions and then announce them	Should make decisions and then sell his or her people on them	Should invite questions on his or her ideas and decisions	Should present tentative decisions subject to change	Should present problems, get suggestions, and make a decision based on this	Should define the limits and ask her or his people to make the decision subject to modification	Should allow his or her people to define the problem, develop alternative solutions, and select a course of action

The second approach involves a continuum of feelings about some object, offering a range of possible degrees of approval or preference. These may be five-point scales or seven-point scales depending upon whichever is appropriate and permits respondents to distinguish between the alternative categories.

Examples: Select the responses which most nearly reflect your opinions and feelings.

A. Executives wearing shirts with open collars and suits at work.

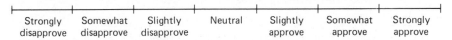

| Strongly disapprove | Somewhat disapprove | Slightly disapprove | Neutral | Slightly approve | Somewhat approve | Strongly approve |

B. What do you think about permitting women employees to wear mini skirts at work?

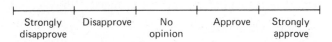

| Strongly disapprove | Disapprove | No opinion | Approve | Strongly approve |

One drawback to these kinds of scales is that some people very rarely, if ever, will select an extreme position, not because it does not most nearly reflect their feeling, but because it is an extreme position, which they prefer not to take.

There are also several standardized instruments that are useful for measuring particular attitudes. These include *How Supervise?* (File and Remmers 1971), "The Leadership Opinion Questionnaire" (Fleishman 1957), *Managerial Philosophies Scale* (Jacoby and Terborg 1957), and Myers' (1970) measure of supervisory style.

How Supervise? asks respondents to indicate whether they agree, disagree, or are undecided with regard to 100 statements about supervision. The L.O.Q. test asks respondents to select a response from a set of five alternatives to how a supervisor should act in forty different situations. *The Managerial Philosophies Scale* assesses the relative strengths of a manager's adherence to and reliance on theory X and theory Y. The Myers' "Belief in People" measures essentially the same thing.

The advantages to the direct approach are that once a good instrument has been developed or secured it is possible to measure a great number of people and a great number of their attitudes and, because of the scaling feature, in a fairly great degree of detail. The biggest drawback is the distortions that are possible for the reasons discussed earlier.

One approach to overcoming these distortions somewhat is the indirect approach. By this method, attitudes are inferred from people's responses to oral or written tests (particularly essay type) or from their behavior in performance tests. This approach is weak, however, in that it does not provide researchers with as much detail about people's attitudes—the best observers might be able to conclude is that people do or do not have a particular attitude, or that they like or approve or dislike or disapprove of something. As a practical matter, however, this may be adequate. The indirect approach is also weak in that the numbers of attitudes measured cannot be very large because of limited time available and the fact that it requires a great deal of time to measure from one to several attitudes via observations of behavior or from testing. And, the indirect approach is weak insofar as the inferences that are made are inaccurate.

Since the indirect approach is particularly susceptible to inference errors, it makes sense to guard against them by structuring the approach in a more scientific fashion. The following steps are suggested:

1.   Clearly identify the particular attitudes that are to be changed. Define and describe those that presently exist and what they should be like when they are changed.

2.   Specify the evidences that must be found to satisfy the requirements necessary to prove that the attitudes are changed in the ways desired.

3.   Plan how these evidences can be collected.

4.   Collect this information and determine whether the objectives have been met.

Sometimes the evidence required will necessitate using small teams of trained observers who can observe behavior and interpret it logically to arrive at accurate inferences about the attitudes in question. Above all else, particularly in this area and method of measurement, it is very important to be able to substantiate logically all inferences made from observed behavior or what people wrote or said.

How much learning is enough?

This is an important question, but all too infrequently asked. Certainly there should be changes that are large enough to be significant and not so slight as to reflect nothing more than random deviations due to variations of measurement. In other words, the average scores of the group on the various measures used should be significant. But what about changes of each of the members in the group? Must everyone who receives training be changed significantly before the training program can be judged to be effective? The answer to this latter question is no. It is unrealistic to think that even an excellent training program will have the same degree of influence on everyone involved and that all participants will learn a substantial amount. There will likely always be a few in any learning setting who will gain perceptibly little if anything at all. At the other extreme, there will be several who will gain a tremendous amount from the same experience. Then there is the "great mass of people in-between." Evaluators need to pay particular attention to what happens to this group. If participants learn significantly, if this amount of learning is acceptable to those who support the training, and if this compares favorably with what other good training programs have been able to generate in the way of increased knowledge and changes in skills and attitudes, then the training program can be judged effective.

Measuring Changes in Job Behavior

When the task of evaluating management training programs is faced, perhaps the most frequently raised question is, "Do the participants behave any differently because of their training?" To many people, the fact that participants return to their jobs after a training program and apply what they were supposed to have learned is sufficient evidence to conclude that the training was beneficial. The difficulty lies in assuring that this happens and then obtaining the evidence that it has.

Most everyone in the field of training has known or at least heard about someone who appeared to have learned the concepts and practices taught at a program, but who returned to the job and continued to manage just as he or she had all along, without applying a single thing that she or he apparently learned. This kind of situation is a good illustration of the fact that a knowledge of principles and techniques is not sufficient to guarantee that the person will use them on his job. There are, of course, many reasons why training can fail to carry over to the work situation. And it is important for those who approach the matter of training evaluation to be fully aware of these reasons so that they will not arrive at an erroneous conclusion that a particular training program was no good because participants did not apply the learning, when in fact they were prevented from doing so because of other reasons.

Katz (1964) has identified five basic requirements if a person is to consciously improve self and change her or his job behavior:

1. He must sincerely want to improve.

2. He must be willing to face-up squarely to his own inadequacies, without rationalizing or minimizing them.

3. He must be provided with a permissive atmosphere which shields out censure or ridicule when he exposes his weaknesses.

4. He must have someone whom he trusts, who is interested in helping him improve his performance, and who is himself sufficiently skilled that he is able to help.

5. He must be provided with direct experiences that enable him to learn and practice applying the knowledge and skills he acquired in the classroom.

These requirements are obviously above and beyond the scope of the typical training program. In short, they comprise what many would consider a "supportive climate," which all good training professionals know is necessary if participants are to apply their newly gained knowledge on their jobs. Nonetheless, it is this very thing which is so badly neglected by organizations and as a result why the potential benefits of training are rarely fully realized. To evaluate a training program in terms of changes in job behavior, without considering the extent to which the organization is supportive by encouraging and rewarding the application of the learning, is to open the door to the possibility of concluding that a program was not effective when, in fact, it might well have been very effective. In spite of the fact that very little attention has been given by organizations to creating supportive climates, most of the empirical investigations of training programs have concluded that they have been effective in causing changes. Perhaps the best review of empirical studies of training effects is the one by Campbell, Dunnette, Lawler, and Weick (1970).

The methodological complications associated with measuring behavioral changes are enormous—so great, in fact, that measurement purists give up on the task and scoff at those who still try. One should not give up on this task just because an uncontaminated, laboratory-like atmosphere for research does not exist. Organizational research and measurements, although not completely free from bias and distortion, can yield useful data for making sound judgments and decisions. And it is this kind of information that top management wants and needs and finds most satisfactory for their purposes. At the same time, sloppy and ill-conceived measurements should not be tolerated either. Every reasonable precaution should be taken to assure that measurements are as thorough and as error free as practical.

As stated a bit earlier in this chapter, the job of evaluating managerial behavior is quite complex. One reason for this is that managers do so many different things and they rarely do the same things twice or in the same way. Thus, if one were to record the behavior of a manager on one day, he or she might be hard pressed to substantiate that this manager was managing any differently at some later date largely because he or she would not be involved with doing the same things.

Another reason why the evaluation of managerial behavior is so difficult is because it does not lend itself to numerical and statistical measurement. How can a manager's communicating, leading, or planning be measured by numbers? It cannot. Qualitative and descriptive approaches must be used instead. The problem with these is that no two observers will see and evaluate the same person in the same situation in the same way. However, this drawback can be minimized to a tolerable level by employing a few checks such as observer training and team evaluations.

A third reason evaluation is difficult stems from the possibility of distortions arising from the fact that people know they are being studied and their behavior is being evaluated. Because of this they behave differently. This may become particularly pronounced during post-training behavior observations. In this regard, Hamblin (1974) raises the interesting point that perhaps this is not all bad. As he sees it, evaluation might be thought of as part of the training process—and if trying to find out how participants have applied their training causes them to use it to make themselves look good, so what? So much the better!

A fourth difficulty associated with evaluations of behavioral change involves the difficulty of establishing conclusively that it was the training itself that has caused these changes and not other factors. Andrews (1966, p. 4–5), fully aware of this, does not address it as a problem because he sees executive development programs as just one of the many factors that lead to change:

> The purpose of executive programs is to produce effects not at the end of the program but at a later time. By then, other developmental forces have affected the maturing of a person and the development of a manager will have so reinforced, contradicted, or in other ways affected the specific contribution of the program that it may no longer be given unshared credit for the consequences.

A fifth problem is the time required for thorough measurement and evaluation of the behaviors of all managers who attend a program. This is usually anywhere from 20 to 40 people. Given the fact that time and resources available for the evaluation of pretraining and post-training behaviors are limited, a dilemma arises. If evaluators study and evaluate the behaviors of all the managers who receive the training plus those in the control group(s) who do not, they will be able to obtain only limited and usually superficial data. If, instead, the pretraining and post-training behaviors of only a few of the people from both groups are made in great depth, then the possibility exists that those few people they study are either those who benefited greatly from the training and exhibited tremendous changes on their job or they are the few who did not benefit from the training and continue to perform their work as they always have. Both of these kinds of extremes are possible.

One way around this dilemma is to obtain information from others in addition to the trained observers, such as supervisors, subordinates, and peers. This may be done by means of interviews and questionnaires. This approach is, of course, subject to error and distortion because it involves untrained observers. However, when well-conceived and carefully administered it can provide reasonably good data.

The following guidelines (adapted from suggestions made by Kirkpatrick 1959) should be observed in studying and evaluating behavioral changes:

1. Systematically study and appraise on-the-job behavior before the training.

2. Clearly determine and specify the behavioral changes sought.

3. Identify and specify the evidences necessary to satisfactorily determine whether or the extent to which changes have occurred.

4. Plan how this evidence will be collected.

5. Systematically study and appraise on-the-job behavior three months or more after the training. This will allow trainees the opportunity to apply what they have learned. Additional studies later on may add to the validity of earlier findings.

6. Obtain evidence from as many of the following groups as practical.

    a) those who receive the training

    b) the trainees' superiors

    c) the trainees' subordinates

    d) the trainees' peers

    e) others in the organization who have frequent contact with the trainees.

7.   Compare before and after training performance. Use both quantitative and qualitative measures.

8.   Relate changes to training. If it is not possible to reason why or how particular changes could be caused by the training, then seriously question whether they were and consider the possibility that they were caused by other factors.

9.   A control group (or groups) not receiving the training should be used. [See "Design of the measurement Process" section of this chapter.]

10.   Use small groups or committees to review evidences and prepare a report on the changes. All claims that changes have occurred should be fully supported by evidences and reasons.

In addition to observations made by trained persons, there are a number of techniques for appraising behavior. Some are more useful than others. It is this factor—usefulness—that should receive primary attention in selecting the particular techniques to be used. In general, this involves specifying the behaviors that are to be changed and then selecting those techniques that can do this best. Many of the behavioral measuring techniques available and reported in the literature are of relatively little use when it comes to measuring those behaviors which are most commonly the targets of change.

Leadership behavior description questionnaire

This instrument is similar to the Leadership Opinion Questionnaire (L.O.Q.). It is an objective type measure completed by a manager's subordinates or others who observe him or her regularly. Like the L.O.Q., it measures the manager's leadership style in terms of initiating structure and consideration. This measure is good in that it contains some forty specific behaviors which respondents are asked to read and tell how frequently the subject in question exhibits each.

Critical incidents

This technique involves asking a manager's superiors, subordinates, or other frequent observers of her or his behavior to think of and describe specific incidents where they thought her or his behavior was effective or ineffective. This technique is useful in identifying training needs too. When used some time after the training program, an evaluation can be made as to whether ineffective behaviors persist and whether new, more effective behaviors are exhibited and can be attributed to the training effort.

Self reports

This approach has trainees tell about as many specific instances as they can of where and how they have put their newly acquired learning to use on the job. It is wise to corroborate these reports with other sources so as to assure the credibility of the evaluation. Management ought to be a deliberate process, and hence essentially consists of an ongoing process of evaluating situations, considering alternative courses of action, and deliberately choosing those which are judged to be most appropriate. To the extent people perform these things consciously, it seems reasonable to believe that they would be able to tell others not only what they did and why they did it, but also whether whatever it was they did and how they chose to do it was influenced by their training experience.

Interviews

A rich quantity of data can be collected by interviews with trainees as well as their subordinates, peers, and superiors. Understandably, this technique is susceptible to error. One kind of error that is possible comes about because interviewees may expect to see behavioral changes in trainees because of their learning experiences. Because of their expectations these observers will attribute effective behavior to the training, when in fact it may not be caused by it at all.

A second kind of possible error is *frozen evaluations* or the tendency to form an opinion of someone or something and never altering it. Once people get to know others fairly well, they tend to see them in pretty much the same way. The need for certainty in interpersonal relationships tends to cause this. As a result people may change, but these changes are not readily perceived by others and consequently may never be reported. To some extent, the problem of frozen evaluations adversely affects the quality of all measures of behavioral change that are based upon obtaining data from others.

One approach that can be followed in formulating interview formats is to develop questions along the same lines as the training purposes. In other words, if the training consisted of topics such as communications, motivation, decision making, planning, and so on, then ask probing questions to determine how those who are being studied behave on their jobs relative to these same areas. Caution should be given so as not to make the questions too leading, which might cause respondents to answer in one way or another. Data collected by means of interviews must be organized and summarized and then analyzed to determine whether the behaviors reported were really caused totally or in part by the training.

Committee opinions

This approach is seen by many as not sufficiently systematic to have adequate validity. Yet it can offer additional information that is helpful in the evaluation process. Committees of interested superiors are formed and charged with the task of identifying how those who have received training have changed in terms of their job behavior. The committee is asked not to simply give off-the-cuff impressions, but to provide examples of specific behaviors plus some reasonable arguments as to how these were caused by the training.

The Organizational Impact of Training

The ultimate aims of management training should be threefold:

1. to improve the performance of the organization in terms of profitability and consumer satisfaction with its products and services;

2. to cause managers to develop and maintain working climates that are richly rewarding and satisfying to their employees; and

3. to help leaders to make their organizations perform as decent, responsible citizens within the economic, social, and political environments in which they function.

These are the three basic responsibilities of all organizations; therefore improved managerial performance should be aimed at enabling organizations to do a better job of meeting them.

The evaluation of training in terms of its impact on the organization is essentially concerned with the question, "Has it assisted the organization to perform better?" More specifically, "Has training assisted the organization in meeting its three basic responsibilities?" While these questions are straightforward, the process of answering them in a satisfactory fashion is enormously complex. The link between improvements in managerial behaviors and improvements in organizational performance is nearly impossible to prove conclusively. It has been stated earlier in this chapter that it is extremely difficult to substantiate conclusively links between managerial behaviors and organizational outcomes. It is even more difficult to make the same kind of connection between improvements in organizational results and changes in managerial behaviors. Moreover, researchers find it very difficult simply to identify the other factors that may have an impact on organizational outcomes, let alone understand how they do have an impact. Investigations and researchers will likely question, "Was the organization's performance caused by managerial actions or by other forces?" Additionally, the evaluation of training in terms of organizational impact is also difficult because the results of improvements in managerial performance are not usually immediate. It may be several years before they begin to occur and even some time beyond this before they become recognized.

Statistical measures and quantifiable evidences cannot be relied upon as the only ways of answering the kinds of evaluation questions mentioned. Opinions and judgments which are substantiated by reasonable evidences have to be used primarily, instead. One should strive to obtain as much quantifiable evidence as possible because it is generally more impressive. However, if unable to do so, one should not feel that qualitative measures cannot demonstrate the values of training adequately.

The "hard-nosed" approach toward evaluating training—that is, insisting that training must prove its worth in terms of profits and costs, production quantity and quality, dollars and cents, should not go unquestioned. Why should training stand alone as the only activity that has to prove its worth? If an organization demands that this kind of justification be given for training, should it not also ask that the same be done for all other expenditures, such as limousine service for its executives, bonus plans, carpeting and walnut desks in the executive offices, vacations, insurance plans, the company jet, liberal pension plans, research and development, advertising, etc.?

Moreover, one should challenge the belief that training, by itself, will cause improvements in managerial performance and, hence, lead to improved organizational effectiveness. Training is just one of the key elements that are needed to bring about these improvements. Alone it is not sufficient to do this. Top management's support and dedication for improvements as well as an organizational climate supportive of change and of sound management practices are also necessary.

When training is done well and when the organization recognizes and rewards the application of the concepts it includes, the benefits accruing to the organization can be numerous and great. More specifically, these may include the following kinds of benefits:

1. Improved viability of the organization through its doing a better job of creating and evaluating possible purposes and directions and then selecting the best ones, formulating policies and plans for attaining its stated goals, and organizing appropriately to meet these

2. Increases in the organization's willingness and ability to change and optimally adapt itself to the economic, social, and political environments in which it operates

3. Greater efficiency in production and other activities carried out by the firm

4. Better quality of products and services to meet the needs and preferences of consumers

5. Improved quality of decisions made throughout the organization

6. More responsible and public-minded actions and policies of the firm

7. Improved supervisory and managerial personnel

8. Improved interdepartmental coordination and cooperation

9. Better union-management relations

10. Better morale, lower turnover and absenteeism, and greater employee satisfaction with jobs and the firm in general

11. Increases in the firm's ability to attract good people and hold them in its employ

12. Better communications throughout the organization

13. Improvements in the career opportunities within the firm for employees

14. Helps to broaden technically oriented people to become managers and think and function from a managerial perspective

15. Improved profitability

16. Keeps people up to date in their technical fields and with the latest management practices; helps them avoid obsolesence as they keep their minds active and alive to new ideas, methods, and challenges

By and large, the choice of the information gathering techniques to be used in assessing the organizational impacts of training largely determine which impacts will be assessed. The choice of techniques, therefore, becomes an important matter because it may cause valuable organizational impacts to go unnoticed. The same may be said for measuring the effects of training at the reaction, learning, and behavior levels.

There may be a tendency to attempt what some would call *evaluation overkill* at the organizational impact level; in other words, an attempt to measure anything and everything possible. Quite obviously, the time and costs associated with this approach will most likely prohibit it. Some degree of judgment is necessary in making the decision as to what to look for and which methods will be used. Those who make this decision should be aware of what it involves and its significance.

For the most part, the techniques used in assessing organizational impact are subjective. Even objective measures such as profit, costs, production, etc., must be interpreted subjectively. As with the other levels of evaluation, this one too requires creativity in designing methods of measurement which are appropriate to the unique aspects of the organization and its management training.

Management audit

This involves an assessment of managerial and supervisory talent throughout the organization. It is usually carried out by task force committees whose members study performance appraisals and other operations reports. The aim of a management audit is to identify the people who have the abilities necessary to fulfill the various management and supervisory positions in the organization. The management audit not only identifies those who are immediately promotable, but it also identifies those who can be prepared to become able to handle these positions. The audit also includes an assessment of strengths and weaknesses of each person studied. These data, particularly the numbers of promotable people and an overall assessment of their strengths and weaknesses, provide one gauge for assessing the impact of training. The basic drawback to this approach is that it takes time, several years usually, to notice changes. One year's data must be compared to past years' data to determine whether changes have occurred. This technique relies on consistency and reliability in the yearly audits.

Surveys

Questionnaires, morale surveys, opinion surveys, and the like, are useful techniques for measuring perceptions of organizational performance and climate from within. Many of the potential benefits listed earlier can be assessed by survey methods.

Analyses of records and performance data

Productivity indices, production records, cost data, profitability measures, and other operating records and data can be studied and analyzed to help assess organizational impacts. Obviously, many other factors will have a direct bearing on these measures of performance. Nonetheless, they ought to be studied and some attempt be made to gauge the impact training has had on them.

Expert's opinion

The services of a capable, outside consultant may be called upon to conduct periodic audits of organizational performance. In essence the outside consultant studies the organization as he or she would analyze a case study. After a few years of repeated visits the consultant should be able to determine whether significant changes have occurred and what they are.

Committee opinions

This essentially involves the same thing as what the outside consultant does, but it is carried out by a task-force committee of managers who have been carefully selected on the basis of their immediate knowledge of the organization and its personnel and of sound management. It is essential that these people be insightful and knowledgeable of good management and that they be given adequate time to conduct systematic audits of the organization.

Additional Outcomes Caused by Training

To some extent, the assessment of additional outcomes will overlap with measures of organizational impact. The distinction between these two areas of evaluation is not important. It is important to recognize additional outcomes and to include them as part of the comprehensive evaluation. Fundamentally, additional outcomes involve benefits to the individuals who received the training and to the groups and organizations to which they belong. It considers questions about those who received the training such as: Are they better people? Do they obtain a greater sense of satisfaction and pride from their work? Do they feel better about themselves? Are they better fathers, mothers, husbands, and wives? Are they better citizens? Can they better serve the various professional, religious, political, and service organizations they are members or leaders of? Are they more mobile and hence better able to work at the job of their choice, and hence more likely to contribute more and to a fuller extent to their nation's economic performance?

A frequently overlooked additional value of training arises because of the fact training takes place. The mere act of engaging in training goes a long way in conveying the message to members of the organization that on-going improvement and personal development are important matters and that the organization values good management. This helps to establish and strengthen desirable organizational norms, such as keeping members up to date in their own fields and encouraging them to remain mentally active. There is a tremendous difference in the climates and the levels of performance of organizations that have these kinds of norms and those that do not.

There are no formal methods for measuring these benefits. Again, a large degree of creativity is needed on the part of those who are charged with the evaluation responsibility in developing approaches to measure the additional outcomes. Opinion surveys and opinion committees are the most logical choice of methods to use.

THE EVALUATION REPORT

Once the evaluation study has been completed, the findings should be communicated to various concerned persons who have an interest and need to know how the program turned out and the impact it had. The careful preparation and timely communication of program evaluation findings is an important responsibility of the training department. To some extent the quality of this report will have an impact upon the level of support in the future for training from influential people in the organization and upon the improvements that, in all likelihood, are necessary.

Although a good evaluation study is quite thorough and encompasses all of the five areas or levels discussed earlier, it ought to be realized that all those who have an interest in the program and its impact do not want or need to know the same information about it. Consequently, it is wise to ascertain exactly what each person who is to receive information about the program evaluation needs and wants to know. And then, just those things should be communicated to these people instead of presenting everyone with the same, massive report to wade through detail by detail. As with most other types of reports, the more concise they are, the better. If someone needs to know more, she or he can always read the complete report from which the one that was prepared for her or him was extracted.

Organization of the Report

A well-organized report is not only impressive and useful, it is appreciated too. It should be typed neatly and reproduced cleanly and attractively. Wording should be straightforward and to the point. Jargon should not be used if possible. When it is used, it should be defined. A well-written report is properly titled, identified, and dated. It should contain the name(s) of the person(s) who prepared it as well as whom to contact in case the reader has questions or wants further information.

It makes good sense to organize the report into the four sections suggested here:

1.   Major findings and conclusions:
Busy managers and executives do not like to wade through piles of details and data. They want "bottom line" answers. So, give them to them. Begin the report with up to a dozen simply worded findings or conclusions. Several examples follow.

a) All participants felt that the program was worthwhile and would recommend it for their peers.

b) Seventy-five percent of the subordinates of the managers who received the training now feel their bosses do a better job of communicating important information.

c) The quality of performance appraisals has improved markedly as a result of the training.

d) Employee morale and motivation are both significantly higher because of the training.

If appropriate, it is a good idea to categorize these major findings and conclusions by the five areas, or levels, of evaluation.

2.   Findings and supporting evidence:
This second section should begin wiht a few brief statements telling how the evaluation data were gathered (e.g., by means of questionnaires, examinations, interviews, observations, study of performance data, etc.)

This section, in effect, reports on how well the program met its objectives. It should, therefore, contain each of the various training objectives accompanied by a statement of how well each was met and the supporting evidence to substantiate each conclusion. Findings should be stated clearly. The supporting evidence may include statistical data accurately tabulated and neatly presented in the form of charts, tables, or graphs. Or they may be a collection of statements or observations. Care must be taken to assure that the findings are logical conclusions drawn from the evidences presented. Two questions will serve to help assure this:

a) What information is sufficient and necessary in order to make a particular conclusion?

b) Can anything different or anything else be concluded from the information obtained?

In some cases the evidences and data need to be interpreted or explained so that readers do not arrive at erroneous conclusions. For example, it may be that the instructor who taught goal setting, or the management of time, or management controls did not receive an exceptionally outstanding rating. From this information alone, some might conclude that this particular instructor is not very good or effective and perhaps should even be replaced on future programs. These conclusions may be totally incorrect and unwarranted since this instructor's comparatively lower rating can be explained by the fact that he or she had to teach a comparatively duller subject.

3.   Significance of the findings:

Surely many of the findings have some significance that is not readily obvious. This should be explored and stated in the third section.

4.   Suggested improvements and recommendations:

Few, if any, programs are perfect. Recommendations and improvements need to be considered and should also be reported. They should be presented in the form of straightforward, simply worded statements. They should be followed by a list of specific actions that will be taken to affect the recommendations and suggested improvements.

EVALUATION: THE PRACTICAL DIMENSION

Throughout this chapter an attempt has been made to encourage people to evaluate training programs as thoroughly as practical. Incidentally, there is a great difference between doing something as thoroughly as possible and as thoroughly as practical. It has also been emphasized that it is important to find out what those who want evaluation information need to know and to obtain this information by the easiest and least costly methods.

One last aspect of being practical in evaluating training has, until now, not been mentioned—namely, not carrying the evaluation effort to the point where it becomes an annoyance and a detriment to the training effort. It is very important, therefore, for those who are engaged in evaluation to be aware of the significance and potential impacts of their activities. The following true incident will hopefully illustrate the kind of thing evaluators should be cautious about.

A few years ago, a company was planning to send several of its managers to a reputable management-development program. The training manager in this firm was quite intent upon evaluating the impact of the training program on these managers. And, being oriented along the lines of objective measures, the training manager laid out an extensive plan involving pretests, post tests, interviews with the managers, and interviews with their superiors and subordinates both before and after the training. From the standpoint of being logical and thorough in evaluating the impact of the training, the training manager's plan was good. But this training manager was very neglectful of a practical dimension. Namely, what was the significance of all these measurements? How would these managers feel about all this testing and checking and interviewing? Would they feel like small children might as a parent figure watched over their every move? Might they feel their company didn't quite trust them to go away to a course and learn? And, to make sure they did learn, would there be measures and reports? How would they feel about all the interviews with their superiors and subordinates? Would they like to be the focus of all these people's attention? And might they even feel as if they're rats in a maze being observed by a scientist or experimenter? In short, would all this evaluation and measuring have a detrimental affect on their attitude and the attitudes of other people in the organization toward training? It is highly possible that it would. As this illustration shows, evaluation needs to be carried out cautiously and with the feelings of those who are being studied in mind.

Another, and frequently neglected, aspect of the evaluation process involves the unnoticed consequence of limiting the evaluation to only the reaction level. While it is desirable for participants to react favorably to the program and to those who presented it, other outcomes should be sought too—particularly attitude changes and learning and behavioral changes on-the-job. If the evaluation process involves only the reactions of participants, it is likely that changes will be made in future presentations of the program, over time, to merely make it more and more pleasing to the participants and not necessarily more educational and impactful. Moreover, an extreme and over concern for merely pleasing participants can lead to a climate or attitude held by participants that training should cater to all their fussy likes and dislikes, and that they are involved in training primarily to be pleased and not to learn. If the evaluation is balanced and involves all five areas or levels, the program will most likely achieve all the aims it was designed to fulfill.

REFERENCES

Andrews, Kenneth. *The Effectiveness of University Management Development Programs.* Boston: Division of Research, Graduate School of Business Administration, Harvard University, 1966.

_____. "Is Management Training Effective?" *Harvard Business Review* **35**, No. 2, 1957, pp. 63–72.

Berry, D. R. *Effective Training.* Scranton, Pa.: ICS-Intext, 1969.

Buchanan, Paul C. "Testing the Validity of an Evaluation Program." *Personnel* **34**, No. 3, 1957, pp. 78–81.

Campbell, John P., Dunnette, Marvin D.; Lawler, Edward E.: III,; and Weick, Karl E., Jr. *Managerial Behavior Performance and Effectiveness.* New York: McGraw-Hill, 1970.

Fast, Dorothy. "A New Approach to Quantifying Training Program Effectiveness." *Training and Development Journal* **28**, No. 9, 1974, pp. 8–15.

File, Quentin W., and Remmers, H. H. *How Supervise?* New York: The Psychological Corp., 1971.

Fleishman, Edwin A. "The Leadership Opinion Questionnaire," in Stogdill, R. M. and A. E. Coons (eds.), *Leader Behavior, Its Description and Measurement.* Columbus, Ohio: Ohio State University Bureau of Business Research, 1957.

Hamblin, A. C. *Evaluation and Control of Training.* London: McGraw-Hill, 1974.

Jacoby, Jacob, and Terborg, James R. *Managerial Philosophies Scale.* Woodstock, Texas: Telemetrics, International.

Katz, Robert. "Human Relations Skills Can Be Sharpened." *Harvard Business Review* **34**, No. 4, 1964, pp. 61–72.

Kirkpatrick, Donald L. "Evaluation of Training," (Chapter 5, pp. 87–112) in Craig, Robert L. and Lester R. Bittel (eds.), *Training and Development Handbook.* New York: McGraw-Hill, 1967. Also published as: "Techniques for Evaluating Training Programs," I–IV, *Journal of the American Society of Training Directors* **13**, 1959, pp. 3–9, 21–26; and **14**, pp. 13–18, 28–32.

Korb, David L. "How to Measure the Results of Supervisory Training." *Personnel* **32**, No. 5, 1956, pp. 378–391.

Kretch, David; Crutchfield, Richard S.; and Ballachey, Egerton L. *Individual in Society.* New York: McGraw-Hill, 1962.

MacKinney, A. C. "Progressive Levels in the Evaluation of Training Programs." *Personnel* **34**, No. 3, 1957, pp. 72–77.

Mahler, Walter R. "Evaluation of Management Development Programs." *Personnel* **30**, No. 2, 1953, pp. 116–122.

Matsushito. "The Matsushito Miracle: How to Build $5.8 Billion in Sales from a $50 Start." *Business Week,* June 6, 1977, pp. 8–9.

Morano, Richard. "Measurement and Evaluation of Training." *Training and Development Journal* **19**, No. 7, 1965, pp. 42–46.

Mosel, James N. "Why Training Programs Fail to Carry Over." *Personnel* **34**, No. 3, 1957, pp. 56–64.

Myers, M. Scott. *Every Employee a Manager.* New York: McGraw-Hill, 1970.

Newman, William H. "Shaping the Master Strategy of Your Firm." *California Management Review* **9**, No. 3, 1967.

Odiorne, George. "The Need for an Economic Approach to Training." *Journal of American Society for Training and Development* 18, No. 3, 1964, pp. 3–12.

_____. "A Systems Approach to Training." *Training Directors Journal* 19, No. 1, 1965, pp. 3–11.

Planty, Earl G. "New Methods for Evaluating Supervisory Training." *Personnel* 21, No. 4, 1945, pp. 235–241.

Randall, L. K. "Evaluation: A Training Dilemma." *Journal of the American Society of Training and Development* 14, No. 5, 1960, pp. 29–35.

Runkel, Philip J., and McGrath, Joseph E. *Research on Human Behavior.* New York: Holt, Rinehart, and Winston, 1972.

Warr, Peter; Bird, Michael; and Rackham, Neil. *Evaluation of Management Training.* London: Gower Press, 1970.

Wolfe, J. "Evaluating the Training Effort." *Training and Development Journal* 27, No. 3, 1973, pp. 20–25.

9

Answers to
Commonly
Asked Questions
About
Management Training

1. What can be done to convince top management of the need for training?

Start by establishing a favorable rapport between yourself and top management. People are influenced most by those whom they know and trust. So the first thing to do is to build a strong and favorable relationship with top management; for without this the channels of communication are pretty much closed. One of the best ways of achieving this aim is by understanding top management and the problems those in top management face and then by acting in helpful ways so that they perceive those responsible for training as being supportive and helpful to their endeavors. Once this kind of rapport is established several things might be tried.

One approach is to suggest to top management what progressive and successful firms are currently doing. Many top-level executives are impressed most by what the managers of prestigious and successful firms do that might account for their success. Simply suggesting to top management that "other firms" are involved in training is not enough; this kind of argument is not sufficiently convincing. You will need to be much more specific, so research the area thoroughly. Find out what other companies are doing so that you will be able to prepare a list of these firms and short descriptions of the training programs they have or use as well as an indication of the numbers of their people who participate.

Another approach is to appeal to top management in a straightforward fashion. Sit down and talk with them about management development and how training is a key part of this process. Focus the discussion on the notion that a firm's long-run success ultimately depends upon the quality of its management. Then raise the question, "What is our firm doing to assure a supply of able and qualified managers?" In cases where the firm's top-level managers are already somewhat sympathetic and favorable toward training, this approach can work. It may, however, only get top management to agree to try out some form of training before making a fuller commitment to it.

Still another approach is to expose some of the firm's managers or supervisors, or better still the top-level managers themselves, to training so they have a chance to discover its value themselves first hand. By all means, make sure that whatever the training experience is, it is of a nature and quality so as to earn support and acceptance. It should be well-planned, well-taught, appropriate and practical.

In one major United States corporation, the director of management development and training could not get top management's commitment for training for upper-level or even middle-level management. They were, however, agreeable to supervisory training for first-line supervisors. The training department was not discouraged but set to work preparing the best quality supervisory-training program they could. Their efforts paid off handsomely. The supervisors who attended the first several sessions liked the training and spoke about it enthusiastically. Soon, other supervisors were clamoring for training. Upper management went along with their request. About the time most of the supervisors had completed the supervisory course, some of the firm's middle-level managers went to their superiors to request a training program for themselves. They felt left out, and hearing about the experiences those below them had with training, wanted to have similar opportunities for self-improvement. These requests increased and within a few months top management was flooded with requests for training from the middle-level managers. This chain of events opened the eyes of the firm's top management, who, a few months later, decided to provide training opportunities for those at the executive level too.

One should bear in mind that, in many cases, apathetic and negative attitudes toward training stem from unfavorable experiences with education and form deepseated fears and feelings of insecurity caused by the perception that others may know more. These people frequently cover up their feeling by saying, "Experience is what really counts. Education is not very useful for me or my people." Training specialists must be sensitive to and understanding of these kinds of feelings. They must never embarrass or intimidate these people. Instead, training professionals should help these people overcome their fears and negative feelings by providing them with useful and rewarding training so they can come to appreciate and value it.

2.   What should I say when people ask, "Can management training do any good?" "After all," they say, "isn't management ability something people are just born with?"

In some cases, management training probably cannot produce observable changes. These situations are few. There are some people with abilities, interests, and personalities that no amount of training can change perceptibly. At the other end of the continuum, however, are those who will profit enormously from training. Then there is the bulk of people in the middle, so to speak. The question is, "Can training cause changes in these people?" The answer is, "yes." And there is adequate research evidence to support this conclusion. If the management training is of the nature described in this book, it can produce change.

Miner's (1965) examination of the evidences concerning the effects of management training programs led him to the following conclusions:

1. Almost all of the research studies done on the impact of management development offer positive evidence of change.

2. There is enough consistency among these results to offer substantial proof of the ability of management development programs to bring about certain types of changes.

3. The most frequently caused changes are the aquisition of human relations attitudes and problem solving skills.

Campbell, Dunnette, Lawler, and Weick's (1970) review of the empirical studies of training effects revealed the following:

1. Approximately 80 percent of the empirical studies done on the effects of general-management and human-relations programs revealed that these programs yielded significant results.

2. There is reasonably convincing evidence that T-group training and the laboratory method do induce changes in the back-home setting.

Quite possibly, those who doubt that management training can bring forth changes in managerial behavior do so because they tend to envision all learning experiences as being pretty much alike. Thus by failing to realize that effective management training involves intellectual as well as emotional learning, they do not see how it can have much of an effect on people.

Observations of managers offer further evidence. Today's enlightened managers—and there are more and more as time goes on—do a far better job than their counterparts in earlier generations. Objectives are more clearly and thoroughly set forth; planning is better; organization structures are better designed; control systems are much improved; leadership is better; work climates are more motivating; communications networks are more effective; and people are being better utilized and developed to a fuller extent today than at any other time. These improvements have not occurred by chance. They have been caused and nurtured by education and by top management's efforts to continually improve the quality of management ability in their organizations.

3.   What is the difference between training and organization development?

Although there is no widely accepted view as to exactly what organization development is, French and Bell's (1973, p. 15) definition appears quite frequently in the literature. According to them:

> Organization development is a long-range effort to improve an organization's problem solving and renewal processes, particularly through a more effective and collaborative management of organization culture—with special emphasis on the culture of formal work teams—with the assistance of a change agent, or catalyst, and the use of the theory and technology of applied behavioral science, including action research.

Organization development is a systematic intervention to bring about some planned change that will improve the functioning of the organization. The goal is to improve the organization's ability to accomplish its goals. The planned changes focus on individual, interpersonal, and intergroup behavior. In general, there are two kinds of interventions—behavioral and structural. The *behavioral interventions* include fulfillment of human needs, improvements in interpersonal relationships, team building, interdepartmental cooperation and coordination. The *structural interventions* include planning, goal setting and M.B.O., improvements in technology, work flows and practices, and control systems.

Training is only a part of organization development. It may be used as an intervention technique in an organization development effort, but by itself it is not organization development. In short, organization development focuses on improving the effectiveness of an organization. Training is only one of the many techniques used to accomplish this.

4.   What are the necessary elements of a management development system? Are things other than training necessary?

Although it plays an important part, training is not the only necessary element of a management-development system. Other activities must be carried out, and carried out well, if an organization is to develop its managerial resources, which include the following:

1.   Managerial manpower planning, including management audits and forecasts

2.   Performance appraisals based upon performance criteria and not traits

3.   Day-to-day coaching and counseling, including career as well as work-performance counseling

4.   Planned on-the-job learning experiences, particularly job rotation, to expose promising managers to opportunities to learn various aspects of the

business, as well as efforts aimed at getting managers to apply in a systematic fashion what they learn in courses and seminars

5.   Planned off-the-job learning experiences, such as courses, workshops, seminars, reading programs, etc.

Perhaps most important is the need for top management's belief in and commitment to the development of employees. An organization may carry out all the above activities, but these may fail to achieve what they should if top management is not 100 percent behind them and does not create and maintain the attitude among employees that training and development are important.

5.   Would it be a wise policy to train just those who can profit from training substantially as can be predicted by pretraining tests? Wouldn't this be a savings for our organization?

There are some people these days who are putting forth the idea of concentrating the training effort on only those who will benefit from it, or benefit from it the most; and to some extent their argument has merit. Certainly, one would not want to spend large sums of money on training in supervisory management hourly employees who have demonstrated little or no supervisory potential. Neither would it make much sense to send all low- and middle-level managers to university or other outside executive-development programs regardless of their career plans or leadership potential. But this kind of screening is not the same as providing training opportunities for only those managers and supervisors who have "passed" some sort of test that claims to predict their success in learning. Tests may exist that can predict learning achievement. However, none does a good job of predicting what really counts—i.e., performance on the job. It would be impossible to tell beforehand what exactly it is that someone might learn in a management training program and successfully use sometime later in her or his work. To exclude some people from training experiences may save the organization training dollars, but it also runs the risk of foregoing substantial benefits as well.

There is a far more important reason for not excluding people from training opportunities that are available to their peers. Those who are excluded from training opportunities that are available to their friends and peers quickly become alienated from the organization. Rightly and understandably so, they feel that they have been "written off" by higher management. When this happens, their dedication to the organization quickly wanes. Worse yet, their self-confidence and motivation for self-improvement can diminish substantially.

Training should be available to everyone. To exclude some and favor others tends to create a caste system of promising hopefuls and "write-offs." This, in turn, can lead to negativism. Still another cost incurred by limiting training opportunities is the effect it will have on the overall organizational attitude toward development and self-improvement. If development is only for a few, then most people will conclude that everyone need not be improvement conscious. This sentiment can adversely influence creativity and innovation.

6.   We used to hear a lot about transactional analysis, and then transcendental meditation and assertiveness training became popular. It seems like every few years another fad comes along and everybody is into it. Should we get involved in these sort of things?

It is difficult to give a simple, categorical yes or no answer to this. It is true that every so many years a new "fad" springs up. There is nothing wrong with this except for the fact that these fads are usually accompanied by the expectation that they will solve all sorts of problems. That is, these fads are viewed as some type of "holy grail," or a panacea for all problems. People expect too much from them. If an organization chooses to get involved in these sorts of things, it should provide its members with realistic expectations as to the demands and the benefits and limitations of these techniques.

A firm also needs to face up to questions such as the following: Is this particular technique or approach useful to us? Can we live with its consequences if it is practiced? For example, many firms found that they could not live with the consequences of sensitivity training, which advocated openness, leveling, and authenticity in interpersonal relationships. Likewise, the question might be raised, can we tolerate everyone becoming more assertive? Naturally, the answers to these and similar questions depend upon the goals and philosophy of the organization.

Even if the immediate benefits of a technique or practice may be small, it may be worthwhile (insofar as training) in that it stimulates thinking and encourages people to remain mentally active. Employees of those firms that provide training in the various fads that come along from time to time may question their value but, at the same time, they also feel that their organization is progressive, up to date, and dedicated to keeping its employees current in management knowledge and skills. The latter is an important ingredient of a climate that nurtures on-going development.

7.   We receive armloads of flyers and brochures announcing all sorts of training programs and workshops. How can we tell if they are any good?

Today's manager is flooded with all sorts of flyers and brochures announcing management courses, seminars, and workshops. Many come from universities and other recognized organizations that present training programs. As a generalization, the better-known universities and professional organizations provide sound programs. Therefore, the question that really needs to be answered in these situations is, "Will this particular training experience be of value to our people?" There are three ways to find out. One is to talk with people who have attended previous sessions of the program. Another way is to study the brochure and the program outline. And the third way is to talk with the program coordinator directly.

But what about program announcements coming from lesser-known universities and training organizations? Here one finds a great variation in quality ranging from excellent to poor. Several questions should be raised when considering these courses.

1.   What are the program's objectives?

2.   Does the course outline make sense? Does it appear to be well thought out?

3.   Who teaches on the program? What are their backgrounds and experiences?

4.   What can the program coordinator tell those who inquire about the course?

5.   What do others who have attended previous sessions say about the course?

6.   What materials (cases, readings, assignments, etc.) are used?

7.   What teaching methods are used?

8.   Who has attended the program? What are the titles and organizations represented?

Many training directors are overly influenced by the name and the prestigious reputations of some universities and therefore tend to give credibility only to the programs offered by these schools. This group misses out on the opportunity to take advantage of many excellent programs presented by lesser-known schools.

8.   How should we go about selecting the right university executive programs for our people to attend?

Today there are over fifty university sponsored executive-development programs in the United States and many others overseas. Most of the ones held in the United States are at least four weeks in length. A few run for six or more weeks. Many of these programs cover roughly the same subject matter. Still, there exists a wide variety of approaches and emphases in terms of content. Some programs are aimed at teaching general management. Based upon the belief that those who attend are already competent in their respective technical fields, these programs stress general management: structure, people, quantitative analysis and methods, and environment. Other programs are aimed at broadening the participants' perspectives through exposing them to the various functional areas of business such as accounting, finance, marketing, economics, quantitative methods, management, and environment. Some university programs emphasize the management-science school of thought and stress quantitative analysis and methods. Others emphasize the behavioral approach.

It is important to recognize that these and other differences exist and that all university executive-development programs are not the same. Moreover, the quality of the various university executive programs is not necessarily related to the prestige of the sponsoring school. Many of the best university programs are not presented by the so-called "elite" universities.

There are many very good university sponsored programs, each with its own unique emphasis and flavor. It makes sense, therefore, for a firm to spend time to carefully select programs that most nearly match the needs and interests of the individual managers they send, as opposed to sending all their managers to the same program or to programs that managers think they would like to attend because of the prestige or snob appeal of this or that university.

A study of developmental needs of the individual slated to attend an outside program is one important prerequisite in effecting a good match. The other important prerequisite is to secure adequate information about the various university programs. There are several good sources. Perhaps the best source is *Bricker's Directory of University Sponsored Executive Development Programs*, written and published by George W. Bricker, a Massachusetts-based management consultant. Other sources are the universities themselves. All that offer programs publish brochures describing their program, which may be obtained by writing to the respective program directors. Information about programs may also be obtained by visiting the universities. Most university executive-program directors will welcome visitors from prospective user companies, provided the visit is short and not distracting. Still other sources of information are past program participants.

In addition to analyzing a program's content and emphasis, other factors should be considered.

1. Length of program

2. Time of year program is offered

3. Geographic location

4. Setting: city, rural, or resort

5. Living accommodations

6. Recreational facilities available

7. Kind of participants: level and type of job

8. Companies represented

Bricker (1975, p. 45) suggests the following principles for firms to keep in mind when selecting and sending people to programs.

1. University executive development programs are not for "problem cases." They simply are not geared for psychiatric therapy.

2. They should not be used as a "reward" or as a sort of "vacation" for a deserving, but no longer "moving" executive.

3. The candidate should be consulted about the choice of program, and should know *why* he is being sent to one, and what he is expected to get out of it.

4. Make sure that the participant is totally relieved of his day-to-day responsibilities while he is attending the program by seeing that these responsibilities are properly delegated to another executive—preferably one who will thereby be experiencing some practical executive development.

5. A participant gets out of one of these programs just about what he puts into it.

9. We would like to set up an in-house supervisory program for our supervisors. Where can we obtain help?

There are several "canned" supervisory-management courses a firm can buy. The problems that users typically encounter with these are:

1. they do not adequately meet the specific needs and interests of their supervisors;

2. they are somewhat dull and boring; many are superficial; and

3. they are structured such that discussion cannot easily dwell upon areas other than what the lesson plan calls for.

Despite these potential problems, a firm might find it useful to investigate what these programs have to offer.

Other sources of information and assistance are the dozen or more books in print on supervisory management. Many of these books contain case studies in each chapter. Any one of these books can serve as the basic structure and training material for a course. Still other sources of help are management professors. Most universities with schools of business have one or two management professors on their staff who have had experience in setting up and running supervisory programs. If a firm attempts to pursue this route, it is a good idea to interview several professors to find the one it likes the best and feels will do the best job for them.

Last, it might be possible to consult other firms to find out what they do in the way of supervisory training. Most people in the training field are willing to share ideas and information.

10. We are setting up a management development program and are faced with a question about scheduling. Is it better to have our course run for one solid week, five days in a row, or should it run one day a week for five weeks?

From the standpoint of learning and attitude change it is better to have the program run for five consecutive days. Participants must be relieved of their normal duties so they can devote their full time and attention to the learning experience. By running the program in one continuous block, the group tends to become more solidified and the benefits of group influences and group learning can be realized. (See Chapter 2 for more information about the importance of the group in the learning process.)

The most obvious difficulty with scheduling a program in one block of time is the impact it might have on organization operations. A firm might not be adequately staffed to permit its managers to be away from work for more than a day or two at a time. In these cases, there is no other choice than to schedule the program one day or even one half a day per week for several weeks. But there are drawbacks to this type of scheduling arrangement. For one thing, it is difficult for people to "shift gears" mentally and get away from pressures and problems at work and get into the learning. For another thing, it is difficult to assure that everyone will be able to attend each session. People have a tendency to skip those days of training when work problems demand their attention and presence. Also, under this type of scheduling participants are not as likely to prepare for each session and to devote adequate time in groups to discuss and analyze case studies. And last, just traveling to and from a conference center can be a nuisance and tiring.

11. Our organization is planning to construct a conference center. Where can we obtain some assistance in designing it?

The best source of help is from others who have conference centers. The more of these you visit and the more you talk with people who use and operate conference centers, the better. Some universities and several of the larger, private firms in the United States have their own conference centers. There are also several privately owned conference centers which rent out space. The latter frequently advertise in training and development periodicals.

When talking with people who run or use these conference centers, it is a good idea to make lists of what they say they like and dislike about their particular facility. Be sure to obtain information about interior furnishings, particularly tables and chairs.

It is also necessary to specify the uses you intend to make of the proposed center. What types of groups and meetings will it serve?

12. What qualities and characteristics should we consider when hiring a training consultant?

Reputation:

1.   What is the consultant known for?

2.   What do the consultant's previous clients think of him or her?

3.   What has the consultant published and accomplished?

Background and experience:

1. What are the consultant's academic credentials?

2. For whom has he or she consulted? What was the nature of these assignments?

3. What are his or her work experiences other than consulting?

Personal characteristics:

1. Does the consultant seem to have all the answers? If so, be leery of her or him. The world is far too complex for quick solutions to work out successfully.

2. Is the consultant innovative or does she or he have "canned" answers to your problems? Does the consultant demonstrate the ability to think and to analyze your problems or does he or she just give out solutions?

3. Does the consultant have a big ego? Can he or she work with others on an *equal* basis? Will others whom the consultant intends to help perceive him or her as being helpful?

4. Is the consultant willing to share knowledge with those whom he or she helps so they will not always have to be dependent upon him or her in the future?

5. Does the consultant have the kind of a personality that invites cooperation and trust so that others will want to implement his or her suggestions and ideas?

6. Will the consultant want to take all the credit or will he or she share credit for success with those whom he or she assists? Will the person or persons with whom the consultant directly works end up with more or less status when the consulting arrangement terminates?

13. Where can we find a reading list of basic books in management for our top-level managers?

Below is a list of what might be considered "classics." Each is a unique contribution to the field. These books are geared to the reading interests of practicing executives.

Allen, Louis. *The Management Profession.* New York: McGraw-Hill, 1961.

Appley, Lawrence. *Management in Action.* American Management Association, 1956.

Argyris, Chris. *Integrating the Individual and the Organization.* New York: Wiley, 1964.

Barnard, Chester. *The Functions of the Executive.* Cambridge, Mass.: Harvard University Press, 1938.

Chandler, Alfred D. Jr. *Strategy and Structure*. Cambridge, Mass.: MIT Press, 1962.

Churchman, C. West; Ackoff, Russell; and Arnoff, E. Leonard. *Introduction to Operations Research*. New York: Wiley, 1957.

Davis, Ralph Currier. *The Fundamentals of Top Management*. Harper and Brothers, 1951.

Drucker, Peter F. *Management: Tasks, Responsibilities, Practices*. New York: Harper & Row, 1973.

Fayerweather, John. *Management of International Operations*. New York: McGraw-Hill, 1960.

Gardner, John W. *Self-Renewal: The Individual and the Innovative Society*. New York: Harper & Row, 1964.

Gellerman, Saul W. *Motivation and Productivity*. American Management Association, 1963.

Haney, William V. *Communication and Organizational Behavior*. Homewood, Ill.: Irwin, 1973.

Kepner, Charles H., and Tregoe, Ben B. *The Rational Manager: A Systematic Approach to Problem Solving and Decision Making*. New York: McGraw-Hill, 1965.

Likert, Rensis. *New Patterns of Management*. New York: McGraw-Hill, 1961.

Likert, Rensis. *The Human Organization*. New York: McGraw-Hill, 1967.

Maier, Norman R. F. *Psychology in Industry*. Boston: Houghton Mifflin, 1955.

McGregor, Douglas M. *The Human Side of Enterprise*. New York: McGraw-Hill, 1960.

Odiorne, George. *Management by Objectives*. New York: Pitman, 1965.

Steiner, George A. *Top Management Planning*. New York: MacMillan, 1969.

Whyte, William F. *Men at Work*. Homewood, Ill.: Richard D. Irwin, Inc., and Dorsey Press, 1961.

14. What are the pros and cons of having an in-house program and the pros and cons of sending managers to outside courses?

In-house programs:

Pros

1. Control over content (can often do a better job of meeting training needs of the group)

2. Can involve key company executives in the teaching

3. Can spend time on company related issues

4. Gives participants a chance to get to know others in the company better

5. The use of the concepts taught is encouraged when all agree upon their desirability and the fact that the company favors their application

    Cons

1. Does not expose participants to outside perspectives and practices of other organizations

2. Too much "shop talk" can distract from learning

3. Sometimes openness and frank discussion and freewheeling thinking is stifled because people do not want to appear odd or foolish among their peers, or superiors and subordinates from their own firm

Outside programs:

Pros

1. Permits exposure to a wide variety of perspectives and practices (this is especially true when there are plenty of opportunities for face-to-face interaction outside of class)

2. Opportunity for participants to get away from their company and to contemplate problems, issues, and own management practices and philosophy from a fresh perspective

3. Provided the "right" outside courses exist and care has been taken in matching people with programs, there is sometimes a greater chance of meeting individual training needs

4. Brings new perspectives to the firm from various sources

    Cons

1. Can be "canned" materials and not entirely applicable to the needs of the audience

2. Sometimes more expensive to send many managers away than it is to have an in-house program

3. Sometimes is difficult to fully know what the course will contain and involve beforehand, thus making the selection of programs a difficult task

15. **How can we prevent our training program from seeming like school?**

1. Treat the group members as adults and equals. Do not talk down to them.

2. Encourage discussion. Do not lecture too much. Instead, draw upon the participants' thinking and experiences. Do not give people "the answers." Allow them to discover them for themselves.

3. Don't give examinations or grades.

4. Refer to the trainees as "participants" and not "students."

5. Refer to the instructors as "discussion leaders."

6. Do not put people "on-the-spot" by asking individuals extremely difficult questions in class. Instead, encourage people to volunteer ideas and answers to questions.

7. Be sure the readings and study assignments and case studies are rigorous and challenging to the group, but not over demanding.

8. Assume that participants will be serious and conscientious. Do not allow it to appear that they are being policed to make sure they do the required work.

9. Do not become upset or annoyed when participants disagree with some of the teaching or when they are critical of the program. Instead, listen to them attentively and with understanding. This is probably just their way of resisting the learning.

10. Start and stop on time. Respect their feelings and their time. Their time is just as important and valuable to them as yours is to you.

16. Why is the case-study method so important? Wouldn't it be faster and easier to simply tell people the right answers?

Teaching isn't telling. Learning isn't listening. People learn best and they learn more when they discover things themselves. To tell people the "right" answers assumes two conditions exist.

1. There are "right" answers, or there is some "right" way to manage.

2. The person who does the telling knows these "right" answers.

Frequently these two conditions do not exist. Moreover, when people are simply told something new they frequently do not accept it because they fail to fully appreciate and accept the logic behind it.

As it was stressed in Chapter 2, management is not simply a process of applying unbending principles or doing things in the "one best" or "right" way. There is no simple formula to follow. Instead, management requires diagnostic and application skills and personal characteristics that support and enable the application of these skills. Telling does not develop either these skills or personal characteristics.

The case-study method teaches both. Moreover it helps people to learn to work in groups with others and to improve their ability in both written and oral expression.

17. Why should there be so much emphasis on the group in management training? After all, don't people pretty much learn on their own?

Individuals can acquire knowledge on their own. They can learn facts, add new data to their storehouses of information, and learn theories. They can do all this by reading, listening to lectures, watching movies, etc. But the ability to manage requires much more than just knowledge. It requires wisdom; and wisdom simply cannot be told. One cannot acquire wisdom passively. It can be acquired only when the trainee is actively involved in the learning process.

The group is particularly useful in helping trainees progress from the first two stages of learning—knowing about and understanding—and through the third and fourth stages of learning—acceptance and the ability to apply. Moreover, in a group setting people can learn from each other as they share ideas and information and help one another sharpen their diagnostic and problem-solving skills through challenging and questioning each other's logic and arguments. In addition, the group is a powerful source of influence in developing the personal characteristics that enable managers to diagnose situations and apply contingent principles.

18. Should we have participants remain in the same case-study buzz groups throughout the entire program or should we have them form into new groups each day?

As groups remain intact over time, they tend to work more efficiently. The first meeting of a group is usually slow and not highly productive. Efficiency improves over time. So, if the objective is to have people zoom through case analyses as fast as possible, then have them remain in the same groups night after night.

If on the other hand the objective is to have people become exposed to a wide variety of perspectives and viewpoints and to develop their abilities in working with many new people, then have them form into different buzz groups each day.

Sometimes participants will voice the desire to remain with the same group for several days. They say things like, "We are just getting to know each other and are starting to feel like a group. Can't we be allowed to remain together?" What they mean is, "We are beginning to level with one another and we are beginning to feel close." Leveling is an important ingredient to the learning process. It is particularly important to the attainment of the third stage of learning—acceptance.

Therefore, it seems to make sense to attempt to obtain some of the advantages of both stability and variety by striking a compromise and have groups remain together for two to four days at a stretch.

19. Why should the daily schedule follow the same pattern throughout the entire program? Wouldn't it be better to have variety?

Don't vary the daily schedule. Keep it the same throughout the entire program.

Participants have to cope with enough new and different things and their energies and tolerances are fairly well depleted in adjusting to these. Learning and trying to accept new ideas, working closely with strangers, living in a group setting far from home, being involved in a full-time learning experience as opposed to working on the job, and concentrated doses of reading and studying are all difficult enough for people to adjust to without the added disruption and confusion of unnecessary daily schedule changes. A fixed, unvarying daily schedule is a source of stability and security. There are enough unknowns in a good program already, there is no sense in adding more. People need a certain amount of predictability in their lives.

20. We would like to use a management game in our executive program. Where can we find a good one?

The first thing you need to do is to identify your purposes and constraints. You will need to answer the following kinds of questions.

1. Who is the audience?

2. What are the objectives for this segment of the course?

3. How much time can be devoted to playing the game?

4. Are computer facilities and resource persons available?

Once you have answered these questions you will be able to eliminate many inappropriate games.

The second thing to do is to locate possible games. One source is the *Business Games Handbook* by Robert G. Graham and Clifford E. Gray (1969). It lists and describes many games and their sources.

Another place to check is with university executive development programs. Many schools use games in their programs. Contact the directors of several programs. These people can put you in touch with the person or persons who conduct games in their programs.

Still another source is management professors, who sometimes use games in teaching college courses, particularly business-policy courses. Letters to the heads of the management departments of several universities can bring helpful information.

21. Suppose one of the instructors we use doesn't receive satisfactory participant evaluations, what should we do? Should we tell her or him?

Generally speaking it is wise to tell the instructor. Let the instructor read the evaluations by himself or herself. If the instructor is the kind of person who wants to improve, he or she will be serious about this and heed the suggestions.

As a program coordinator, bear in mind that nobody who has taught many programs has never had a bad showing. Even the best of instructors have "bombed-out." Try to discover the reasons for the poor performance. Approach it as a problem. Try to solve the problem. Don't just blame the person who failed to get a good evaluation. By all means, earn your keep as a competent program coordinator by coming up with several concrete suggestions of do's and don'ts for the instructor to follow, so that she or he will get a better rating next time.

22. Is there a fundamental message or philosophy that training and development professionals ought to convey to those they serve?

Yes. Keep mentally active and alive. We are all vulnerable to rigidity and narrowness of thought and action, mental deterioration, and eventual stagnation. Even the best of us can permit ourselves to become obsolete. Unwanted and unnoticed forces are at work daily pushing us in this direction—unthinking habit, fear of failure, doing just enough to get by, the tendency to procrastinate, exclusive reliance on old solutions and methods, the avoidance of opportunities and new endeavors because they seem too complex or difficult, unchanging routine void of new experience, and the attitude, "I already know enough to get by."

What's the answer? Self-renewal—a process of regeneration to keep our minds alive and growing. There are many ways—new experiences, new hobbies, travel, new friends and acquaintances, continuing education, etc. The aim should always be in view and pursued deliberately and conscientiously: to avoid mental and emotional death through ongoing learning and new experiences. This will enable us to live richer, fuller, more productive, and more satisfying lives.

REFERENCES

Bricker, George W. "University Executive Education: How to get the Most out of Campus-Based Programs." *Training* 13, No. 10, 1975, p. 45.

Campbell, John P.; Dunnette, Marvin D.; Lawler, Edward E., III; and Weick, Karl E., Jr. *Managerial Behavior Performance and Effectiveness.* New York: McGraw-Hill, 1970.

French, Wendell L., and Bell, Cecil H., Jr. *Organization Development: Behavioral Science Interventions for Organization Improvement.* Englewood Cliffs, N.J.: Prentice-Hall, 1973.

Graham, Robert G., and Gray, Clifford E. *Business Games Handbook.* New York: American Management Association, 1969.

Miner, John B. *Studies in Management Education.* New York: Springer, 1965.

Index